Adobe® PhotoDeluxe® For Dummies®

Cheat Sheet

File Menu Shortcuts

To Do This	Windows Shortcut Keys	Macintosh Shortcut Keys
Open a file	Ctrl+O	⌘+O
Open the PhotoDeluxe clip art	Ctrl+\	⌘+\
Close a file	Ctrl+W	⌘+W
Save an image in PDD format	Ctrl+S	⌘+S
Print an image	Ctrl+P	⌘+P
Preview before printing	Ctrl+/	⌘+/
Open Cursors dialog box	Ctrl+K	⌘+K
Shut down PhotoDeluxe	Ctrl+Q	⌘+Q

Selection Shortcuts

To Do This	Windows Shortcut Keys	Macintosh Shortcut Keys
Select entire image	Ctrl+A	⌘+A
Deselect entire image	Ctrl+D	⌘+D
Invert existing selection outline	Ctrl+I	⌘+I
Select Trace tool	Ctrl+L	⌘+L
Select Rectangle tool	Ctrl+M	⌘+M
Select Color Wand	Ctrl+F	⌘+F
Relocate selection outline	Ctrl+Alt drag with Move tool selected	⌘+Option+drag with Move tool selected
Select Move tool	Ctrl+G	⌘+G

Painting Shortcuts

To Do This	Windows Shortcut Keys	Macintosh Shortcut Keys
Select Brush tool	Ctrl+J	⌘+J
Select Text tool	Ctrl+T	⌘+T
Select Eraser tool	Ctrl+E	⌘+E
Adjust tool opacity	Press a number key	Press a number key
Selection Fill command	Ctrl+9	⌘+9
Gradient Fill command	Ctrl+8	⌘+8
Fill selection with foreground color	Alt+Backspace	Option+Backspace

...For Dummies®: Bestselling Book Series for Beginners

Adobe® PhotoDeluxe™ For Dummies®

Cheat Sheet

Color Correction Shortcuts

To Do This	Windows Shortcut Keys	Macintosh Shortcut Keys
Adjust color balance	Ctrl+Y	⌘+Y
Adjust contrast/brightness	Ctrl+B	⌘+B
Adjust hue/saturation	Ctrl+U	⌘+U
Convert to grayscale image	Ctrl+0	⌘+0

Basic Editing Shortcuts

To Do This	Windows Shortcut Keys	Macintosh Shortcut Keys
Undo last editing action	Ctrl+Z	⌘+Z
Crop an image (Trim tool)	Ctrl+7	⌘+7
Cut selection to Clipboard	Ctrl+X	⌘+X
Copy selection to Clipboard	Ctrl+C	⌘+C
Paste selection from Clipboard	Ctrl+V	⌘+V
Move selection	Drag with Move tool	Drag with Move tool
Copy and move selection	Alt+drag with Move tool	Option + drag with Move tool

Miscellaneous Shortcuts

To Do This	Windows Shortcut Keys	Macintosh Shortcut Keys
Zoom in	Ctrl+plus	⌘+plus
Zoom out	Ctrl+minus	⌘+minus
Show/hide rulers	Ctrl+R	⌘+R
Duplicate image	Ctrl+;	⌘+;
Rotate right (clockwise)	Ctrl+>	⌘+>
Rotate left (counterclockwise)	Ctrl+<	⌘+<
Flip horizontal	Ctrl+[	⌘+[
Flip vertical	Ctrl+]	⌘+]
Display distortion handles	Ctrl+2	⌘+2
Display perspective handles	Ctrl+5	⌘+5

...For Dummies®: Bestselling Book Series for Beginners

 ™

References for the Rest of Us!®

BESTSELLING BOOK SERIES

Are you intimidated and confused by computers? Do you find that traditional manuals are overloaded with technical details you'll never use? Do your friends and family always call you to fix simple problems on their PCs? Then the *...For Dummies*® computer book series from IDG Books Worldwide is for you.

...For Dummies books are written for those frustrated computer users who know they aren't really dumb but find that PC hardware, software, and indeed the unique vocabulary of computing make them feel helpless. *...For Dummies* books use a lighthearted approach, a down-to-earth style, and even cartoons and humorous icons to dispel computer novices' fears and build their confidence. Lighthearted but not lightweight, these books are a perfect survival guide for anyone forced to use a computer.

> *"I like my copy so much I told friends; now they bought copies."*
>
> — **Irene C., Orwell, Ohio**

> *"Quick, concise, nontechnical, and humorous."*
>
> — **Jay A., Elburn, Illinois**

> *"Thanks, I needed this book. Now I can sleep at night."*
>
> — **Robin F., British Columbia, Canada**

Already, millions of satisfied readers agree. They have made *...For Dummies* books the #1 introductory level computer book series and have written asking for more. So, if you're looking for the most fun and easy way to learn about computers, look to *...For Dummies* books to give you a helping hand.

ADOBE® PHOTODELUXE™ FOR DUMMIES®

by Julie Adair King

IDG Books Worldwide, Inc.
An International Data Group Company

Foster City, CA ♦ Chicago, IL ♦ Indianapolis, IN ♦ New York, NY

Adobe® PhotoDeluxe™ For Dummies®

Published by
IDG Books Worldwide, Inc.
An International Data Group Company
919 E. Hillsdale Blvd.
Suite 400
Foster City, CA 94404
www.idgbooks.com (IDG Books Worldwide Web site)
www.dummies.com (Dummies Press Web site)

Library of Congress Catalog Card No.: 98-86184

ISBN: 0-7645-0426-6

Printed in the United States of America

10 9 8 7 6 5 4 3

1B/ST/QT/ZZ/IN

Distributed in the United States by IDG Books Worldwide, Inc.

Distributed by CDG Books Canada Inc. for Canada; by Transworld Publishers Limited in the United Kingdom; by IDG Norge Books for Norway; by IDG Sweden Books for Sweden; by Woodslane Pty. Ltd. for Australia; by Woodslane (NZ) Ltd. for New Zealand; by TransQuest Publishers Pte Ltd. for Singapore, Malaysia, Thailand, Indonesia, and Hong Kong; by ICG Muse, Inc. for Japan; by Norma Comunicaciones S.A. for Colombia; by Intersoft for South Africa; by Le Monde en Tique for France; by International Thomson Publishing for Germany, Austria and Switzerland; by Distribuidora Cuspide for Argentina; by Livraria Cultura for Brazil; by Ediciones ZETA S.C.R. Ltda. for Peru; by WS Computer Publishing Corporation, Inc., for the Philippines; by Contemporanea de Ediciones for Venezuela; by Express Computer Distributors for the Caribbean and West Indies; by Micronesia Media Distributor, Inc. for Micronesia; by Grupo Editorial Norma S.A. for Guatemala; by Chips Computadoras S.A. de C.V. for Mexico; by Editorial Norma de Panama S.A. for Panama; by American Bookshops for Finland. Authorized Sales Agent: Anthony Rudkin Associates for the Middle East and North Africa.

For general information on IDG Books Worldwide's books in the U.S., please call our Consumer Customer Service department at 800-762-2974. For reseller information, including discounts and premium sales, please call our Reseller Customer Service department at 800-434-3422.

For information on where to purchase IDG Books Worldwide's books outside the U.S., please contact our International Sales department at 317-596-5530 or fax 317-596-5692.

For consumer information on foreign language translations, please contact our Customer Service department at 1-800-434-3422, fax 317-596-5692, or e-mail rights@idgbooks.com.

For information on licensing foreign or domestic rights, please phone +1-650-655-3109.

For sales inquiries and special prices for bulk quantities, please contact our Sales department at 650-655-3200 or write to the address above.

For information on using IDG Books Worldwide's books in the classroom or for ordering examination copies, please contact our Educational Sales department at 800-434-2086 or fax 317-596-5499.

For press review copies, author interviews, or other publicity information, please contact our Public Relations department at 650-655-3000 or fax 650-655-3299.

For authorization to photocopy items for corporate, personal, or educational use, please contact Copyright Clearance Center, 222 Rosewood Drive, Danvers, MA 01923, or fax 978-750-4470.

About the Author

Julie Adair King is the author of *Digital Photography For Dummies* and has contributed to many other books on digital imaging and computer graphics, including *Photoshop 4 Bible, Photoshop 4 For Dummies, CorelDRAW! 7 For Dummies,* and *PageMaker 6 For Dummies.* She is also the author of *WordPerfect Suite 7 For Dummies* and *Corel WordPerfect Suite 8 For Dummies.*

ABOUT IDG BOOKS WORLDWIDE

Welcome to the world of IDG Books Worldwide.

IDG Books Worldwide, Inc., is a subsidiary of International Data Group, the world's largest publisher of computer-related information and the leading global provider of information services on information technology. IDG was founded more than 30 years ago by Patrick J. McGovern and now employs more than 9,000 people worldwide. IDG publishes more than 290 computer publications in over 75 countries. More than 90 million people read one or more IDG publications each month.

Launched in 1990, IDG Books Worldwide is today the #1 publisher of best-selling computer books in the United States. We are proud to have received eight awards from the Computer Press Association in recognition of editorial excellence and three from Computer Currents' First Annual Readers' Choice Awards. Our best-selling *...For Dummies®* series has more than 50 million copies in print with translations in 31 languages. IDG Books Worldwide, through a joint venture with IDG's Hi-Tech Beijing, became the first U.S. publisher to publish a computer book in the People's Republic of China. In record time, IDG Books Worldwide has become the first choice for millions of readers around the world who want to learn how to better manage their businesses.

Our mission is simple: Every one of our books is designed to bring extra value and skill-building instructions to the reader. Our books are written by experts who understand and care about our readers. The knowledge base of our editorial staff comes from years of experience in publishing, education, and journalism — experience we use to produce books to carry us into the new millennium. In short, we care about books, so we attract the best people. We devote special attention to details such as audience, interior design, use of icons, and illustrations. And because we use an efficient process of authoring, editing, and desktop publishing our books electronically, we can spend more time ensuring superior content and less time on the technicalities of making books.

You can count on our commitment to deliver high-quality books at competitive prices on topics you want to read about. At IDG Books Worldwide, we continue in the IDG tradition of delivering quality for more than 30 years. You'll find no better book on a subject than one from IDG Books Worldwide.

John Kilcullen
Chairman and CEO
IDG Books Worldwide, Inc.

Steven Berkowitz
President and Publisher
IDG Books Worldwide, Inc.

*Eighth Annual
Computer Press
Awards ≥1992*

*Ninth Annual
Computer Press
Awards ≥1993*

*Tenth Annual
Computer Press
Awards ≥1994*

*Eleventh Annual
Computer Press
Awards ≥1995*

IDG is the world's leading IT media, research and exposition company. Founded in 1964, IDG had 1997 revenues of $2.05 billion and has more than 9,000 employees worldwide. IDG offers the widest range of media options that reach IT buyers in 75 countries representing 95% of worldwide IT spending. IDG's diverse product and services portfolio spans six key areas including print publishing, online publishing, expositions and conferences, market research, education and training, and global marketing services. More than 90 million people read one or more of IDG's 290 magazines and newspapers, including IDG's leading global brands — Computerworld, PC World, Network World, Macworld and the Channel World family of publications. IDG Books Worldwide is one of the fastest-growing computer book publishers in the world, with more than 700 titles in 36 languages. The "...For Dummies®" series alone has more than 50 million copies in print. IDG offers online users the largest network of technology-specific Web sites around the world through IDG.net (http://www.idg.net), which comprises more than 225 targeted Web sites in 55 countries worldwide. International Data Corporation (IDC) is the world's largest provider of information technology data, analysis and consulting, with research centers in over 41 countries and more than 400 research analysts worldwide. IDG World Expo is a leading producer of more than 168 globally branded conferences and expositions in 35 countries including E3 (Electronic Entertainment Expo), Macworld Expo, ComNet, Windows World Expo, ICE (Internet Commerce Expo), Agenda, DEMO, and Spotlight. IDG's training subsidiary, ExecuTrain, is the world's largest computer training company, with more than 230 locations worldwide and 785 training courses. IDG Marketing Services helps industry-leading IT companies build international brand recognition by developing global integrated marketing programs via IDG's print, online and exposition products worldwide. Further information about the company can be found at www.idg.com.   1/24/99

Dedication

This book is dedicated to the memory of George E. Harris, the best grandfather a girl could have.

Acknowledgments

Like all books, this one would be languishing in a digital dustbin somewhere were it not for the efforts of a terrific team of editors and production professionals. I am fortunate to have on my side a wonderful group of people from IDG Books Worldwide, including copy editor Linda Stark, who also contributed some exceptional photographs to this book; acquisitions editor Mike Kelly; Shelly Lea, Lou Boudreau, Karen York, and Cindy Phipps (among others) in the Production department; Carmen Krikorian, Marita Ellixson, and Heather Dismore in the Media Development department; and last, but not least, the always unflappable, understanding, and exceptional project editor Jennifer Ehrlich.

In addition to those thoughtful and talented folks, I would like to thank technical editors Lee Musick and Ben Barbante. Your willingness to lend your expertise to this effort is appreciated more than you know. Special thanks also to Loni Singer and Mark Dahm at Adobe, as well as all the vendors who provided material for the CD-ROM that accompanies this book.

Finally, continued gratitude to my family, especially to my mother and father, Barbara and Dale King, for giving my raw manuscript the once-over and for their unwavering support; to my sisters April and Rachel, for putting up with my whining whenever things get to be too much — which is just about always; and to my wonderful nieces and nephews, Kristen, Matt, Adam, Brandon, and Laura, for posing patiently whenever I come around with camera in hand.

Photo Credits

All images in this book are ©1998 Julie King Creative, Inc., with the exception of the following:

Image	*Photographer/Source*
Figures 1-8, 4-7, 4-10, 6-2, 8-2, 8-4, 8-7, 9-8, 9-10, 11-2, 14-1 through 14-13; Color Plates 3-1, 9-2, 9-3, and 9-4	Adobe PhotoDeluxe (Adobe Systems Inc.)
Figures 7-2, 7-3, 8-10; Color Plates 6-2, 7-4, and 12-4	Linda S. Stark
Figure 9-6 and Color Plate 9-1	George E. Harris
Figures 13-6 and 13-7	Spin Panorama (Picture Works Technology, Inc.)

Publisher's Acknowledgments

We're proud of this book; please register your comments through our IDG Books Worldwide Online Registration Form located at http://my2cents.dummies.com.

Some of the people who helped bring this book to market include the following:

Acquisitions, Editorial, and Media Development

Senior Project Editor: Jennifer Ehrlich

Acquisitions Editor: Michael Kelly

Copy Editors: Linda S. Stark, Christine Meloy Beck

Technical Editors: Ben Barbante, Lee Musick

Media Development Technical Editor: Marita Ellixson

Associate Permissions Editor: Carmen Krikorian

Editorial Manager: Mary C. Corder

Media Development Manager: Heather Heath Dismore

Editorial Assistant: Donna Love

Production

Project Coordinator: Karen York

Layout and Graphics: Lou Boudreau, Angela F. Hunckler, Jane E. Martin, Brent Savage, Deirdre Smith, Rashell Smith, Michael A. Sullivan

Proofreaders: Kelli Botta, Michelle Croninger, Henry Lazarek, Janet M. Withers

Indexer: Anne Leach

Special Help
Elizabeth Netedu Kuball
Access Technology, Inc.

General and Administrative

IDG Books Worldwide, Inc.: John Kilcullen, CEO; Steven Berkowitz, President and Publisher

IDG Books Technology Publishing: Brenda McLaughlin, Senior Vice President and Group Publisher

Dummies Technology Press and Dummies Editorial: Diane Graves Steele, Vice President and Associate Publisher; Mary Bednarek, Director of Acquisitions and Product Development; Kristin A. Cocks, Editorial Director

Dummies Trade Press: Kathleen A. Welton, Vice President and Publisher; Kevin Thornton, Acquisitions Manager

IDG Books Production for Dummies Press: Michael R. Britton, Vice President of Production and Creative Services; Cindy L. Phipps, Manager of Project Coordination, Production Proofreading, and Indexing; Kathie S. Schutte, Supervisor of Page Layout; Shelley Lea, Supervisor of Graphics and Design; Debbie J. Gates, Production Systems Specialist; Robert Springer, Supervisor of Proofreading; Debbie Stailey, Special Projects Coordinator; Tony Augsburger, Supervisor of Reprints and Bluelines

Dummies Packaging and Book Design: Patty Page, Manager, Promotions Marketing

♦

The publisher would like to give special thanks to Patrick J. McGovern, without whom this book would not have been possible.

♦

Contents at a Glance

Cartoons at a Glance

By Rich Tennant

page 129

page 197

page 9

page 317

page 285

Fax: 978-546-7747 • E-mail: the5wave@tiac.net

Table of Contents

Introduction

*I*f you were to eavesdrop on a roomful of computer-industry marketing gurus, you'd hear the phrase *out-of-box experience* flung about on a regular basis. This buzzword — or, more accurately, buzz phrase — refers to how easily an ordinary mortal can get up and running with a new piece of software or hardware. In the ideal out-of-box scenario, you can install your new program or gadget and make it productive in minutes, without even having to (gasp!) read the instruction manual.

As computer programs go, Adobe PhotoDeluxe delivers a fairly decent out-of-box experience. Designed for those with little or no background in digital artistry, this entry-level program enables you to open a scanned photograph or image from a digital camera and perform a variety of retouching and special-effects maneuvers. Without exerting much mental energy at all, you can create some pretty cool images and even put your photographic creations on calendars, greeting cards, business cards, and the like. PhotoDeluxe is stocked with templates and wizards, so all you have to do is follow the on-screen prompts and do as you're told.

Well — almost, anyway. Where the out-of-box experience breaks down is when you stop being dazzled by the colorful effects that you can produce in PhotoDeluxe and start looking closely at the *quality* of your digital art. The truth is that despite the generous amount of hand-holding that PhotoDeluxe provides, image editing is still fairly complex stuff. Even when you use the PhotoDeluxe wizards to get things done, you have to make decisions about which way you want the program to implement your ideas. And unless you take a few moments here and there to acquire some fundamental image-editing knowledge, you can easily choose the wrong fork in the road. The result is images that look amateurish at best — and downright embarrassing at worst.

That's where *Adobe PhotoDeluxe For Dummies* comes in. This book explains the science behind the art of PhotoDeluxe so that you can use the program to its fullest advantage. In simple, easy-to-read language, *Adobe PhotoDeluxe For Dummies* helps you wrap your brain around such perplexing subjects as choosing the right image resolution, selecting a file format, and other topics that are essential to creating good-looking images.

Beyond that, you gain the information you need to venture past the surface level of the program and explore its considerable hidden talents. Almost obscured by the consumer-friendly PhotoDeluxe interface are some very powerful image-editing tools — the kind that you may expect to find only in professional (read that, expensive) graphics software. This book shows you how to exploit those tools and even how to work around some built-in limitations to get a bit more flexibility than the program's designers likely intended. (Adobe has to give you *some* reason to pay a few hundred dollars to upgrade to its professional image editor, Photoshop, right?)

Finally, this book gives you the know-how to put your own personal, creative stamp on your images instead of relying solely on the prefab templates and wizards that PhotoDeluxe provides. The templates and wizards are great as a starting point, and they're very useful for those quick-and-dirty, every-day projects. But for those times when you really want your image to stand out — which is *always* if you're creating images for business use — you need to abandon the automatic, cookie-cutter approach and start wielding the editing tools with a bit more individuality. Let's face it, you can't create the kind of unique images that attract an audience to your company's Web page or product brochure if you're using the same design templates as millions of other PhotoDeluxe users. But you can if you follow the techniques provided in this book.

In short, by heading out of the PhotoDeluxe box and into this book, you can get more from a $50 image-editing program than most people get from far more expensive software. You not only get tons of artistic ideas, but you also gain the technical background you need to make sure that the quality of your finished images is as impressive as your creative vision.

About This Book

PhotoDeluxe has evolved through several incarnations in its short life. This book covers four of them, including:

- ✔ Version 2, for Windows and Macintosh
- ✔ Business Edition 1.0, for Windows only
- ✔ Version 3, which Adobe refers to as Home Edition 3.0 and makes available for Windows only

If you're a Macintosh user, don't be dismayed by the fact that most of the screen shots in this book were taken on a PC. In almost every case, your menus, dialog boxes, and screens offer the exact same options as on the PC side, so don't worry that you're being left out of the action. If a program component acts differently on a Mac than on a PC, I give you specific instructions for the Macintosh platform.

On the other side of the operating system war, Version 3 and the Business Edition of PhotoDeluxe run on Windows NT as well as Windows 98. This book focuses on Windows 95 and does not specifically address Windows 98 and NT. If you're running 98 or NT, you may find a few areas where things work differently than described here, but the majority of the information is absolutely the same no matter what flavor of Windows you fed your computer.

Finally, if you're wondering what level of experience you need to understand the goings-on in this book, the answer is: almost none. The book is designed for those who are at the beginner or intermediate level when it comes to image editing. However, I do assume that you have at least a basic understanding of how to use your computer. For example, you know what it means to click and drag with a mouse; you understand how to move through file folders, hard drives, and the like; and you know just where to whack your computer when it misbehaves. If you need help with these fundamentals, pick up a copy of the *...For Dummies* book for your specific operating system.

Sneak Preview

If I had to give a one-sentence synopsis of this book, I'd say "Everything you ever wanted to know about PhotoDeluxe — and then some." Fortunately, I'm not limited to one sentence; in fact, my editors have graciously allotted me several paragraphs to give you a brief summary of the topics covered in each part of the book. As they say in those late-night infomercials, "Just look at all you get for one low, low price!"

Part I: It's a Brave New (Digital) World

This part of the book gives you a firm foundation for working with digital images and PhotoDeluxe, whether you want to create an attention-getting image for your company's customer newsletter or simply apply goofy special effects to a photo of your pesky brother-in-law.

Chapters 1 and 2 familiarize you with the PhotoDeluxe interface (the on-screen components that you use to control the program), and Chapter 3 covers the inner workings of a digital image, explaining vital technical issues such as resolution and pixels. Chapters 4 and 5 show you how to save and print your masterpieces and also offer some advice about choosing removable storage media and color printers.

Part II: Editing Boot Camp

Don't be put off by the title of this part — you're not subjected to any grueling calisthenics or hard-nosed drill sergeants. This is boot camp Dummies-style, where you acquire important image-editing skills in a fun, relaxed fashion.

Chapter 6 shows you how to do simple, everyday edits such as cropping an image and correcting brightness and contrast. Chapter 7 covers more-complicated image-correction tasks, such as covering up photographic flaws and removing red-eye from snapshots. Chapter 8 explains how to use the PhotoDeluxe selection tools, which enable you to limit the effects of your edits to one portion of your image.

With the basic training provided in this part, you're well-prepared for the rest of your image-editing life. And you don't even have to break a sweat to earn your stripes.

Part III: Amazing Feats of Digital Trickery

If Part II is boot camp, Part III is summer camp — a really great summer camp, not the kind where you sing dopey songs and make lame crafts out of sticks and yarn. Here, you find out about all the really fun games you can play with digital images.

Chapter 9 shows you how to paint on your photographs and replace one image color with another. Chapter 10 introduces you to the wonderful world of image layers, which enable you to combine images into photographic collages and perform other neat tricks with surprising ease.

Chapter 11 explains how to add basic text to your image and also gives you a top-secret recipe for creating special text effects, such as semitransparent text and text filled with an image. In Chapter 12, you experiment with all kinds of fun and interesting special effects, and Chapter 13 gives you ideas for putting the images you create to good use. Suffice it to say, you're going to be one happy camper exploring this part.

Part IV: The Part of Tens

In the time-honored ...For Dummies tradition, this part of the book contains short chapters that follow the popular "Top Ten List" format. Turn here when you're in short-attention-span mode or just want a quick bit of information or inspiration.

Chapter 14 shows you ten ways to distort an image using the PhotoDeluxe distortion filters, which are always good for a laugh. Chapter 15 answers the ten most frequently asked questions — FAQs, as they're known in Internet lingo — about image editing and PhotoDeluxe. Chapter 16 helps you shave minutes off your image-editing projects by listing ten groups of keyboard shortcuts, and Chapter 17 points you toward ten online resources where you can get even more pointers and ideas about image editing.

Appendixes and CD

Not sure how to install PhotoDeluxe on your computer? Check out Appendix A, which explains how to get started and which installation options to choose.

After you install the program, take a gander at Appendix B, which describes all the goodies found on the CD-ROM that's included on the inside back cover of this book. The CD is brimming with demos and trials of programs that make terrific partners to PhotoDeluxe. You can try out programs that help you organize your images, display images in an on-screen photo album, turn any image into a jigsaw puzzle, and more. You even get a full working version of Spin Panorama, from PictureWorks Technology, Inc., which you can use to stitch multiple images together into a panoramic photograph. And you thought that the back of a book was just a repository for leftover, inconsequential stuff!

Conventions Used in This Book

As you probably already know, ...*For Dummies* books are anything but conventional. But this book, like others in the series, does follow a few conventions — stylistic guidelines, if you will — in how it presents information.

First, two or more words linked by an arrow represent a command or commands that you choose from a menu. The instruction "Choose File⇨Open," for example, means that you need to choose the Open command from the File menu.

Second, if you see words and letters joined by a plus sign — as in *Ctrl+A* or *⌘+A* — you're looking at a keyboard shortcut. Keyboard shortcuts enable you to select a command using your keyboard rather than a mouse. Pressing the Ctrl key and then the A key on a PC, for example, is the same as choosing the Select⇨All command. On a Mac, you press the ⌘ key along with the A key to accomplish the same thing. When I mention a keyboard shortcut, the PC version is listed first, followed by the Mac version in parentheses, as in "Press Ctrl+A (⌘+A on the Mac)."

You can read more about both these subjects in Chapter 1, so don't worry about them now. I just wanted to mention them so that you wouldn't freak out if you noticed these odd-looking bits of text as you flipped through the book.

Icons Used in This Book

On just about every page in this book, you're likely to encounter an *icon* — a little circular graphic in the margin. Although icons certainly spice up the page from a design standpoint, they also have a practical purpose: to let you know that you're about to read something especially useful, important, or otherwise noteworthy.

The Tip icon flags information that you can use to get a job done faster, better, and easier. Don't read these paragraphs if you have way too much time on your hands or if you like doing things the long way.

Pay extra attention to paragraphs marked with a Remember icon. You'll need this information often during your image-editing adventures, so give it a prominent place in your memory bank.

This icon is akin to a "Danger Ahead!" road sign. When you see the Warning icon, slow down, hang up the cell phone, and read the corresponding paragraph carefully to avoid making a horrible, life-altering mistake. Well, a mistake you may live to regret, anyway.

If you want to be able to carry on a meaningful conversation with digital imaging fanatics or impress the neighborhood computer geek, look for the Technical Stuff icon. This icon marks paragraphs that provide background information about technical concepts, as well as explanations of all those gobbledygook acronyms that the computer industry loves so much.

Check out paragraphs marked with this icon for a preview about the products included on the CD in the back of this book. (Flip to Appendix B for a complete listing of the freebies on the CD.)

Using PhotoDeluxe Version 2 for the Macintosh? If so, the Mac icons point out information specifically for you. Keep in mind that almost everything else in the book applies to you, too — the icon simply alerts you to special circumstances related to the Macintosh platform.

Those using the latest home edition of PhotoDeluxe, Version 3, should keep an eye out for this icon. It highlights new features in Version 3 and changes from earlier versions of the program.

 Similarly, the Business Edition icon signals information about features that are unique to the Business Edition or work differently than in other versions of PhotoDeluxe.

 When you see this icon, you're about to read information that applies to both the Business Edition and Version 3. If you're using Version 2, you have my permission to ignore text marked with this icon — unless you want to know what you're missing, of course.

Where Do I Go from Here?

The answer to that question depends on you. If you're a neat, orderly, step-by-step sort of person who wants to find out about PhotoDeluxe in a neat, orderly, step-by-step sort of way, start with Chapter 1 and read straight through to the end of the book.

If, on the other hand, you have neither the time nor inclination to give this book a traditional read — or you're trying to solve a specific image-editing problem — simply turn to the section of the book that interests you. This book is designed so that it works both for those who want to take the beginning-to-end reading path and those who prefer the reference-book approach, where you can find out about a particular subject without having to read all the pages that come before.

Whichever route you choose, *Adobe PhotoDeluxe For Dummies* leads you safely along the sometimes-rocky image-editing trail, gets you out of jams when necessary, and even offers you some entertainment along the way. In short, it's the perfect companion for your PhotoDeluxe journey.

Part I

It's a Brave New (Digital) World

In this part . . .

Sometime during my childhood, a well-meaning teacher introduced the notion of the daily food pyramid. You know, the chart that prescribes how many servings of this and how many servings of that you should eat in order to maintain good health.

In the realm of my daily food intake, this theory has been completely wasted on me. Not in this lifetime or any other am I going to ingest the recommended amount of fruits and vegetables — unless, of course, you count microwave popcorn as a vegetable and grape suckers as fruit.

But the food pyramid concept does serve me well (hey, a pun!) as the perfect analogy for describing this part of the book. If this scintillating tome were a smorgasbord, this first part would be the fruit and vegetables. Like lima beans and brussels sprouts, the chapters in this part aren't the tastiest, most appetizing offerings on the menu. You find out how to open, save, and print images, and you get a thorough explanation of important technical issues such as pixels, resolution, and file formats. Although I've done my best to sauce up these dissertations, they're hardly as mouthwatering as later chapters, which dish out such juicy topics as using special effects and creating photo collages.

Without the information in this part, though, your images can never be healthy, well-balanced, or long-lived. In fact, they're going to be downright sickly and may even disappear on you altogether. On top of that, PhotoDeluxe won't perform at peak capacity, either.

So skip ahead to the dessert section if you must, or make a run for the sushi bar. But at some point, come back and get your required portions of fruit and vegetables. This stuff may not be as fun to swallow as other parts of the book, but I guarantee that it can save you a major case of indigestion down the line.

Chapter 1

Blasting onto the Image-Editing Freeway

*R*emember the last time you bought a new car? After you maneuvered your pride and joy into the driveway, you spent a glorious hour inhaling that new car smell and exploring all the car's bells and whistles. You figured out how to boost the bass on the stereo, how to blast your horn at all those idiot drivers, and, most important, how to work the cup holders.

This chapter and the one that follows offer you a similar get-acquainted session with PhotoDeluxe. You get a quick introduction to the PhotoDeluxe interface, including an explanation of the Guided Activities and other features designed to guide you gently into the sometimes confusing world of image editing. You also find out how to open an image, which is an essential task if you plan on doing something more than staring at the PhotoDeluxe background screen all day long.

While this chapter familiarizes you with the basics of PhotoDeluxe, Chapter 2 shows you how to customize the program's interface according to your preferences, just as you give a new car your personal touch. Sadly, PhotoDeluxe doesn't have an option that enables you to slip on a wooden-bead seatcover or hang fuzzy dice from the rearview mirror. But if you have a really big monitor, you can stick one of those stuffed animals with suction-cup feet to your screen if you want. Good taste has never been a requirement for driving on the image-editing highway, as a quick scan of any supermarket-aisle tabloid reveals.

Unlocking Your Image-Editing Vehicle

I trust that if you're advanced enough to be venturing into image editing, you're far enough down the technology highway to know how to start PhotoDeluxe. But just in case you're new to the whole computer thing, here's a quick review:

✔ In Windows 95, click the Start button on the taskbar. Then choose Programs⇨Adobe⇨PhotoDeluxe⇨Adobe PhotoDeluxe. (The number and name of the version you're using appears on the menus after the PhotoDeluxe name.) Whew, this stuff is hard work. Five clicks just to start the program!

The Business Edition and Version 3 install a shortcut icon on the Windows 95 desktop. You can simply double-click the icon if you want to avoid all the Start menu rigmarole.

On a Mac, go to the Finder level. Double-click the desktop icon for the hard drive on which you installed the program. Track down the Adobe PhotoDeluxe folder and double-click it. Then double-click the Adobe PhotoDeluxe icon. Hmm . . . one fewer clicking maneuver on a Mac than on a PC, but you have to double-click instead of single-click. It appears that the age-old question of Mac versus Windows is not to be resolved today.

PhotoDeluxe requires plenty of memory (RAM) to maneuver. Refer to Appendix A for the exact memory requirement for your operating system and version of PhotoDeluxe. Depending on your operating system, you may be able to get by with a little less RAM, but only if you're working on really small images and performing very uncomplicated edits — otherwise, be prepared for some trouble. If you're working with minimal RAM, shut down any other programs that are running and restart your computer before you launch PhotoDeluxe. Restarting your computer ensures that the maximum amount of RAM is available for the program to use.

You also need a fair amount of empty space on your hard drive, because PhotoDeluxe writes some image data to the hard drive when you process an image. For more on the subject of hard drive and RAM requirements, read "Boosting Your Memory" and "Telling PhotoDeluxe Where to Scratch" in Chapter 2.

After you launch PhotoDeluxe, you're greeted by a window like the one shown in Figure 1-1, assuming that you're using Version 2 on a PC. The Macintosh Version 2 screen is nearly identical, except that it lacks the Windows 95 window control buttons, and a few items on the menu bar are configured a little differently. (I explain these differences in upcoming sections.)

The Business Edition opening screen also resembles the one in Figure 1-1, except that a few buttons have different names and the background design is different. For a look at the Version 3 opening screen, which has a more space-age look than its predecessor, see Figure 1-2.

Regardless of which version you're using, the opening screen is pretty but not too exciting. If you want to explore the real action, you need to open an image, a process that I explain in mind-numbing detail a little later in this chapter. After you open an image, the image-editing area (labeled in Figures 1-1 and 1-2) becomes a hotbed of activity, but until then, you may get more enjoyment from watching your grass grow.

Menu bar   Guided Activities panel   Image-editing area

Figure 1-1:
The initial
PhotoDeluxe
Version 2
program
window.

Menu bar   Guided Activities panel   Image-editing area

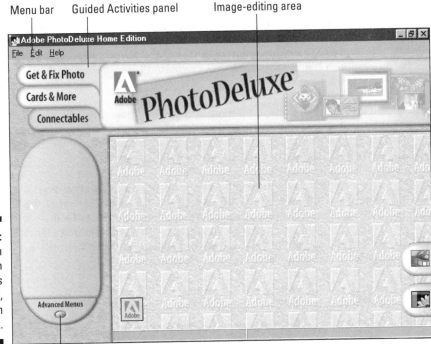

Figure 1-2:
The Version
3 program
window has
a sleeker,
high-tech
look.

Click to display hidden menus

The Adobe technical support documents note that PhotoDeluxe may not get along with Quarterdeck CleanSweep Version 3.0.7. If you're running CleanSweep, you may experience all sorts of problems, from missing filters to scary-sounding error messages. To solve the problem, upgrade to Version 3.0.8. Also check the ReadMe files on the PhotoDeluxe CD-ROM to find out about other potential software conflicts, especially if you experience frequent problems running the program.

Working the Controls

You can access the various PhotoDeluxe tools, filters, and features in three ways:

✔ You can choose commands from the menu bar, labeled in Figures 1-1 and 1-2. Click the menu name to display a list of commands and then click the desired command. In some cases, choosing a command results in a submenu of additional commands. Again, just click the command that you want to use.

✔ You can click the buttons on the Guided Activities panel, also labeled in the figures. The buttons access the PhotoDeluxe Guided Activities, which provide you with on-screen instructions that guide you through various editing projects. Computer gurus refer to these on-screen help functions as *wizards*.

✔ To access some commands, you can use *keyboard shortcuts* — that is, press one or two keys on your keyboard.

You may find the Guided Activities helpful and even necessary on some occasions, such as when you're creating a calendar featuring your family's favorite photographs. But for ordinary editing, choosing commands from menus or pressing a keyboard shortcut is almost always quicker. And many of the Guided Activities buttons simply display the same dialog box that you get when you choose the corresponding menu command — you're not provided with any additional on-screen assistance.

However, some program features are accessible only via the Guided Activities panel. Others are available only by using menu commands or keyboard shortcuts. The following sections explain how to use all three approaches to put PhotoDeluxe to work.

Turning on hidden menus

In this book, a chain of words separated by arrows indicates a series of menu commands that you follow to reach a chosen destination (sort of like a map that points out scenic stops along your vacation route). For example, if I tell you to "choose File⇨Preferences⇨Long Menus," you click File in the menu bar to display the File menu, click the Preferences command on the File menu, and then click the Long Menus command on the Preferences submenu.

In fact, go ahead and take those very steps right now, unless you're using Version 3. By default, PhotoDeluxe presents you with only three menus: File, Edit, and Help, as shown in Figures 1-1 and 1-2. But if you choose File⇨Preferences⇨Long Menus, the program displays a slew of other menu choices. You need to dig into these additional menus to take advantage of many PhotoDeluxe features. (The additional menu choices also appear if you click the Advanced button on the Guided Activities panel in Version 2 and the Business Edition. When you click the button, some Guided Activities options also appear at the top of the screen. These options are explained later.)

If you use Version 3, click the Advanced Menus button, labeled in Figure 1-2, to display the hidden menus.

Frankly, I don't understand why Adobe chose to hide some of your options in this fashion. Perhaps the program designers feared that you would be intimidated by so many menu choices. Well, ours is not to reason why, as they say. Just turn on the hidden menus and leave them on.

Note that on a Mac, the Help menu shown in Figures 1-1 and 1-2 does not appear on the menu bar. Instead, the Help options are found on the Apple menu on the left end of the menu bar.

Trying out the Guided Activities

Throughout this book, I explain how to do most things by using menus and keyboard shortcuts rather than Guided Activities. As mentioned earlier, choosing commands from the menus is almost always faster than working your way through the Guided Activities. In addition, although many Guided Activities do provide valuable on-screen help, a fair share simply open a dialog box and leave you hanging. You don't get any advice on which options to select inside the dialog box.

Finally, getting to know the menu commands gives you a head start if you decide to move up to Adobe Photoshop, the professional image editor from which PhotoDeluxe was spawned. Many of the commands are exactly the same in both programs, in fact.

That said, you do need the Guided Activities if you want to create greeting cards, calendars, and other projects using the templates on the PhotoDeluxe CD-ROM. The templates offer fun ways to use your images, and I certainly urge you to explore them.

Using the Guided Activities is simple. On the Guided Activities panel, click the button corresponding to the task that you want to do. If you want to open an image, for example, click the Get Photo button (labeled Get & Fix Photo in Version 3 and the Business Edition). After you click a button, one of two things happens, depending on whether you're using Version 3 or one of the other editions of PhotoDeluxe.

In Version 3, you see a row of icons representing different categories of projects — Get Photo, Rotate & Size, Adjust Quality, and so on. Click an icon to display a drop-down list of options within each category. Click the option that you want to use.

In other versions of PhotoDeluxe, clicking a button on the Guided Activities panel displays a row of project tabs, as shown in Figure 1-3. The tabs are organized by category, as in Version 3, and each tab contains buttons representing options related to the category. Again, just click the button for the option that interests you.

Project tab

Project button

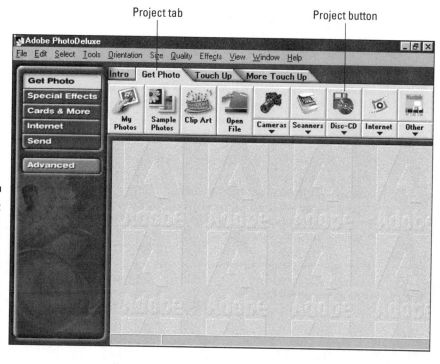

Figure 1-3:
The Guided
Activities
buttons
walk you
through
various
editing
projects.

In most cases, PhotoDeluxe displays on-screen prompts to explain each step in the editing process. If you decide to bail midway through a project, you may need to click the Done panel to exit the wizard.

Windows users who have Internet access can download additional Guided Activities templates from the Adobe Web site. You must be connected to the Internet and have Internet Explorer installed for this feature to work. In addition, you must be using a Windows version of PhotoDeluxe; unfortunately, Adobe doesn't provide additional activities on the Macintosh platform.

The process for accessing the Guided Activities at the Adobe Web site varies depending on whether you're using Version 2, the Business Edition, or Version 3. For specific how-to's, check the online help system. But before you attempt to download more activities, pay a visit to the Adobe Web site at www.adobe.com and check for updated information about the process. In some cases, you may need to download updates to your program before you can get more activities. Version 2, for example, requires a patch that corrects a problem that occurs when you attempt to download Guided Activities using some versions of Internet Explorer.

Using keyboard shortcuts

Many frequently used commands have been assigned *keyboard shortcuts*. Instead of clicking menus or Guided Activities buttons to apply a command, you can press just one or two keys on your keyboard. For example, if you want to open the Cursors dialog box to change the on-screen appearance of your cursor, you can choose File⇨Preferences⇨Cursors. Or, if you're using a PC, you can press the Ctrl key along with the K key. On a Mac, you press ⌘ and K.

The available keyboard shortcuts are listed in the menus, to the right of the corresponding command. I also include shortcuts when I give you instructions in this book. I list the PC shortcut first, followed by the Mac shortcut in parentheses, like so: "Press Ctrl+K (⌘+K on the Mac)." For a list of my favorite shortcuts all in one place, flip to the Cheat Sheet at the front of this book and also to Chapter 16.

In most cases, "translating" a PC shortcut to a Mac shortcut or vice versa is a simple matter of swapping the Ctrl and Alt keys on a PC for the ⌘ and Option keys on a Mac.

Pulling Out of the Driveway:
Opening Images

Opening images in PhotoDeluxe is a fairly straightforward process, which is covered from several different angles in upcoming sections. But a few aspects of working with images in PhotoDeluxe may cause you some confusion, especially if you've used other image editors:

✔ PhotoDeluxe can open RGB images only. As explained more thoroughly in Chapter 5, RGB images are images created by mixing red, green, and blue light. (Such images are also said to use the RGB *color model.*) If you need to work on an image that was created using some other color model — CMYK or LAB, for example — you must convert the image to RGB in another program if you want to edit it in PhotoDeluxe. You can read more about color models in Chapter 5.

✔ After you issue the Open File command, PhotoDeluxe determines the image file format (the method used to store the image data on disk). Common file formats for images include TIFF, JPEG, and GIF. These and other formats are explored in Chapter 4.

If the image was saved using any format except the native PhotoDeluxe format, PDD, the program creates a copy of the image, converts the copy to the PDD format, and opens that PDD copy for you to view and edit. The copy is named *Untitled-1* (or *Untitled-2,* or *-3,* depending on how many images you have open).

PhotoDeluxe insists on working on PDD images because the PDD format is optimized to take best advantage of the program's features and to speed up editing operations. But if you're used to other image editors that work with the image file in its original format, the PhotoDeluxe approach can be a little confusing, especially when it comes time to save your work. For more information, read the section "Saving Rules!" in Chapter 4.

✔ PDD images are always 24-bit, 16 million-color images. Even if you open an 8-bit, 256-color or grayscale image, the PDD copy that PhotoDeluxe creates is a full-color image. You have access to all 16 million colors for your painting and editing tools. For more about bit depth and colors, read "How deep are your bits?" in Chapter 3. If you're working with grayscale images, be sure to also review "Playing with Gray" in Chapter 12.

Now that you've survived your initial driver training course, you're ready to pull out of the driveway and onto the image-editing expressway. Well, maybe not the expressway yet — how about exploring that nice farm road outside of town? Come to think of it, maybe we should just do a few spins around the school parking lot and see how you do. We don't want any innocent bystanders to get hurt in the event of a crash, you know. (My, isn't the automobile metaphor holding up nicely?)

Opening the sample images

The PhotoDeluxe CD-ROM includes a slew of sample photographs as well as many clip-art images, which are drawings that have been converted to a format that PhotoDeluxe can open. The program also ships with EasyPhoto, an image browser from Storm Technology, Inc. The image browser enables you to see thumbnail previews of the sample photos and clip-art images before you open them.

Here's how to preview the samples and open them:

1. **Put the PhotoDeluxe CD-ROM in your CD-ROM drive.**

   If your computer's autoplay feature is enabled, the PhotoDeluxe installation program may overtake your screen. Press the Esc key on your keyboard to shut the installation program down.

2. **To preview the sample photographs, choose File⇨Open Special⇨Get Sample Photo.**

   PhotoDeluxe displays thumbnail previews of the sample photographs inside an EasyPhoto browser window, as shown in the middle of Figure 1-4.

Browser windows

Figure 1-4:
The
EasyPhoto
browser
enables you
to preview
the sample
images and
clip art.

3. **To preview the sample clip art, choose File⇨Open Special⇨Clip Art.**

Or, for a quicker approach, press Ctrl+\ (⌘+\ on the Mac).

PhotoDeluxe opens a second EasyPhoto browser window displaying available clip-art images, as shown at the bottom of the screen in Figure 1-4. Figure 1-5 offers a close-up view of the browser window.

4. **Find just the right image.**

Scroll box

Title bar   Category tab   Click to scroll categories

Figure 1-5:
A closer
look at the
EasyPhoto
browser
window.

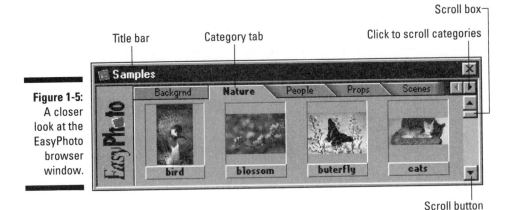

Scroll button

The images are organized into categories: People, Animals, and so on. You may see different categories than those shown in Figure 1-5 depending on what version of the program you use.

Drag the scroll box or click the scroll buttons on the right side of the browser window to see images in the current category. Click the tabs at the top of the window to display other categories. And click the scroll arrows in the top-right corner of the window to display more categories. (If the scroll arrows are grayed out, all available categories are currently visible.)

In Windows, you can enlarge or shrink the EasyPhoto active window by placing your cursor over a corner of the window. When your cursor changes into a two-headed arrow, drag to resize the window.

On a Mac, resize the window by dragging the resize box in the lower-right corner of the window, just as you do any Macintosh window. Click the box in the upper-right corner of the browser window — known as the zoom box in some circles — to expand and collapse the window.

5. **Double-click the image that you want to open.**

Or just drag the image onto an empty spot in the image-editing area. PhotoDeluxe opens the image, which may be hidden behind the EasyPhoto window. To close the browser window, click the window close button. Or drag the window by its title bar to move it out of the way.

If you want to add a sample photo or piece of clip art to an existing image, just drag the thumbnail from the EasyPhoto browser onto the existing image. The sample art is pasted onto your image as a separate layer. You can find out more about working with layers in Chapter 10.

Opening images in an EasyPhoto gallery

You can also use EasyPhoto to store thumbnails of your own images so that you can preview them just as you preview the PhotoDeluxe samples. To find out how to add your own thumbnails to EasyPhoto, travel to "A Few EasyPhoto Tricks" in Chapter 4.

To preview your personal thumbnails, choose File➪My Photos➪Show My Photos. The EasyPhoto browser window opens, this time containing any thumbnails that you created as well as some for the PhotoDeluxe samples. You can browse through your thumbnails, as explained in the preceding section. Double-click the image you want to open or drag the image into the editing window.

To display a bit of information about the image, including the image file size and the exact filename, Windows users can press and hold on the image title in the EasyPhoto gallery, as illustrated in Figure 1-6. Mac users can display the same information by simply placing the mouse cursor over the title — you don't need to click. On either platform, you can also display the information by choosing File➪My Photos➪Get Photo Information. Chapter 4 offers details about how to add this kind of information to your thumbnails. You can use this same tip in any EasyPhoto browser window, by the way.

Figure 1-6:
Press and hold on the image name to display details about the image file.

Opening images directly from disk

If you know the exact name and location of the image file that you want to open, you don't have to bother with the EasyPhoto browser. You can open the image file more efficiently by following these steps:

1. **Choose File➪Open File.**

   Or press Ctrl+O (the letter *oh,* not zero) on a PC. On a Mac, press ⌘+O.

   PhotoDeluxe responds by displaying the Open dialog box. Figure 1-7 shows the dialog box as it appears in Windows 95. If you're using the Mac, the dialog box offers similar controls but looks a little different. Figure 1-8 shows the Macintosh version of the dialog box.

2. **Find the file that you want to open.**

   In Windows, choose a drive name in the Look In drop-down list to display the contents of the drive inside the file list box. For example, to see all the folders on your C drive, select that drive from the Look In drop-down list. Double-click a folder in the file list box to display the contents of that folder. Click the Up One Level button (labeled in Figure 1-7) to move up one level in the folder/drive hierarchy. Be sure to select All Formats From The Files Of Type drop-down list to display all available files in the file list box.

   On a Mac, choose the folder or drive from the Folder bar (labeled in Figure 1-8).

3. **Click the filename in the file list box.**

File list box   Up One Level

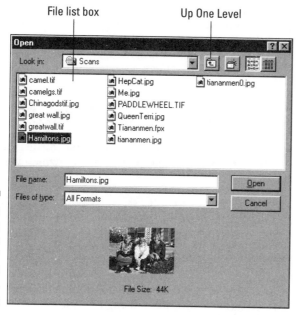

Figure 1-7:
The Open
dialog box
for
Windows
95.

Folder bar

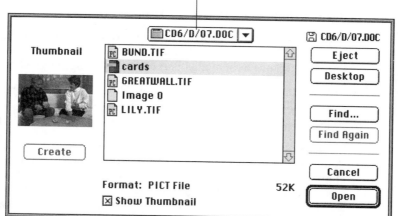

Figure 1-8:
The Open
dialog box
on a
Macintosh.

If you previously opened and saved the image in PhotoDeluxe,
PhotoDeluxe shows you a preview of the image inside the dialog box. (On
a Mac, you must have Apple's QuickTime extension loaded. Additionally,
thumbnails are not displayed for images saved in some file formats.)

4. Click the Open button.

Or double-click the filename.

The Open dialog box used in PhotoDeluxe is the same one used in most PC and Mac programs. If you need more help understanding how to navigate this dialog box, grab a copy of *Windows 95 For Dummies* or *Windows 98 For Dummies,* both by Andy Rathbone, or *Macs For Dummies,* 2nd Edition, by David Pogue (IDG Books Worldwide, Inc.).

Scanning images into PhotoDeluxe

If you have a scanner hooked up to your computer, you can scan an image directly into PhotoDeluxe. The steps vary depending on which version of the program you use.

For recommendations on the input resolution setting to use when you scan images, read "Input Resolution" in Chapter 3.

Scanning in Version 2

The following steps explain how to scan for the first time inside PhotoDeluxe Version 2 (the steps for scanning in the Business Edition and Version 3 are provided later). In this case, using the Guided Activities is the quickest route to success:

1. **Click the Get Photo button and then click the Get Photo tab.**

2. **Click the bottom portion of the Scanners button.**

   Click the down-pointing arrow at the bottom of the button. PhotoDeluxe opens a dialog box that asks you to specify your scanning source. Choose the option recommended by your scanner manual and click OK.

   After you scan the first time, you can skip this step unless you need to select a different scanning source for some reason.

3. **Click the top portion of the Scanners button.**

   If you're working your way through this book in sequential order — that is, if you've been following along with all the steps so far in this chapter — you may at this point encounter something called a Clue Card. Clue Cards are little pop-up windows that offer words of advice. Chapter 2 discusses these entities in more detail, but for now, just click the close button on the Clue Card window to put it away.

   PhotoDeluxe first opens the EasyPhoto browser window for your personal image gallery, discussed earlier in this chapter, in "Opening images in an EasyPhoto gallery." Then it launches your scanner software. You can now scan your image as described in your scanner manual.

4. **Name your image.**

   PhotoDeluxe displays a dialog box asking you to name your new image. Enter the name and click OK.

Your scanned image appears in the EasyPhoto browser on the Acquire tab and is stored on disk in the PhotoDeluxe/EZPhoto/Photo folder. To open the image, double-click its thumbnail in the EasyPhoto browser. (With some scanners, you may need to close the scanner software first.)

The scanned image is saved to disk in the JPEG format, and JPEG compression is applied in the process. Depending on how you plan to use your image, you may not want to apply JPEG compression (see "JPEG: the incredible shrinking format" in Chapter 4 for details). If so, don't scan directly into PhotoDeluxe. Instead, use your scanner software to scan the image to your hard disk and then open the file inside PhotoDeluxe as usual.

After you select your scanner source for the first time, as described in the steps, you can bypass the Guided Activities and simply choose File⇨Open Special⇨Scan Photo.

Scanning in the Business Edition

If you're using the Business Edition, the scanning process works a little differently — and better, in my humble opinion. Here's the drill:

1. **Click the Get & Fix Photo button.**

2. **Click the Get Photo tab.**

   A row of buttons appears.

3. **Click the bottom portion of the Scanners button.**

   PhotoDeluxe opens a dialog box that asks you to specify your scanning source. Choose the option recommended by your scanner manual and click OK.

   You only have to take this step the first time you scan inside PhotoDeluxe or when you need to select a different scanning source.

4. **Click the top portion of the Scanners button.**

   The Guided Activities panel changes and advises you that you can scan by using either your scanner's own software or the PhotoDeluxe scanning wizard. I suggest that you do the former because the scanner's software usually gives you more control over your scanning options. But you may want to try the wizard to see for yourself.

5. **Click the Mode tab.**

   To scan using your scanner software, click the Custom button. Your scanner software launches; scan as usual. To use the PhotoDeluxe wizard, click the Guided button and then work your way through the steps as explained in "Trying out the Guided Activities," earlier in this chapter.

Whichever option you choose, your scanned image appears inside a PhotoDeluxe image window. Be sure to save the image directly to disk before you do anything else (see Chapter 4 for the how-to's), because PhotoDeluxe doesn't save the image for you during the scanning process as it does in Version 2.

After you identify your scanner source, you don't have to keep using the Guided Activities to scan using your scanner's own software. You can simply choose File⇨Open Special⇨Scan Photo.

Scanning in Version 3

Version 3 users follow yet another procedure for scanning:

1. **Click the Get & Fix Photo button.**

2. **Click the Get Photo icon.**

   A drop-down menu appears.

3. **Click the Scanners option.**

   The Guided Activities area changes to display several panels related to scanning.

4. **Click the Scanner tab.**

5. **Click the Choose Scanner icon.**

   A dialog box appears, listing all the input sources installed in your computer. Select the option that your scanner manual recommends.

6. **Click the Mode tab.**

   The Mode tab contains two options. The Guided option launches a PhotoDeluxe scanning wizard. I recommend that you choose the Custom option instead, which enables you to scan using your scanner's own software. But you may want to try the Guided option if you're not fond of your own scanning software or have poor results with the Custom option.

7. **Click the Custom icon.**

   PhotoDeluxe fires up your scanner software. Scan the image as you normally do.

   The scanned image appears inside a PhotoDeluxe image window.

8. **Click the Done tab.**

   Don't forget to save your image right away. The scanned image is temporary until you save it to disk. (Chapter 4 contains file-saving information.)

After you scan for the first time, you can skip the step of choosing your scanner unless you need to change the scanner setting. You can initiate a scan by simply clicking the Custom icon or choosing File⇨Open Special⇨ Scan Photo.

Opening a Photo CD image

Images stored on CD-ROM are frequently saved in the Kodak Photo CD format. You may encounter the Photo CD format if you buy an image collection from a stock photo agency, such as Digital Stock, or have your own images scanned to CD at a professional image-processing lab.

As discussed in more detail in Chapter 3, the Photo CD format stores the same image at several different pixel dimensions (number of pixels wide by number of pixels tall) to give users the choice of working with very small or very large versions of the picture. When you open the image file, you specify which size you want to use.

To open a Photo CD image, press Ctrl+O (⌘+O on the Mac) or choose File⇨File Open. You see the standard Open dialog box, discussed in the section "Opening images directly from disk," earlier in this chapter. Track down your file in the normal fashion, click it, and click Open. PhotoDeluxe shows you a dialog box similar to the one shown in Figure 1-9.

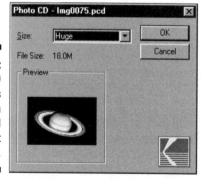

Figure 1-9: Photo CD images come in several different sizes.

Select the image size that you want to use from the Size drop-down list. Your choices are Tiny, Small, Default, Large, and Huge, which translate to the five standard sizes of Photo CD images. The respective pixel dimensions and file sizes for each option are listed in Table 1-1. For an explanation of this pixel stuff, including recommendations on which size option is appropriate for your project, head for Chapter 3. Note that you can't open the ultra-high-resolution image size provided on a Kodak Pro Photo CD (4096 x 6144 ppi).

Table 1-1	Photo CD Image Sizes		
Official Name	*PhotoDeluxe Name*	*Pixel Dimensions*	*File Size*
Base/16	Tiny	192 x 128	72K
Base/4	Small	384 x 256	288K
Base	Default	768 x 512	1.13MB
4 Base	Large	1536 x 1024	4.5MB
16 Base	Huge	3072 x 2048	18MB

Opening a FlashPix image

PhotoDeluxe can also open images stored in the new FlashPix file format, which is described in Chapter 4. Like the Photo CD format, the FlashPix format stores the same image at several different image sizes. The different versions are stacked in a sort of pyramid inside the file, with the largest version sitting at the bottom of the pyramid.

To open a FlashPix image, follow the steps outlined in "Opening images directly from disk," earlier in this chapter. After you click the Open button inside the Open dialog box, PhotoDeluxe asks you which image size you want to access. At least, that's the case in Version 2. The program makes the choice for you in Version 3 and the Business Edition.

Why the change? Well, the problem is that if you open and edit the smallest version of the image and then resave the image under its original name, you wipe out the larger versions of the image. When you save the image, PhotoDeluxe rebuilds the FlashPix pyramid, using the open image as the bottom layer in the stack. Should you ever need the image at a larger size, you're sunk.

(The same crisis can't occur with Photo CD images, because you can't save to the Photo CD format. So after you open and edit a Photo CD image, you're forced to save the image as a new file, using a different image format. The original image always remains intact.)

If you're using Version 2, feel free to open the image at the size that best fits your project (see "Input Resolution," Chapter 2 for more information.) Ignore the Advanced options: Stick with the default settings. But be careful to save the image under a new name when you're done editing; you may want the image at its largest size some day.

In the Business Edition and Version 3, PhotoDeluxe always opens the image at the largest size, so you don't have to worry about screwing up your image. Of course, if you resample your image (as discussed in Chapter 3) and you want to retain a copy at the original size, you must give the edited version a new name when you save the file.

Creating an image from scratch

PhotoDeluxe, like other image editors, is designed primarily for editing existing images. The program doesn't offer many tools for painting an image from scratch because most folks don't have the need — or patience — for that kind of project. If you want to create a logo or some other piece of art from scratch, you're better off using a drawing program such as CorelDraw or Adobe Illustrator. (Read the sidebar "Can I edit drawings in PhotoDeluxe?" in Chapter 3 for more information on why drawing programs are typically better than image-editing programs for creating simple graphics.)

But on occasion, you may want to start with a blank image canvas. To do so, choose File⇨New or press Ctrl+N (⌘+N on the Mac). PhotoDeluxe displays the New dialog box, shown in Figure 1-10. Here you can set the size and resolution of your new image. The Width, Height, and Resolution options work just as they do inside the Photo Size dialog box, which is covered fully in Chapter 3.

Figure 1-10:
Create a
blank
canvas via
the New
dialog box.

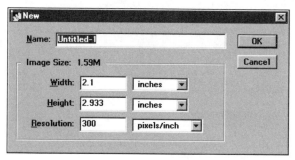

Touring the Image Window

Regardless of which path you follow to open an image, the image appears inside its very own image window. Figure 1-11 gives you a peek at the image window as it appears in Windows in Version 2; the image window looks almost exactly the same in the other Windows editions. Figure 1-12 presents the Macintosh version of the image window.

The following list covers what you need to know about working with an image window. If you're an old hand at this computing business, you may recognize most of the controls in the image window.

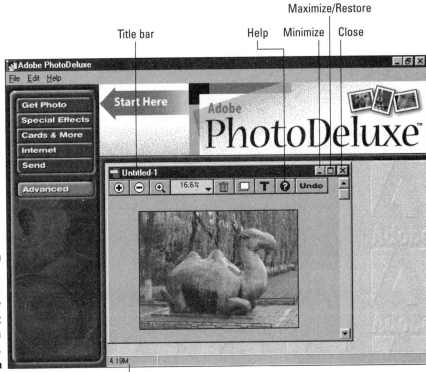

Title bar

Help Minimize Close

Maximize/Restore

File Information box

Figure 1-11:
The image
window
as it
appears in
Windows 95.

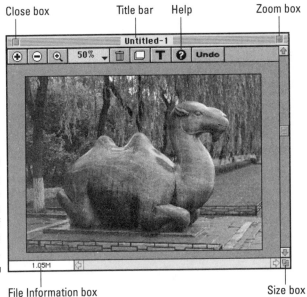

Close box Title bar Help Zoom box

Figure 1-12:
The
Macintosh
version of
the image
window.

File Information box Size box

✔ The title bar displays the name of the image. Until you save the image for the first time in the PhotoDeluxe file format (PDD), as explained in Chapter 4, PhotoDeluxe assigns the image a meaningless name like *Untitled-1*.

✔ Drag the title bar to move the image window.

✔ You can shrink or enlarge the size of the image window just as you can any program window. If you're a Windows user, click the Minimize button (labeled in Figure 1-11) to reduce the window so that just the title bar is visible. The Minimize button changes to display two little boxes. Click the button again to return the window to its former size.

To enlarge the window so that it fills all the available space on the PhotoDeluxe screen, click the Maximize/Restore button (labeled in the figure). To reduce the window to its former size, click the button again.

You can also resize the window by placing your cursor over a corner of the window until it becomes a two-headed arrow and then dragging.

On a Mac, drag the size box in the lower-right corner of the window (labeled in Figure 1-12) to enlarge or reduce the window. Click the zoom box to resize the window so that it more closely matches the size of the image display. Click the zoom box again to restore the window to its former size.

✔ The File Information box shows you how much RAM your image is using. In Windows, the box is located at the bottom of the program window; on a Mac, it appears at the bottom of the image window. For more about this feature, read "The Top-Secret Image Information Box" in Chapter 3.

✔ In Version 3, the File Information box also displays the current print dimensions of the image — that is, the size at which the image will print if you choose the Print command.

✔ To close an image, click the Close button. PhotoDeluxe may ask whether you want to save the image before you close. For more information about saving images, read Chapter 4. Alternatively, you can choose File⇨Close or press Ctrl+W (⌘+W on a Mac).

✔ Like just about every other program on the planet, PhotoDeluxe offers a built-in Help system, which is quite good compared to those offered by many other programs. You can fire up the Help system by clicking the Help button in the image window, labeled in Figures 1-11 and 1-12. Alternatively, you can use the commands on the Help menu in Windows or choose the Help command from the Apple menu on a Mac.

Of course, with this book at your side, you're not likely to need the Help system, but you may find it handy if you're away from home and didn't tote the book along with you. If you need an explanation of how to find information in the Help system, choose Help⇨How to Use Help in Windows. On a Mac, open the Help system and then display the Help, How to Use item from the Index tab of the help window.

Zooming in and out

When you first open an image, PhotoDeluxe displays the image at the largest size at which the entire image fits on-screen. To zoom in or out on your image, you can use the following techniques:

✔ The value in the Zoom menu, labeled in Figure 1-13, reflects the current level of magnification. At 100 percent, one screen pixel is used to display one image pixel. For an explanation of this pixel stuff, check out Chapter 3.

✔ Remember that the on-screen size of the image at 100 percent is *not* equal to the printed size of your image unless you set the image resolution in the Photo Size dialog box to match the resolution of your monitor. Again, check out Chapter 3 for more information about screen resolution, image resolution, and image size.

✔ To zoom in on your image, choose a value higher than 100 percent from the Zoom menu or click the Zoom In button, labeled in Figure 1-13.

✔ To zoom out, choose a value lower than 100 percent from the Zoom menu or click the Zoom Out button, also labeled in the figure.

Figure 1-13: PhotoDeluxe offers you several different ways to zoom in and out on your image.

✔ If you want to zoom in on a specific portion of your image, click the Zoom tool. (Yep, that one's labeled in Figure 1-13, too.) Then drag around the area you want to magnify. As you move the mouse, a dotted outline, known as a *marquee,* appears to indicate the scope of your drag, as shown in Figure 1-13. After you release the mouse button, PhotoDeluxe fills the image window with the portion of your image that was enclosed in the marquee.

✔ Tired of clicking or dragging to zoom? Here's an alternative: To zoom in, press the Ctrl key along with the plus key on your keyboard. (On a Mac, press ⌘ instead of Ctrl.) To zoom out, press Ctrl (or ⌘) along with the minus key. You can use the plus and minus keys either on your numeric keypad or the ones that lie above all your letter keys. If you do the latter, you may think that you need to press Shift to make the zoom-in shortcut work, because you ordinarily need to press Shift to access the plus symbol. In the wonderful world of Adobe shortcuts, though, the Shift key isn't required.

Viewing hidden areas of the image

When you zoom in on an image or work with a very large image, portions of the image may be hidden from view. To scroll the display so that you can see the hidden areas, you can do any of the following:

✔ Drag the scroll boxes along the bottom and right side of the window, labeled in Figure 1-13.

✔ To scroll in smaller increments, click the scroll arrows, also labeled in the figure.

✔ Using the scroll boxes and arrows can be a little clumsy. To move quickly to a certain part of your image, try this method instead: Place your mouse cursor inside the image window and then press and hold the spacebar on your keyboard. The cursor turns into a little hand, which is officially known as the Hand tool. While keeping the spacebar depressed, drag inside your image. The hand tugs at your image, pulling the area that you want to see into view.

Changing the image orientation

If your image opens up lying on its side, you can rotate it to the proper orientation by choosing Orientation⇨Rotate Right or Orientation⇨Rotate Left, depending on which way you want to spin the picture.

Should you need to flip the image from left to right or top to bottom, choose the Flip Horizontal or Flip Vertical commands, respectively. Both commands are also found on the Orientation menu.

If you find yourself rotating or flipping lots of images, you may want to commit these keyboard shortcuts to memory:

✔ Rotate Left: Ctrl+< (⌘+< on a Mac)

✔ Rotate Right: Ctrl+> (⌘+>)

✔ Flip Horizontal: Ctrl+[(⌘+[ )

✔ Flip Vertical: Ctrl+] (⌘=])

For the first two shortcuts to work, you must press the Shift key (the greater than and less than symbols are accessible by pressing the comma and period keys along with the Shift key).

The Free Rotate command, by the way, displays the same rotate handles you get when you click an image or selection with the Object Selection tool. For more information on this feature, make your way to Chapter 8.

Communicating with a Dialog Box

When you choose some PhotoDeluxe commands, the program responds by displaying a dialog box. Inside the dialog box, you can specify how you want PhotoDeluxe to apply that command.

For the most part, a PhotoDeluxe dialog box works like any other dialog box. But some PhotoDeluxe dialog boxes, like the one shown in Figure 1-14, offer special features that you can use to make your editing easier.

Preview area

Hand cursor   Option box

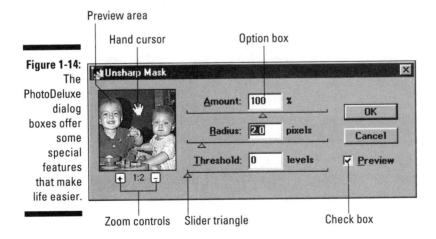

Figure 1-14: The PhotoDeluxe dialog boxes offer some special features that make life easier.

Zoom controls   Slider triangle   Check box

The following list offers the insider's guide to these dialog boxes:

✔ In many cases, you can change the value for a particular option in several ways. You can drag a slider triangle, labeled in Figure 1-14, or you can double-click the corresponding option box and type in a value.

After you double-click the option box to make it active, you press the up- or down-arrow keys to raise or lower the value by 1, .1, or .001 (depending on the values permitted for the option). Press Shift plus the up- or down-arrow key to raise or lower the value by 10, 1, or .1 (again, depending on the parameters of the particular value). All of that means that if the option allows only whole number values, pressing the key raises or lowers the value by 1. If the option allows values in tenths of a whole number — for example, 12.1, the key press changes the value by one tenth. And so on.

✔ Click a check box to turn the corresponding option on or off. A check mark or X in the box means that the option is turned on.

✔ The preview area shows you how the values you set will affect your image. If you select the Preview check box in the lower-right corner of the dialog box, you can also see the effects of your changes in the main image window. A blinking line appears underneath the check box while PhotoDeluxe updates the previews.

To magnify or reduce the view shown in the dialog box, click the zoom controls beneath the preview area. Click the plus button to zoom in and the minus button to zoom out.

You can use the two preview options to display both a close-up view and a big-picture view at the same time. Before you open the dialog box, zoom out on your image so that you can see the entire picture in the image window. Then magnify the view shown in the dialog box to see small details.

✔ To display a different portion of your image in the preview area, move your cursor into the preview. The cursor changes into the Hand cursor, as shown in Figure 1-14. Drag to pull a hidden area of the image into view.

✔ Alternatively, move your cursor into the image window. The cursor takes on a square shape. Click with the cursor to display the area you click inside the dialog box.

✔ To compare how the image looks now and how it will look if you apply the command, click the Preview check box and watch the image window. With the check box off, you see the "before" version of the image; with the check box on, you see the "after" version.

Another way to accomplish the same thing is to place the cursor in the image preview inside the dialog box. Press and hold on the preview to display the "before" view. Let up on the mouse button to see the "after" view.

> ✔ If you Alt+click the Cancel button, it transforms itself into a Reset button. (Option+click the Cancel button on a Mac.) You can then click the Reset button to return all values to the settings that were in place when you first opened the dialog box.

Parking PhotoDeluxe

To shut down PhotoDeluxe, choose File⇨Exit on a PC and File⇨Quit on a Mac. For even quicker results, press Ctrl+Q on a PC and ⌘+Q on a Mac. And for the fastest exit possible, click the Close button (the one marked with an X) in the upper-right corner of the program window if you're using Windows.

If you have an image open and you haven't yet saved it to disk in the PhotoDeluxe file format (PDD), PhotoDeluxe asks whether you want to do so. If you do, click Yes and follow the saving instructions outlined in Chapter 4. If you don't, click No and say good riddance to bad rubbish.

Before PhotoDeluxe curtsies and exits the room for good, it may tell you that the Clipboard contains image data and ask whether you want that data to be available to other programs. For more about this tantalizing offer, read "Exploring the Clipboard (or Not)" in Chapter 2. But in short, if you want to paste the Clipboard contents into a document that you're creating in another program, click the Yes button when PhotoDeluxe prompts you. Otherwise, click No.

Chapter 2
Customizing Your Darkroom

· ·

In This Chapter

▶ Displaying more than one image on-screen at a time

▶ Changing the size and shape of your cursor

▶Turning the rulers on and off

▶ Setting your preferred unit of measurement

▶ Changing the image canvas color and size

▶ Itching the scratch disk and managing memory

▶ Getting rid of Clue Cards and the Assistant Drawer

▶ Setting other obscure preferences

· ·

*A*lmost every computer program these days gives you the option of customizing the program interface to suit your own taste. PhotoDeluxe is no exception. You can change several different aspects of how the program looks and behaves, if you like.

This chapter explains all your options and offers advice on which ones are best in certain situations. Don't you wish it were this easy to make the rest of the world conform to your personal whims?

Opening Multiple Images at a Time

By default, PhotoDeluxe Version 2 restricts you from having more than one image open at a time. If you want to open more than one image, the fix is easy, though: Just choose File➪Preferences➪Allow Multiple Document Windows. Now you can keep as many as 30 images at a time. Remember that each open image makes additional demands on your system's resources.

The Business Edition and Version 3 automatically enable you to open as many images as you want at a time. So you don't find the Allow Multiple Document Windows on your Preferences submenu.

In Windows, you can open several images with only one trip to the Open dialog box (explored in Chapter 1). Choose File⇨Open File, click the first image that you want to open, Ctrl+click on any additional images you want to open, and then click Open.

Working with multiple image windows is just like dealing with multiple document windows in any other program. Here's a refresher course:

- ✔ To see all your open images side by side in Windows, choose Window⇨Tile. To stack the image windows vertically, choose Window⇨Cascade. (If you don't see a Window menu, choose File⇨Preferences⇨Long Menus, as discussed in Chapter 1.

- ✔ On a Mac, drag the title bars of the image windows to arrange the windows on-screen.

- ✔ You can also rearrange windows by dragging the title bars in Windows, too.

- ✔ Only one image is active — that is, affected by your edits — at a time. The title bars on the inactive image windows are grayed out (dimmed). In Figure 2-1, for example, the image Untitled-1 is active; image Untitled-2 is inactive.

Thumbnails

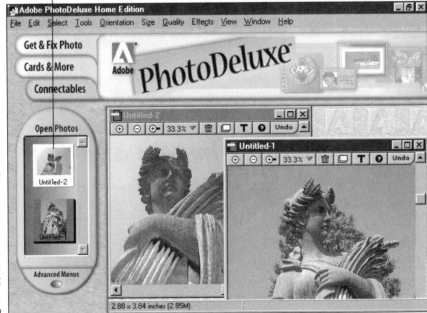

Figure 2-1: You can have more than one image open, but only one is active at a time.

✔ To make an image become the active image, click anywhere on its image window. Or choose the image name from the bottom of the Window menu.

 ✔ In Version 3, the Open Photos area on the left side of the image window displays a thumbnail view of every open image, as shown in Figure 2-1. You can double-click on a thumbnail to make that image the active image. This feature comes in handy when you have one of the open windows maximized so that the other open windows aren't visible to click.

✔ For the scoop on how to resize windows, see Chapter 1.

✔ To close all open windows with one swift motion on a PC, choose Window➪Close All.

 The most common reason to have multiple images open at the same time is to cut and paste elements from one image into another. If you're working on this type of project and your computer isn't sufficiently powered to enable you to have several images open at once, you may want to take advantage of the Hold Photo feature, discussed next. This feature is available in Version 2 and the Business Edition; the Open Photos area replaces the Hold Photo feature in Version 3.

Putting Images on Hold

 If you use Version 3, you can skip this section. The Hold Photo feature has been eliminated in Version 3. The Open Photos feature, discussed in the preceding section, replaces Hold Photo.

For those Version 2 and Business Edition users whose system memory isn't sufficient to handle more than one open image at a time, PhotoDeluxe provides a Hold Photo command. Essentially, Hold Photo enables you to have quick access to several images without tying up too much of your computer's resources. (You can take advantage of this option whether or not you have the Version 2 Allow Multiple Document Windows feature enabled.) Certain Guided Activities projects, described in Chapter 1, involve the Hold Photo command as well.

The Hold Photo command makes a copy of the on-screen image, stores the image on disk, and displays a thumbnail of the image in the Hold Photo window, on the left side of the program window, as shown in Figure 2-2.

Figure 2-2:
Drag
images
from the
Hold Photo
window
into the
image
window to
edit them.

Hold Photo window

After you put an image on hold, you can retrieve the image as follows:

- ✔ If you want to copy the Hold Photo image into an existing image, drag the thumbnail into the image window. Your Hold Photo image is automatically resized to match the open image.

  Your Hold Photo image is placed on a separate layer from the open image. For more about working with image layers, read Chapter 10.

- ✔ To open the Hold Photo image by itself, double-click the thumbnail. You can also drag the thumbnail into an empty spot in the editing workspace — that is, anywhere but inside another image window.

- ✔ Click the scroll arrows on the right side of the Hold Photo window to browse through all the images that you've put on hold.

To send an image to the Hold Photo window, choose File➪Send To➪ Hold Photo. Or press Ctrl+H (⌘+H on a Mac). A dialog box appears, listing the names of all the photos currently on hold. Enter a name for your image in the File Name option box and click OK if you're using Windows or Save if you're working on a Mac. PhotoDeluxe stores the copy of your image in the PhotoDeluxe/Hold folder and displays the thumbnail in the Hold Photo window.

After you're done working with an image, delete the image from the Hold folder to free up hard disk space. In fact, if you have too many images in the folder, PhotoDeluxe gently suggests that you do some housecleaning.

To delete an image from the Hold folder, click the image thumbnail and press Delete. You don't delete your original image file — just the copy that PhotoDeluxe stored in the Hold folder. PhotoDeluxe may ask you whether you're sure you want to delete the image; go ahead and confirm your decision.

If you delete all images from the folder, the Hold Photo window disappears.

Changing the Cursor Style

PhotoDeluxe offers you a choice of cursor designs, which you select in the Cursors dialog box, shown in Figure 2-3. To open the dialog box, press Ctrl+K (⌘+K on a Mac). Or, if you like doing things the long way, choose File⇨Preferences⇨Cursors.

Figure 2-3: Choices you make here determine how your cursor looks.

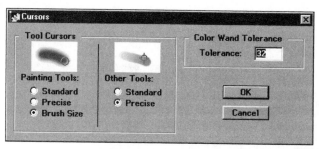

The Painting Tools options affect the Eraser, Line, Brush, Clone, and Smudge tools; the Other Tools options control the Paint Bucket tool and all the selection tools. The options result in different sizes and shapes of cursors, as follows:

✔ **Standard:** If you click this option, your cursor resembles a tiny replica of the tool. If you select the Brush tool, for example, your cursor looks like a paintbrush. Folks who tend to forget what tool they're using may find this option helpful.

✔ **Precise:** Choose this option, and you get a simple crosshair cursor regardless of what tool you use. The crosshair cursor is best for making precise edits (hence the name), when the larger, standard cursors can obscure your view.

✔ **Brush Size:** Available for the painting tools only, this option results in a round cursor that represents the actual size of the brush you select in the Brushes palette. (Changing brush sizes is discussed in Chapter 8.) When you're using a large brush size, this option helps you get an idea of how much image territory your next swipe of the tool will cover.

You can switch back and forth between some cursor options by pressing the Caps Lock key on your keyboard. If you select the Standard or Brush Size option in the Cursors dialog box, pressing Caps Lock switches you to the Precise (crosshairs) cursor. If you select Precise as the Painting Tools option, Caps Lock turns on the Brush Size cursor when you're working with a painting tool. Turn off Caps Lock to return to the cursor option that you selected in the Cursors dialog box.

Turning Rulers On and Off

You may find it helpful to display rulers in the image window, as shown in Figure 2-4, if you want to place an image element at a specific position in your image — for example, to put a line of text exactly 2 inches from the top of the picture.

Zero point marker   Rulers

Figure 2-4:
Turning on the rulers can help you position elements precisely.

The rulers appear along the left and top sides of the image window when you choose View➪Show Rulers or press Ctrl+R (⌘+R on the Mac). To turn the rulers off, choose View➪Hide Rulers or press Ctrl+R (⌘+R).

If the View menu doesn't appear on your screen, choose File➪Preferences➪ Long menus in Version 2 and the Business Edition. In Version 3, click the Advanced Menus button at the bottom of the Open Photos area.

By default, PhotoDeluxe aligns the rulers so that the zero point is at the top left corner of your image. The *zero point* is the point at which the zero tick mark on the horizontal ruler intersects with the zero tick mark on the vertical ruler. But you can relocate the zero point by dragging the zero point marker, labeled in Figure 2-4. As you drag, dotted lines extend from each ruler to indicate the new position of the zero point, as shown in the figure (I added the arrow for emphasis). When you let up on the mouse button, the rulers reflect the new zero point.

The ruler uses inches as the unit of measurement by default, but you can change the unit by heading for the Unit Preferences dialog box, which is explained just inches from here.

Choosing Your Measuring Stick

Do you prefer to size things up in terms of inches? picas? pixels? PhotoDeluxe, ever so accommodating, offers you all these options and a few more.

Inside the Unit Preferences dialog box, shown in Figure 2-5, you specify the default unit of measurement that PhotoDeluxe uses in the Photo Size and Canvas Size dialog boxes, as well as on the rulers in the image window. To open the dialog box, choose File➪Preferences➪Units.

The following list explains your measuring options:

✔ Choose the unit of measure that you prefer from the Ruler Units drop-down list. If you plan to print most of your images, you probably want

Figure 2-5: Set your preferred unit of measure in this dialog box.

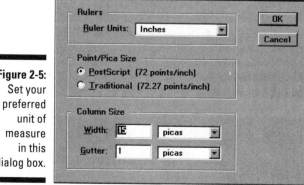

to choose a traditional print measure, such as inches, centimeters, points, or picas. If you're going to create images primarily for on-screen display, though, pixels is a better option, for reasons discussed in Chapter 3.

✔ The Point/Pica Size option tells PhotoDeluxe precisely how big you want your points to be. (Points and picas, by the way, are units of measure used in the print publishing business. Twelve points equal 1 pica, just as 12 inches equal 1 foot.)

The old-world school of publishing says that 72.27 points equal 1 inch. But the new-world school of publishing — that is, the one that uses PostScript printing devices — considers a point to be exactly $1/72$ inch. (Dealing with that extra 0.27 of a point is just too cumbersome, you know.) If you're printing to a PostScript device, make sure that the PostScript option in the Unit Preferences dialog box is selected. Otherwise, use whatever points-to-inches conversion makes you feel good about yourself.

✔ The Column Size options may be useful if you regularly create images for use in a newsletter or other publication that features a columnar layout. You can size your images to match precisely the width of a column (or to span several columns, if you really want to get wild and crazy).

First, specify the width of the column in the Width option box. Enter the width of the gutter (the space between columns) in the Gutter option box. You can choose from several units of measurement from the adjacent drop-down lists.

When sizing your image inside the Photo Size dialog box, as explained in Chapter 3, choose Columns as the unit of measurement for the Width option. Enter the number of columns that you want the image to occupy as the Width value. For example, if you want the image to stretch across three columns, enter 3 as the Width value. You can also use the same approach when sizing your image canvas in the Canvas Size dialog box, covered in Chapter 6, or creating a new image via the New dialog box, explained in Chapter 1.

Exporting the Clipboard

One of the more obscure options on the File⇨Preferences submenu is Export Clipboard. This option, when turned on, enables you to copy and paste an image or part of an image from PhotoDeluxe into another program.

When you use the Cut or Copy commands discussed in Chapter 6, the image data that you copy or cut is sent to the Clipboard, a temporary holding tank for data. If the Export Clipboard option is turned off, the contents of the Clipboard are deleted when you shut down PhotoDeluxe. When the option is turned on, the image data is converted into a format that enables you to paste the copied or cut image into a document or graphic that you're creating in another program. On a Mac, the process happens automatically; in Windows, you're asked whether you want the Clipboard information to be retained, even though you have the Export Clipboard option turned on.

I recommend that you leave the option turned on, especially if you use Windows and switch back and forth between applications frequently. Turning off the Export Clipboard option can speed things up a bit, however, because the computer doesn't have to process the Clipboard information.

Export Clipboard is one of those options that you toggle on and off simply by clicking the option name in the menu. A check mark next to the option name means that the feature is turned on.

Getting Helpful Hints

When you first install and start PhotoDeluxe, little windows of helpful information pop up out of nowhere every so often. In Version 2 and the Business Edition, the pop-up advice appears inside little windows known as Clue Cards, shown in Figure 2-6.

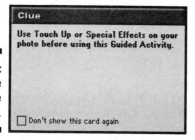

Figure 2-6:
An example
of a Clue
Card.

After you read the insights offered in the box, if you decide that you never want to see that particular piece of information again, click the Don't Show This Card Again check box. Then click anywhere inside the program window to send the Clue Card packing. If you don't click the Don't Show This Card Again box, the card reappears whenever PhotoDeluxe deems appropriate.

In Version 3, the pop-up advice feature is called the Assistant Drawer because the information slides out from the right side of the program window like a file drawer, as shown in Figure 2-7. Click anywhere on the Assistant Drawer thingie to slide the drawer back into its digital filing cabinet.

When the Clue Cards become tiresome, choose File⇨Preferences⇨Turn Off All Clue Cards to prevent any more from popping up. Choose Turn On All Clue Cards if you miss the little guys and want them back. In Version 3, toggle the File⇨Preferences⇨Show Assistant Drawer option on and off to display and hide the Assistant Drawer advice. (A check mark next to the option name means that the option is turned on; click the option name to turn the option off.)

Changing the Background Display

Every image in PhotoDeluxe rests atop a transparent background, known as the image *canvas*. Normally, the canvas is completely hidden from view, and you needn't think a thing about it. But when you're creating a photo collage, cutting and pasting the elements of several images together, you may want to enlarge the canvas, as discussed in Chapter 6. When you enlarge the canvas, portions of it may become visible, as in Figure 2-8. In the figure, the gray checkerboard area is the canvas.

By default, the canvas is white. But you can set the canvas to appear as a checkerboard-like grid, as I did in Figure 2-8. Displaying the checkerboard grid can be helpful in some editing projects. For example, if you have an

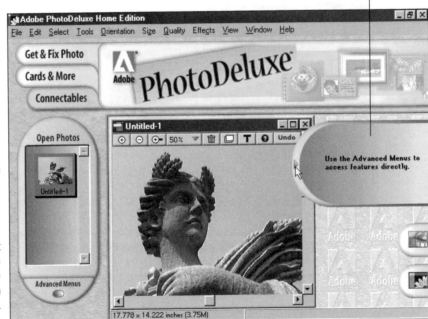

Figure 2-7:
In Version 3, pop-up advice slides out from the side of the program window.

Figure 2-8:
Every image
rests on a
transparent
canvas,
represented
here by
the gray
checkerboard
area.

image with a white border and you enlarge the canvas, you will have a tough time telling where the image ends and the canvas begins if you have the canvas color set to solid white.

Changing the canvas color can also come in handy when you're working on an image that has multiple layers, as discussed in Chapter 10. PhotoDeluxe uses the background pattern that you specify to represent transparent areas of a layer, as well as the image canvas. Again, switching to the checkerboard area makes it easier to distinguish the transparent portions of the image.

The following steps explain how to change the canvas display from the default setting — solid white — to a checkerboard pattern:

1. **Choose File⇨Preferences⇨Background.**

   The Background Options dialog box, shown in Figure 2-9, rushes on-screen.

2. **Choose a Grid Size option.**

   Choose Small to make your checkerboard squares, er, small. Choose Medium or Large if you want the squares to be bigger than small. (Aren't you glad you have me to decipher these high-tech options?)

3. **Set your checkerboard colors.**

   You can select one of the predefined color patterns from the Set drop-down list, as I did in Figure 2-9, or you can create a custom pattern. (Fussy, fussy.) Choose Custom from the Set drop-down list and then click one of the color swatches above the drop-down list. PhotoDeluxe

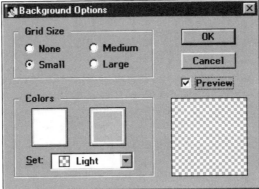

Figure 2-9:
In this
dialog box,
specify how
you want
the canvas
to appear.

opens the Color Picker dialog box, where you can choose a new color using the instructions laid out in Chapter 9. Click the other color swatch to set the second color in the grid.

If you select the Preview option, PhotoDeluxe displays your grid design in your on-screen image as well as in the dialog box. If the dialog box is obscuring the image window, you can drag the dialog box title bar to move the box aside. If you don't check the Preview option, you have to rely on the preview box in the dialog box. The Preview option only controls the image window; the preview in the dialog box is turned on regardless.

   4. Click OK.

To revert to the default solid-white canvas, head back to the Background Options dialog box, select None as your Grid Size option, and then click OK.

Keep in mind that even though the canvas is transparent inside PhotoDeluxe, it appears solid white when you open the image in other programs. For example, if you place the image on a Web page, any visible canvas areas appear white. Ditto for images that you place into a page layout program. If you want the image background (canvas) to have some other color when you export the image, you must fill the empty canvas area with the color, as explained in Chapter 9.

Displaying the Macintosh Desktop

If you're using PhotoDeluxe on a Mac, you can control whether the desktop is visible when you run PhotoDeluxe.

The Show Desktop option, when turned on, displays the desktop around any portions of the screen not occupied by the Guided Activities panel or the image window. This setup can be handy if you frequently need access to desktop elements while you're editing.

To switch between seeing the desktop and not seeing the desktop, choose File⇨Preferences⇨Show Desktop. A check mark next to the option name means that the option is turned on. Click the option name to toggle the option on and off.

Telling PhotoDeluxe Where to Scratch

PhotoDeluxe needs lots of computer memory — known as RAM *(random access memory)* — in order to carry out your image-editing requests. At times, the program needs more RAM than is available, even on computers that have gigantic memory banks. To get around this limitation, PhotoDeluxe uses *virtual memory.*

Despite the intimidating name, virtual memory is nothing more than empty hard drive space. When PhotoDeluxe runs out of memory to store image data, it puts that data temporarily in some empty portion of your computer's hard drive. Just to confuse you thoroughly, PhotoDeluxe (and other image-editing programs) refer to the drive it uses as virtual memory as the *scratch disk.*

To specify what drive you want to use as your scratch disk, choose File⇨ Preferences⇨ Scratch Disks in Version 2 and the Business Edition; choose File⇨Preferences⇨Memory Prefences in Version 3. Choosing the command displays the Memory Preferences dialog box, shown in Figure 2-10, where you can specify what drive you want to use as your scratch disk. (On a Mac, you see only the Scratch Disk options, not the memory options at the bottom of the dialog box.)

Here's a little scratch disk advice:

✔ You have the opportunity to choose both a primary and secondary scratch disk. PhotoDeluxe turns to the secondary scratch disk only if your primary scratch disk is full.

✔ If you have only one hard drive, choose Startup from the Primary drop-down list and choose None from the Secondary drop-down list. Chances are, PhotoDeluxe made these choices automatically for you when you installed the program.

✔ If you have more than one hard drive, choose the drive that offers the best combination of empty space and access speed as your primary scratch disk. You want the computer to be able to read and write

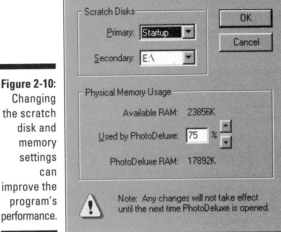

Figure 2-10:
Changing
the scratch
disk and
memory
settings
can
improve the
program's
performance.

information to the disk as quickly as possible to cut down the time
PhotoDeluxe needs to carry out your editing commands.

✔ Note that even if you have only one physical hard drive, it may be
partitioned into several virtual drives on your system. That is, your
system may think that you have several drives, even though you have
only one drive device. For example, my machine has a 4GB hard drive,
but Windows 95 separated those 4GB into three drives named C, E, and
F. Again, select the drive that has the most free space (the speed of the
drives is the same in this case).

✔ In a pinch, Mac users can set a removable drive, such as a Zip drive, to
serve as a scratch disk. But expect your processing speed to suffer
unless the drive is as fast or faster than a standard internal hard drive.

✔ When PhotoDeluxe can't find any empty scratch disk space, it announces that your scratch disk is full and refuses to do anything else
until you free up some disk space. Unfortunately, I can't offer you a
magic bullet for fixing this problem — you simply have to dump some
of the data that's living on your hard drive.

If you used the Copy or Cut commands to put a large image on the
Clipboard, you can sometimes free up a little RAM and get PhotoDeluxe
to work again by replacing the Clipboard contents. The Clipboard, you
see, needs RAM to operate, and the more you put in the Clipboard, the
more required RAM.

Using one of the selection tools explained in Chapter 8, copy a very small selection to the Clipboard, thereby replacing the large, memory-hogging image with the smaller, less-memory-intensive selection. Of course, you can't get the previous contents of the Clipboard back later, so make sure that you don't need them before you take this step.

Boosting Your Memory

If you work with very large image files — or an underpowered computer — PhotoDeluxe may occasionally complain that it doesn't have enough memory to complete certain operations. The following two sections offer a few techniques that you can try in order to placate PhotoDeluxe and get on with your work. But ultimately, you may need to install more memory or be content with smaller images.

Managing a tight memory supply

Your computer, like me, may be short on memory. Keep these tips in mind to get the most out of your available RAM:

✔ **Defragment the computer's memory by restarting your machine.** Each program that you're using consumes a portion of the system's RAM. So if you're having a memory shortage, you simply shut down all the other open programs, right? Maybe, and maybe not.

If you start and shut down several programs during a computer session, the system RAM can become fragmented. Instead of having a large, uninterrupted block of RAM, you have little bits of RAM scattered here and there. PhotoDeluxe requires uninterrupted RAM to do its thing, which is why closing all other programs often doesn't satisfy PhotoDeluxe when it demands more memory.

To correct the situation, close down all programs — including PhotoDeluxe — and restart your computer. Then open PhotoDeluxe again to see whether you've resolved your memory crisis.

✔ **Turn off extensions and background applications.** Even small utilities that run in the background may eat up RAM that PhotoDeluxe needs. To find out whether shutting down your background applications will enable PhotoDeluxe to proceed with your editing project, restart the computer with the applications disabled.

In Windows, hold down the Ctrl key as you restart the computer. This technique starts Windows without opening any of the applications in your StartUp folder.

On a Mac, turn off any nonessential extensions and Control Panels. Keep the QuickTime, Apple Guide, and AppleScript extensions loaded, or the EasyPhoto browser incorporated in PhotoDeluxe doesn't function.

✔ **Merge image layers.** If you're creating a layered image, use the Merge Layers command to flatten all the layers into one, as discussed in Chapter 10. Images with layers require more RAM to process than flattened ones. Of course, you don't want to use this approach unless you're sure that you no longer need the layered version of the image.

Assigning memory to PhotoDeluxe

By default, PhotoDeluxe restricts itself to using only a certain portion of your computer's memory, graciously leaving some RAM untouched for things like, oh, running Windows or the Mac operating system. You have the option of telling PhotoDeluxe that it can use more or less of the available RAM.

In all likelihood, you want to increase the RAM allocation rather than decrease it. But if you're having trouble running other applications at the same time as PhotoDeluxe and your image-editing projects typically involve small images that don't require huge amounts of RAM, you may want to trim back the PhotoDeluxe memory usage. If you do, however, PhotoDeluxe may run more slowly and balk at some memory-intensive commands.

Changing the memory allocation in Windows

You can allot a maximum of 75 percent of the system RAM to PhotoDeluxe. To set the RAM allocation, choose File⇨Preferences⇨Scratch Disks in Version 2 and the Business Edition and File⇨Preferences⇨Memory Preferences in Version 3. PhotoDeluxe unfurls the Memory Preferences dialog box (refer to Figure 2-10). Raise or lower the Used by PhotoDeluxe value by clicking the arrows next to the option box or by typing in a new value. Don't raise the value above 75 percent, or you may degrade the program's performance. Your changes take effect the next time you start PhotoDeluxe.

Assigning RAM on a Mac

Assigning RAM to PhotoDeluxe on a Mac involves some notetaking and number-crunching. Here's the drill:

1. **Shut down PhotoDeluxe and any other applications that are running.**

2. **Choose About The Macintosh from the Apple menu.**

   The resulting dialog box shows you how much total memory you have on your system, how much memory each open program is currently using, and the size of the largest unused block of RAM.

3. **Jot down the Largest Unused Block value.**

4. **Close the dialog box.**

5. **Locate and click the PhotoDeluxe application icon at the Finder level.**

   This is the same icon that you double-click to start the program.

6. **Choose File⇨Get Info.**

   You see the Adobe PhotoDeluxe Info dialog box.

7. **Increase the Preferred Size value.**

   Don't raise the value to more than 90 percent of the value that you wrote down in Step 3. Also, leave the Minimum Size value alone.

8. **Close the Info dialog box.**

Setting the Plug-Ins Directory

Many companies create filters and special-effects routines that work with PhotoDeluxe. Collectively, these add-ons are known as *plug-ins*. When you install plug-ins, the installation program usually asks you where you want to store the plug-ins. Be sure to put any plug-ins in the appropriately named Plug-Ins folder, which is inside the main PhotoDeluxe folder. Otherwise, PhotoDeluxe can't access or run the plug-ins.

If you choose the File⇨Preferences⇨Plug-Ins command in PhotoDeluxe, the program displays a dialog box in which you can specify the location of all your plug-ins. Don't change the location from the default setting (the Plug-Ins folder) unless you actually move your plug-ins to some other folder or drive.

Keep in mind that PhotoDeluxe stores files that are necessary to run many of its own filters and effects in the Plug-Ins folder. So if you decide to move your plug-ins, be sure to move *all* the files in the Plug-Ins folder, not just the third-party add-ons you've installed.

Many, but not all, plug-ins created for Adobe Photoshop also work with PhotoDeluxe. The CD at the back of this book includes demo versions of several Photoshop plug-ins from ULead; these plug-ins cooperate beautifully with PhotoDeluxe and enable you to do some cool tricks, too.

Dumping Your Custom Preferences

If you decide that you want to return all the settings in PhotoDeluxe back to the defaults that were in force when you installed the program, follow these steps:

1. **Shut down PhotoDeluxe.**

2. **Find the program's preferences file.**

   In Windows, fire up Explorer. (Choose Start➪Programs➪Windows Explorer.) Track down the main PhotoDeluxe folder. Unless you changed the default installation settings, you can find the folder in the Program Files folder on your hard drive. Open the PhotoDeluxe folder, which contains a Prefs folder. The PhotoDeluxe preferences file is located inside that Prefs folder; the file is named PD20.PSP in Version 2 and PBE10.PSP in the Business Edition.

   On a Mac, the file is named Adobe PhotoDeluxe 2.0 Prefs. You can find the file in the Preferences folder, which is inside the System Folder.

3. **Delete the file.**

   You heard me — trash the thing.

4. **Restart PhotoDeluxe.**

   The program reappears in its original, untouched state.

Dumping your preferences file is also a good option to try if PhotoDeluxe starts behaving strangely, you start getting a slew of disk error messages, or you can't get the program to launch at all. Sometimes the file gets corrupted and causes problems. Of course, you have to reset all your custom preferences, but doing that is better than not being able to use the program at all, right? Unless, of course, you're looking for a good excuse to skip out on that screwy image-editing project your manager dreamed up while on vacation.

Using Other Version 3 Gizmos

Version 3 comes with a few other options that don't seem to fit logically in any other discussions, so I decided to tack them on here. I'm not sure that decision was logical either, but I was hoping you could cut me a break, seeing as how you're such a forgiving person and all. At any rate, if you're wondering about some of the new Version 3 bells and whistles and you don't find them covered anywhere else, this is the place to be.

Those little icons in the lower-right corner

First, in the lower-right corner of the image window, you see two colorful icons. Click either icon, and a menu full of other icons slides out, as shown in Figure 2-11. These icons are actually links to different Web sites. If you connect to the Internet and then click an icon, you're taken directly to the corresponding Web site. These Internet links are in addition to the ones you find if you click the Internet or Connectables buttons on the Guided Activities panel, discussed in Chapter 1.

The top row of icons links you to companies that offer online photo process-ing, image scanning, and the like. You can read more about these kinds of services in Chapter 17. Links on the bottom row of icons connect you to the Adobe Web site home page, the PhotoDeluxe main page, the technical support page, and to other companies that provide products related to PhotoDeluxe. To scroll through the available links, click the little green right- and left-pointing triangles (labeled *scroll arrow* in Figure 2-11).

Note that in order for the links to work, you must have Microsoft Internet Explorer installed. Internet Explorer is provided on the PhotoDeluxe CD-ROM.

You can keep the links displayed as you work if you want; to hide them, click the leftmost icon on the row (the one you clicked to display the row in the first place). If you have the image window maximized, you don't see the links icons at all. Shrink the window to get to the icons if you want to use them.

That tricky Adobe icon

Of all the features I could live without in Version 3, the one I'm about to describe has to top the list. But Adobe provided this option, so you may as well take a look and judge for yourself.

Close all your open images or reduce the size of the image window so that you can see the little Adobe logo in the lower-left corner of the image-editing

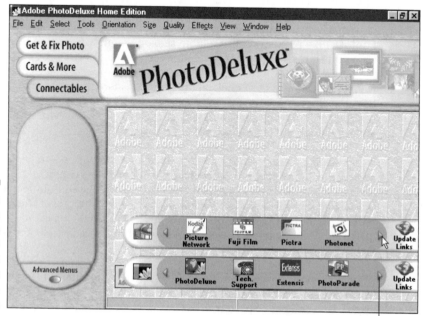

Figure 2-11:
Click an
icon to
connect to
a Web site
related to
PhotoDeluxe.

Scroll arrow

area — right above the File Information box and just to the left of the Advanced Menus button. If you click the logo, a dialog box appears with a few different icons. The icons represent different designs that you can display as the window background in the image-editing area. By default, you get a windowful of gray Adobe logos. But you can pick something more interesting — a beach scene, for example, if you're easily bored.

And if you're the really picky sort, you can download additional background coverings — known in the computer business as *wallpaper* — from the Adobe Web site. Connect to the Internet and then click the Download Wallpaper icon at the bottom of the dialog box. Additionally, you can install more wallpaper patterns from the PhotoDeluxe CD-ROM, as I explain in the next section.

Seasonal stuff

Version 3 also offers a new feature called Seasonal Activities. These are special templates for creating projects related to the time of year — Christmas cards, Father's Day cards, Halloween party invitations, and so on.

PhotoDeluxe offers the activities to you automatically according to the date on your computer's system clock. When fall comes around, for example, you're offered activities related to that time of year.

In order for PhotoDeluxe to bring the seasonal options to your attention, you must have the Allow Seasonal Activities option turned on in the File⇨ Preferences submenu. A check mark next to the option name means that the option is turned on. Click the option name to toggle the option on and off.

PhotoDeluxe presents the available seasonal activities to you the second time you start the program. That is, after you install the program, open it for the first time, shut it down, and then reopen. Choose the activities that you want to install and then click Install. You can also choose to install additional wallpaper for the program window if you like (see the preceding section for more on this topic). Select the activities that you want to install and then click the Install button.

If you want to take a gander at all the seasonal activities you can install at some other time, close PhotoDeluxe. Then set your system clock one year ahead (in Windows 95, choose Start⇨Control Panel and double-click the Date/Time icon). Open PhotoDeluxe and close it. Then reset the clock to the correct year, put the PhotoDeluxe CD in your CD-ROM drive, and restart the program. A dialog box appears, asking which of the seasonal activities you want to install.

After you install the seasonal activities, click the Connectables button on the Guided Activities panel to use them. Any additional wallpaper you install appears on the list of patterns displayed when you click the Adobe icon, as explained in the preceding section.

Chapter 3

Put a Pixel in Your Pocket

*I*f you're wired into the Internet, you may have discovered the world of online *newsgroups,* also known as *discussion groups.* For the uninitiated, newsgroups are like digital bulletin boards where people exchange information about a common interest. If you have a question about which digital camera to buy, for example, you can post a message asking for advice in the `rec.photo.digital` newsgroup. Within a few hours, helpful folks from all over the world reply with their recommendations.

I read several newsgroups every morning, including those mentioned in Chapter 17. One reason I adopted this practice is that it gives me a legitimate excuse to enjoy another cup of coffee and put off doing anything really productive for 30 minutes or so. But reading the digital imaging newsgroups also gives me a clue as to what kind of problems people are having with their image-editing projects.

At any rate, my unofficial tally of newsgroup postings suggests that the top questions baffling image-editing newcomers are:

✔ Why does my image look fine on-screen but like garbage when I print it?

✔ Why does my snapshot-size image get all fuzzy and yucky when I blow it up to an 8 x 10?

✔ What image resolution do I choose when scanning? When printing? When creating images for a Web page?

To understand the answers to these questions, you need a bit of knowledge about how digital images work, which is what you find in this chapter. You come face-to-face with the essential building block of every digital image, the *pixel.* You also get acquainted with a bunch of other important techie terms, including *resolution, ppi,* and *dpi,* all of which are critical to predicting whether your images will look sharp and beautiful or soft and cruddy when you display or print them.

I'll warn you straight away, this stuff can be a little perplexing and, compared with the topics covered in the rest of the book, pretty dry and scientific. You even have to do some math here and there. But trust me, if you don't take some time to explore this information, you're going to be disappointed with the quality of your images. Not only that, but you'll be exposed as a naive, uninformed "newbie" when you post messages in your digital imaging newsgroup, which can only lead to deep feelings of inadequacy and shame. And really, don't we all have enough of those already?

Pixels Exposed

All digital images, whether they come from a scanner, digital camera, or some other device, are made up of tiny colored squares known as *pixels.* Pixel is shorthand for *picture element,* if you care, which you probably shouldn't. What *is* critical to know is how pixels operate.

Pixels work like the tiles in a mosaic. If you stand far away from a mosaic, you can't distinguish the individual tiles, and the image appears seamless. Only when you move closer can you see that the picture is indeed composed of tiles. The same thing is true with a digital image. If you print the picture at a relatively small size, as in the left image in Figure 3-1, the pixels blend together into a seamless photograph. But when you enlarge the picture, as I did with the eye in the upper-right portion of Figure 3-1, you can see the individual pixels.

To see this phenomenon in action for yourself, follow these steps:

1. **Fire up PhotoDeluxe and open an image.**

   Chapter 1 provides detailed information about opening images.

2. **Click the Zoom In button at the top of the image window.**

   The Zoom In button is the left-most button on the toolbar at the top of the image window. (The button looks like a plus sign inside a circle.) PhotoDeluxe magnifies the view of your image.

3. **Click, click, and click again.**

   Keep clicking on that button until you can make out the individual pixels in your image, as you can see in the upper-right portion of Figure 3-1.

Figure 3-1:
Zooming in on a digital image reveals that it's nothing more than a bunch of colored squares.

Another way to zoom in is by pressing the Ctrl key together with the plus key. (On a Mac, press ⌘ and the plus key instead.) To zoom out, press Ctrl (⌘) and the minus key.

Having earlier made an analogy between a digital image and a mosaic, I should point out two subtle but important differences between the two:

- ✔ In a mosaic, the dimensions of individual tiles may vary. One tile may be slightly larger or have corners that are slightly more round, for example. But all pixels in a digital image are perfectly square and exactly the same size.

- ✔ Although you may see some color variations within a single tile in a mosaic, each pixel in a digital image can represent only one specific color. A pixel can't be half red and half blue, for example. Nor can a pixel be dark blue in one area and light blue in another. You get exactly one hue and brightness level per pixel.

Of course, you can change the color of any pixel by using an image-editing program such as PhotoDeluxe. You also can change the number of pixels in your image and alter the size of all the pixels. You're the master of your pixel domain, as it were.

Can I edit drawings in PhotoDeluxe?

Computer artwork comes in two forms. *Digital images,* also referred to as *bitmap images,* are composed of pixels, as explained in "Pixels Exposed," in this chapter. PhotoDeluxe and its big brother, Adobe Photoshop, are designed to edit this kind of picture, as are competing programs such as Corel Photo-Paint.

Other programs, including CorelDraw and Adobe Illustrator, enable you to create and edit *vector graphics,* often referred to as *drawings.* Vector graphics are made up of lines and curves that can be defined by mathematical equations. (Drawing software is sometimes called *object-oriented software* because every shape is considered a mathematical object.) You draw a line, for example, and the computer translates the distance and angle between the beginning and end points of the line into an equation. When you print the drawing, the drawing software sends the equation to the printer, which renders the line on paper as the equation dictates.

Because of the way vector graphics work, you can enlarge or reduce them as much as you want without any loss in print quality. This feature makes drawing software ideal for creating text, logos, and similar graphics that you need to output at several different sizes. But drawing programs don't do a good job of re-creating photographic images; for that task, pixels are a better way to go. The downside to pixel-based graphics is that they deteriorate in quality when you enlarge them. (See "Higher resolution = better image quality" in this chapter for an explanation.)

Although you usually can open a vector graphic in an image-editing program and vice versa, you can't do any serious editing without converting the artwork to the type the program is designed to handle. Some programs perform the conversion automatically when you open the picture file, whereas others require you to do the conversion manually by saving the picture in a specific file format. (See the discussion of file formats in Chapter 4 for some additional information.)

The moral of this long and incredibly geeky story is this: If you're serious about computer graphics, you need both a drawing program and an image-editing program. Don't edit images in a drawing program, and don't edit drawings in PhotoDeluxe.

Other chapters in this book discuss ways you can play with pixel color to enhance reality or completely obliterate it, depending on your mood. The rest of this chapter is devoted largely to a discussion of how the number and size of your pixels affects the appearance of your images when you print them or display them on-screen. If you want people to say, "Ooh! You're an artistic genius!" instead of "Ick, what's that blurry mess?" when you show them your images, don't skip these pages.

Pixel Math

One of my favorite mottos is "Friends don't let friends do math." To say that I am numerically challenged is an understatement. Unfortunately, working with digital images requires that you remember a few critical equations, which are explained in the next few sections. If you're a math-hater like me, don't worry too much, though — if I can grasp this stuff, you surely can as well.

Pixels ÷ image size = resolution

Every digital image begins life with a specified number of pixels. Entry-level digital cameras, for example, typically create images that are 640 pixels wide by 480 pixels tall, for a total of 307,200 pixels. Higher-priced cameras create *megapixel* images, which are images with 1 million or more pixels. The number of pixels across by the number of pixels down is called the image *pixel dimensions.*

The term *image resolution* indicates the number of pixels used to represent a specific area of the picture when you print it or display it on-screen. Resolution is usually measured in pixels per linear inch, or *ppi* for short. Note that I said *linear inch* — you count the number of pixels across or down, but not both. The image resolution is constant throughout the entire image; in other words, you never have more pixels per inch in one area of your image than in another.

To determine the image resolution, you divide the horizontal pixel dimensions by the width of the picture. Or you divide the vertical pixel dimensions by the picture height. For example, if your image is 640 pixels across by 480 pixels high, and you set the image size at 4 inches wide by 3 inches tall, the image resolution is 160 ppi. (640 ÷ 4 = 160 or 480 ÷ 3 = 160.)

Now that you know how to calculate the resolution of your image, you're no doubt wondering why you might want to do so. The answer is that resolution determines whether your image looks lovely or lousy, as explained in the next section.

Higher resolution = better image quality

Generally speaking, the higher the resolution, the better the quality of your images, especially with printed images (as opposed to on-screen images). Figures 3-2 through 3-4 illustrate this point. The first figure has a resolution of 266 ppi; the second, 133 ppi; and the third, 72 ppi.

Figure 3-2:
A 226-ppi image looks smooth and detailed.

Figure 3-3:
When the resolution is cut in half, to 133 ppi, image quality suffers.

Figure 3-4:
A resolution
of 72 ppi is
fine for
on-screen
display, but
inadequate
for printing.

Why does the 72 ppi image look so much worse than the others? For one thing, with only 72 pixels per inch, fewer distinctly colored squares are available to represent the scene, which means that small details get lost. In Figure 3-4, the effect is particularly noticeable in the center of the daisy.

In addition, when you reduce the number of pixels per inch, the pixels have to grow in order to cover the same image ground. The bigger the pixel, the easier it is for the eye to distinguish the individual tiles, and the more the image looks like a bunch of squares rather than a continuous scene. Compare the edges of the petals around the bottom of the flower in Figure 3-2 with the same petals in Figure 3-4, and you can see how smooth, seamless edges turn to jaggedy, stair-steppy edges when printed at a lower resolution. In image-editing lingo, the image in Figure 3-4 suffers from *the jaggies,* or, in more technical terms, *pixelation.*

For another illustration of how resolution affects pixel size, take a look at the black borders around Figures 3-2 through 3-4. I applied the borders using the Effects⇨Outline command in PhotoDeluxe, as explained in Chapter 6. The border around Figure 3-2 is 2 pixels wide, as is the border around Figure 3-3. But the border in Figure 3-3 appears twice as thick because at 133 ppi, the pixels are twice as big as those in Figure 3-2, which has a resolution of 266 ppi. In Figure 3-4 (the 72-ppi image), I applied a 1-pixel border to create a border that's roughly the same size as the 2-pixel border in Figure 3-3 (the 133-ppi image).

Now that I've publicly recognized the effects of packing lots of pixels into your image, allow me to note that ultra-high-resolution images aren't always necessary or even desirable. For on-screen images, including those that you use on Web pages, anything more than 96 ppi is overkill, and 72 ppi is usually adequate. Why? Because most computer monitors aren't set up to display more pixels per inch than that anyway. Too high a resolution can also confuse some printers, which are designed to handle a certain number of pixels and no more. In fact, PhotoDeluxe protects you from this pitfall by limiting the number of pixels you can send to the printer. For more on the thorny question of how many pixels are enough, check out the section "So How Many Pixels Do I Need?" later in this chapter. And for more on other printing issues, read Chapter 5.

More pixels = bigger files

For every pixel in your image, a certain amount of computer data is stored in the image file. The more pixels you have, the bigger the image file, and the more room you need to save the image on your computer's hard drive or a removable storage disk (such as a floppy disk or Zip disk).

Just to give you a frame of reference, the 266-ppi image in Figure 3-2 contains more than a million pixels and consumes 864 kilobytes (K) on disk. The 133-ppi version in Figure 3-3 contains roughly 265,000 pixels and eats up 221K. Figure 3-4, at 72 ppi, contains approximately 77,500 pixels and requires a mere 68K of disk space.

When thinking about file size, remember that the total number of pixels, and not the image resolution (pixels per inch), is the important factor. A 4-x-3 image with a resolution of 144 ppi has the same number of pixels as an 8-x-6 image at 72 ppi — each image is 576 pixels wide by 432 pixels tall. Therefore, the file sizes of the two images are the same.

Image file size is most important when you're creating images for the Internet, whether you want to place them on a Web page or e-mail them to a friend. The bigger the file, the longer it takes the viewer to download and display the image. Few Web surfers are patient enough to sit and wait while huge image files come trickling down the data line, so try to keep your Web images under 20K in size. Your e-mail buddies may be slightly more forgiving — but not much. If your image files are overly large, you can slim them down by reducing the number of pixels, as explained later in this chapter, or by saving the image in the JPEG or GIF format, discussed in Chapter 4.

File size is also important from an everyday storage and file transfer point of view. After you create that mondo-resolution, poster-size image, where are you going to keep it? Is your hard drive really so big that you can afford to fill it up with dozens of 10MB images? And if you decide to have your image professionally printed, how are you going to get the image to the print shop?

Your old floppy disk drive isn't going to cut it — a floppy holds about 1.4MB of data. You're going to need a Zip drive or some other larger storage device for those big image files. (Chapter 4 includes a brief discussion on various storage options, by the way.)

Additionally, large image files tax your computer's mental resources. The larger the file, the more memory (RAM) you need to open and edit the file. If you're working with less than 32MB RAM, applying a filter or performing other editing tricks to a large image file can take a *loooonnng* time. Your computer may even refuse to carry out your instructions altogether.

Even an image file that doesn't consume a huge amount of storage space on disk can give your computer fits. That's because the amount of memory required to open and edit an image is greater than the size of the file on disk. For example, Figure 3-2 occupies 864K on disk, but when opened in PhotoDeluxe, it uses 3.03MB (megabytes) of memory.

Finally, the bigger the image file, the longer it takes to print. Most home-office printers use the computer's memory in order to print images, which means that you can't do anything else while your image prints. And printers that come with their own stash of memory instead of relying on system resources may not have enough memory to handle really big image files.

So before you crank up the pixel machine, be sure that you really need all those little squares and that your system can handle the strain. For a review of how many pixels are enough, see "So How Many Pixels Do I Need?" later in this chapter.

Adding pixels ≠ better pictures

Some image-editing programs, including PhotoDeluxe, enable you to change the image pixel dimensions — that is, to add or subtract pixels from your image. This process is known as *resampling*. The idea is that if you need more pixels, the software can simply add them. Similarly, if you want to reduce the number of pixels, PhotoDeluxe can weed out the excess for you. (For specifics on how to add or subtract pixels, see "Resampling your image," later in this chapter.)

Why would you want to add or subtract pixels? Well, one reason to dump pixels is to reduce file size, as discussed in the preceding section. Another reason is to change the size at which the image is displayed on-screen. If you have a 640-x-480-pixel image and you want it to occupy one-half of a monitor that's set to display 640 x 480 pixels, you need to trim the image pixel dimensions by 50 percent. (This issue is explained more thoroughly in "Sizing images for the screen," later in this chapter.) Finally, you may want to adjust the number of pixels in order to achieve the right resolution for printing.

Resampling *sounds* like a good idea. But in practice, resampling can turn your image to mud. When you add pixels, the image-editing program makes a calculated guess at the color and brightness of the new pixels. The results are usually poor, whether you're using an entry-level image editor such as PhotoDeluxe or a professional-grade program such as Photoshop.

For proof, take a look at Figure 3-5. On the left is a 133-ppi image of a statue at the Ming Tombs near Beijing. At 133 ppi, the image is pretty fuzzy. But when I double the number of pixels, thereby doubling the resolution, the image doesn't get any better. In fact, the resampled image looks slighty less sharp than the original.

Downsampling — the techie term for tossing away unwanted pixels — is generally safer than upsampling (adding pixels). But any time you delete pixels, you're deleting image information. Throw away too many pixels, and you can lose important image details and reduce your image quality.

Whenever possible, avoid downsampling by more than 25 percent and avoid upsampling altogether. If you need to raise the image resolution, the only good way to do it is to reduce the image size, as explained in "Sizing an image for printing," later in this chapter.

Figure 3-5:
Resampling a 133-ppi image (left) up to 266 ppi results in an even fuzzier image (right).

Some image-editing gurus say that you can safely upsample by as much as 25 percent, too, but that figure depends on the image subject matter. Large expanses of color look better after upsampling than areas of intricate detail. And an image that's exceptionally sharp doesn't suffer as much from a pixel infusion as one that's already a little soft in the focus department.

For specifics on how to add or subtract pixels, see "Resampling your image," later in this chapter.

Ppi ≠ dpi

If you've ever shopped for a printer, you've no doubt encountered the term *dpi*. Dpi stands for *dots per inch* and refers to the number of dots of color the printer creates to represent each portion of the image.

Many people assume that dpi and ppi mean the same thing, and the terms are often used interchangeably. But dots per inch is *not* the same as pixels per inch, so don't confuse the two. The term ppi refers to the number of pixels in the image; dpi refers to the number of ink dots a printer uses to reproduce those pixels on paper.

Most printers create dots that are smaller than pixels, which means that the printer lays down several dots to reproduce each pixel (a technology known as *dithering* or *halftoning*). Each printer has an optimum pixel-to-dot ratio. Most 600-dpi inkjet printers, for example, do their best work when the image resolution is set to 300 ppi.

Sometimes dpi is used to describe the capabilities of monitors, scanners, and digital cameras as well. In all three cases, the term is a misnomer because these devices create images by using pixels, not printer dots.

For more on this issue, read "So How Many Pixels Do I Need?" and "Input Resolution," both of which are just around the bend, as well as the sidebar "Shopping tips" in Chapter 5.

So How Many Pixels Do I Need?

Ah, the $64,000 question. The answer depends on what you want to do with your finished image — print it or view it on-screen? You need far more pixels for the former than the latter, as explained in the sections about to jump out and grab you by the collar.

The right ppi for printing

For best results when printing, check your printer's manual for information about the ideal image resolution (pixels per inch) to use. If you're having your image professionally printed at a copy shop or commercial printer, ask the printer's sales rep for the correct resolution. Each printer is engineered to deliver its best prints at a certain image resolution.

Don't confuse the printer's resolution, stated in dpi (dots per inch) with the image resolution you need to specify in PhotoDeluxe. If you have a 600-dpi inkjet, for example, don't assume that you should set your image resolution to 600 ppi. For more on this subject, see "Ppi ≠ dpi," earlier in this chapter.

Consumer-level color inkjets typically deliver the best prints when the image resolution is in the 250- to 300-ppi neighborhood. A resolution of 300 ppi is also the norm for color images that are printed commercially, like the ones in this book. These same values apply for grayscale images as well, although you can often get away with a lower resolution for screen shots such as the ones you see in this book (most have a resolution of 140 ppi).

If you snapped your image with a digital camera, you may not have enough pixels to get both the print size and the image resolution that you want. An entry-level digital camera typically delivers images that are 640 pixels wide by 480 pixels tall, which means that you can print an image about $2^1/_4$ inches wide by $1^1/_2$ inches tall at a resolution of 300 ppi. (To determine the image size, divide the number of pixels across or down by the resolution.) In this case, you simply have to make a decision: Which is more important, size or quality? Strike the balance that's most suited to your printing project.

If you scanned your image or are working with an image from a commercial image collection, though, you may have more pixels than you need. You may think that if 300 ppi is required for a good printout, 450 ppi should be even better. But the truth is that when the printer gets more pixels than it's designed to handle, it just dumps the excess. Your image doesn't look any better than it would at 300 ppi, and it may even look worse because the printer may not pick the best pixels to eliminate. For instructions on how to rid yourself of a pixel overpopulation, see "Resampling your image," later in this chapter.

The right ppi for on-screen display

If you're preparing an image for use on a Web page, or in a multimedia presentation, or for some other on-screen use, your resolution needs are much lower than for printed images.

You see, the monitor's capabilities limit the on-screen resolution of your image. Screen displays, like digital images, are composed of nothing more than squares of color. And every monitor has a maximum screen resolution, which is the number of pixels that it can display per linear inch. The typical screen resolution ranges from 72 to 96 ppi. Even if you set your image resolution to 300 ppi, you don't see any more than 72 to 96 ppi on-screen.

Where did I come up with that vague "72 to 96 ppi" recommendation? I'm afraid the answer involves still more math. Here's the deal: Most monitors enable you to choose between several different display settings. Typically, you can select from the following options: 640 x 480, 800 x 600, 1,024 x 768, and 1,280 x 1,024. The first number represents the number of pixels displayed across the screen, while the second number indicates the number of pixels displayed vertically.

The effective resolution of the monitor depends on the actual screen size. A 15-inch monitor set to display 640 x 480 pixels has a resolution of about 57 ppi, for example, whereas a 21-inch monitor has a resolution of around 41 ppi at the same setting. (If you're doing the math, remember that the actual screen space of monitors is much less than the stated monitor size. I based my resolution numbers on a screen size of $11^1/_4$ inches for the 15-inch monitor and $15^3/_4$ inches for the 17-inch monitor.)

I could provide you with a chart of all possible monitor sizes and available screen resolutions, but that would only confound you and send me straight to the nuthouse. So I'll just give you a general rule regarding screen resolutions: When they are shipped from the factory, most PC monitors are set to a screen resolution of 96 ppi, and most Macintosh monitors are set to 72 ppi. Of course, some people do change the monitor settings from the factory default. But even when set to the highest display setting, screen resolution rarely exceeds 100 ppi, and a 72-ppi image usually looks just fine at that resolution.

Now that I've taken the time to explain screen resolution and drilled the 72-to-96 ppi thing into your head, I should fess up and tell you that when you're preparing images for on-screen use, you really don't need to worry about image resolution if you don't want to. Instead, you can simply focus on the image pixel dimensions, as explained in "Sizing images for the screen," later in this chapter.

The Top-Secret File Information Box

For a quick way to check the current size and resolution of your image, place your cursor on the File Information box at the bottom of the program window and hold down the left mouse button. (On a Mac, the File Information box is at the bottom-left of the image window, not the program window.) A second, bigger box appears out of nowhere, as shown in Figure 3-6. The box lists the image size, pixel dimensions, and resolution.

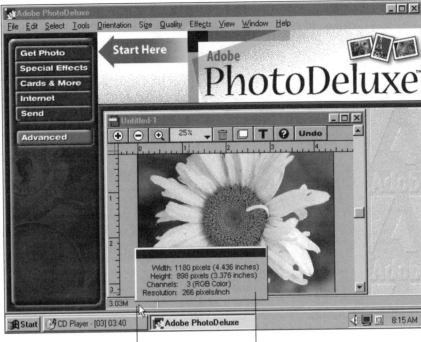

Figure 3-6:
This box
displays
information
about the
image.

Press and hold   File Information box

You can safely ignore the other piece of information in the box: the number
of channels and image color model (RGB Color in Figure 3-6). Like many
other controls in PhotoDeluxe, this information is a carryover from the more
sophisticated Adobe Photoshop. In that program, you can view and edit the
independent color channels in an image and convert an image from one
color model to another, which makes the channel and model information
useful. You can't do either in PhotoDeluxe, though. For more on color
models, see Chapter 5.

Field Guide to the Photo Size Dialog Box

If you want to make changes to your image size, pixel dimensions, or
resolution, head for the Photo Size dialog box, shown in Figure 3-7. To open
the dialog box, choose Size⇨Photo Size. Figure 3-7 shows the photo size
data for the daisy image in Figure 3-2, earlier in this chapter.

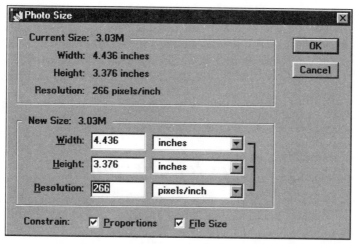

Figure 3-7:
To size or resample your image, the Photo Size dialog box is the place to go.

Upcoming sections walk you through the process of using the dialog box to accomplish various tasks. But here's an overview of the components inside the dialog box:

✔ The top section of the dialog box shows you the current dimensions and resolution of the image. You make your changes in the option boxes in the bottom half of the dialog box.

✔ The Current Size and New Size values indicate how much room the image consumes in your computer's memory *while the image is open for editing in PhotoDeluxe.* This value is not the same thing as how much space the image consumes on disk when you save it to your hard drive or a removable disk. For example, the daisy image in Figure 3-2 consumes 864K when saved to disk but requires 3.03MB of memory to edit.

✔ To enter a new value in the Width, Height, or Resolution option box, double-click the box and type a number. After you double-click, you also can press the up- and down-arrow keys on your keyboard to raise and lower the value. Depending on what unit of measurement is being used, each press of an arrow key changes the value by 1, 0.1, or 0.001. Press Shift along with the up- or down-arrow key to raise or lower the value in increments of 10.

✔ You can select from several units of measurement by using the pop-up menus beside the Width and Height option boxes. To see the pixel dimensions of your image, choose pixels from the pop-up menus.

✔ To change the unit of measurement that appears by default when you open the Photo Size dialog box, choose File➪Preferences➪Units. Select the unit that you want to use from the Ruler Units pop-up menu and click OK. Bear in mind that your choice affects the rulers running along the top and left side of your image window. (Turn the rulers on and off by pressing Ctrl+R on a PC and ⌘+R on a Mac.)

✔ Select the pixels/inch option from the Resolution pop-up menu unless you're working with an output device (printer or monitor) that requires you to set resolution in terms of pixels per centimeter. In that case, choose pixels/centimeter.

✔ If you press the Alt key (Option key on a Mac) while clicking the Cancel button, the button changes into a Reset button. Click the Reset button to return to the original values that were in place when you first opened the Photo Size dialog box.

Sizing an image for printing

PhotoDeluxe displays your image on-screen at the size you specify with the zoom controls, discussed in Chapter 1. To find out what size your image will be if printed in Version 3, just glance at the File Information box in the bottom-left corner of the program window. For other versions of PhotoDeluxe, press and hold on the File Information box, as shown earlier, in Figure 3-6.

Alternatively, choose View⇨Show Rulers to display a ruler along the top and left side of your image. To turn the rulers on and off quickly, press Ctrl+R (⌘+R on a Mac). No matter what view size you choose using the zoom controls, the rulers always reflect the print size of your image. To change the unit of measure shown on the rulers, choose File⇨Preferences⇨Units and make a selection from the Ruler Units pop-up menu.

If you're not happy with the print size of the image, you have two options for resizing:

1. You can retain the current number of pixels, in which case the image resolution and pixel size go up or down accordingly. If you enlarge the picture, the resolution goes down and pixels get bigger. If you reduce the picture, the resolution goes up and pixels get smaller. (Remember, image size divided by the pixel dimensions equals the resolution. So when the image size changes, resolution and pixel size have to change if the number of pixels doesn't.)

2. You can add or subtract pixels — known as *resampling* the image — so that the image resolution and pixel size remain the same. If you enlarge the image, the software creates new pixels to fill in the new image area. If you reduce the image, the software tosses out the unwanted pixels.

As discussed earlier, in "Adding pixels ≠ better pictures," option #2 can be a dangerous move. You can generally downsample (delete pixels) by about 25 percent without much change in image quality, and you may even be able to resample up slightly. But for best results, avoid adding pixels to your image and limit the number of pixels you subtract.

For information on how to resample your image, see "I Took on the Mob and Won!" later in this chapter. Er, hold that — got distracted by my *National Enquirer* for a moment. The section you want for resampling information is the much more dull-sounding "Resampling your image."

The following steps explain how to change your print size *without* resampling:

1. **Choose Size⇨Photo Size to open the File Size dialog box.**

2. **Select the Proportions check box, as shown in Figure 3-7.**

   This option, when turned on, ensures that your image is resized proportionately. If you change the Width value, the Height value changes, too.

3. **Check the File Size check box, as you see in Figure 3-7.**

   When File Size is turned on, the number of pixels in your image can't be changed. If you raise the Width and Height values, the Resolution value goes down automatically. If you decrease the Width and Height values, the Resolution value goes up. To hammer home this fact, PhotoDeluxe displays a line linking the Width, Height, and Resolution options, as shown in Figure 3-7.

4. **Set the Width and Height values as desired.**

   Double-click inside either option box and type in the new dimensions. Or press the down and up arrows on your keyboard to change the values. Select the unit of measurement you want to use from the adjacent pop-up menu.

   But don't choose Percent as your unit of measure! When this option is selected, your image is resampled automatically. PhotoDeluxe automatically deselects the File Size check box when you enter a new value in the Width or Height option box.

   The same is true when you select Pixels as your unit of measurement. Select the Pixels and Percent options only when sizing images for on-screen display or when you want to resample your image, as discussed later in this chapter.

5. **Click OK.**

   Don't be alarmed that the on-screen size of your image doesn't change. Remember, the on-screen display size is determined by the zoom level you set with the PhotoDeluxe zoom controls, not by the size you set in the Photo Size dialog box. To verify that your image is indeed the correct size, turn on the rulers (Ctrl+R or ⌘+R). Or check the File Information box, as shown in Figure 3-6. Now you can see that PhotoDeluxe did indeed resize your image as requested.

   If your image *did* change size on-screen, you didn't select the File Size option box as instructed in Step 3. Press Ctrl+Z (⌘+Z on a Mac) to undo the resizing, and try again.

For more information on printing, take a spin through Chapter 5, which is devoted entirely to that subject.

Sizing images for the screen

If you're sizing an image for use on a Web page, a multimedia show, or some other on-screen use, you need to take a little different approach than if you are sizing an image for printing.

When you size an image for printing, you think in terms of inches, picas, or whatever other traditional unit of measurement you may use. But when sizing an image for the screen, you should think in terms of pixel dimensions instead.

Before diving into an explanation of exactly how to size images for the screen, I want to recap two important pieces of information presented earlier in this chapter:

✔ When an image is displayed on-screen, the image resolution defaults to that of the monitor. Most monitor displays are set to a resolution of 72 to 96 ppi. Even if you set the image resolution to 300 ppi in PhotoDeluxe, the image is displayed at the screen resolution, with one screen pixel devoted to every image pixel.

This arrangement often causes some confusion for image-editing newcomers, who can't understand why an image that they've sized to be, say, 3 inches square at 300 ppi, appears substantially larger than 3 inches square on-screen. The reason is that the monitor automatically lowers the resolution for display purposes, which means that the image grows in size. (As resolution goes down, image size has to grow if the pixel count stays the same.)

✔ Most monitors can be set to several different display settings: 640 x 480 pixels, 800 x 600 pixels, 1,024 x 768 pixels, and 1,280 x 1,024 pixels, for example. The effective screen resolution depends on the size of the screen. (Screen area divided by number of pixels equals screen resolution.)

To size an image for on-screen display, you simply figure out how much of the screen you want to cover and set your pixel dimensions accordingly. Remember, the monitor uses one screen pixel to represent one image pixel. So if you want to fill the whole screen on a monitor that's set to display 640 x 480 pixels, you change the pixel dimensions of your image to 640 x 480 pixels. If you want to fill half the screen on that same monitor, you change the pixel dimensions to 320 x 240.

The one difficulty you face when sizing images for on-screen display — especially Web images — is that you have no way to know what size monitors and display settings your viewers will use when they view your image. You may create a 640 x 480 image, expecting it to fill the viewers' screens. But if some of those viewers are running their monitors at 1,024 x 768, their screens are only half-filled by the image, as illustrated in Figures 3-8 and 3-9. Figure 3-8 shows a 640 x 480 image displayed on a 17-inch monitor set to the 640-x-480-pixel display option. Figure 3-9 shows the same image when the display setting is changed to 1,024 x 768.

Because you can't predict the monitor situation for all your viewers, the best idea is to go with the lowest common denominator and size your images for a 640-x-480-pixel screen.

Now that you've got the background scoop, the following steps give you the 1-2-3, or, in this case, the 1-2-3-4-5, for resizing your images for screen display.

Figure 3-8:
A 640-x-480-pixel image consumes the entire screen when the monitor display is set to 640 x 480.

Figure 3-9:
When the monitor setting is 1,024 x 768 pixels, the 640 x 480 image consumes roughly one-fourth of the screen.

Before you take these steps, save a backup copy of your image in case you ever need the image at its original pixel dimensions.

1. **Choose Size⇨Photo Size to open the Photo Size dialog box.**

2. **Check the Proportions check box.**

   This option maintains the current proportions of your image. If you change the Height value, the Width value changes accordingly.

3. **Choose pixels as the unit of measurement for both the Width and Height option boxes.**

4. **Change the pixel dimensions as desired.**

   When you begin typing a new value in the Width or Height option box, the File Size check box is automatically deselected, enabling you to add or delete pixels.

   If you increase the Width and Height values, you may not like the results. You're adding pixels, which usually doesn't work very well. For an explanation, see "Adding pixels ≠ better pictures," earlier in this chapter.

5. Click OK.

As an alternative, you can choose Percent as your unit of measurement from the Width and Height pop-up menus and resize the image by a percentage of its current size. Setting the Width and Height values to 50 with Percent selected as the unit of measurement dumps exactly half of the image pixels.

"But what about resolution?" you ask. "Don't I have to worry about that value?" The answer is, as long as you size your image using Pixels or Percent as your unit of measurement, you don't have to worry about resolution. Only if you can't think in terms of pixels and want to use inches or picas or whatever as your unit of measurement do you need to adjust the resolution for screen display. In that case, deselect the File Size check box, set the desired Width and Height values, and set the Resolution value to match the screen resolution of your display, if you know it. Otherwise, a resolution in the range of 72 to 96 ppi range is appropriate.

Changing the image resolution

If you want to raise or lower the image resolution, you have two choices. You can add or delete pixels to the image, also known as resampling. Adding pixels — up sampling — isn't recommended, for reasons explained earlier in this chapter. But if you want to try to it anyway or need to downsample the image (delete pixels), see the next section for instructions.

Alternatively, you can change the image size and retain the current number of pixels. As you enlarge the image, the resolution goes down; as you reduce the image, the resolution goes up. Reducing the size of the image is the only good way to raise the image resolution, by the way.

To walk the safer, better, resolution-changing path, follow the steps given in "Sizing an image for printing," earlier in this chapter. But instead of changing the Width and Height values, change the Resolution value. PhotoDeluxe automatically adjusts the width and height of your image as needed. Be sure that the File Size option is checked! Otherwise, PhotoDeluxe adds or deletes pixels to achieve the Resolution value that you specify.

Resampling your image

Resampling an image means adding or deleting pixels — also known as changing the pixel dimensions. You may need to resample your image to change the size at which an image is displayed on a Web page. Or you may want to trim excess pixels to lower the image resolution and reduce file size.

As mentioned ad nauseam throughout this chapter, adding pixels (upsampling) is seldom a good idea. If your image is very sharp and contains mostly large areas of flat color, you may be able to get away with a small amount of upsampling. Otherwise, you're likely to do your image more harm than good.

Downsampling — deleting pixels — can also destroy an image when done to excess. For best results, don't downsample more than 25 percent. And before you resample an image at all, be sure to save a backup copy of the original. You may need the image at its original pixel count some day.

Now that the important legal disclaimers are out of the way, here's how to resample an image:

1. **Choose Size⇨Photo Size to open the Photo Size dialog box.**

2. **Check the Proportions check box.**

   This option ensures that when you change the image height, the image width changes proportionately.

3. **Deselect the File Size check box.**

   If the check box is turned on, PhotoDeluxe doesn't let you change the number of image pixels.

4. **Change the Width/Height or Resolution values.**

   You're free to change the Width/Height values independently of the Resolution value, and vice versa. If you want to dump pixels, choose a print unit of measurement (inches, picas, and so on) and lower the Resolution value. Or choose Pixels or Percent as your unit of measurement and lower the Width or Height value.

   To add pixels — and don't say I didn't warn you against it — raise the Resolution value while using a print unit of measurement for the Width and Height values. Or increase the Width and Height values while using Pixels or Percent as your unit of measurement.

5. **Click OK.**

   If you don't like the results — I *told* you so — press Ctrl+Z (⌘+Z on a Mac) to undo the resampling. Or click the Undo button in the image window.

Applying the Unsharp Mask filter can sometimes improve the appearance of a resampled image. For how-to's, chart a course to Chapter 7.

Input Resolution

Before I put the topic of resolution to rest for good, I want to add a few final tips about *input resolution* — which is a fancy way of referring to the resolution used when you scan an image, capture it with a digital camera, or open it from a Photo CD. The general guidelines are as follows:

- **Scanning:** When you set the image resolution in your scanning software, consider the final use of the image. If you're going to print the image, set the resolution to match the optimum resolution for the printer. (See "The right ppi for printing," earlier in this chapter, for more information.) If the image is destined for stardom as a Web image or as part of a multimedia presentation, set the scan resolution to match the monitor's screen resolution — typically, 72 to 96 ppi.

- **Capturing with a digital camera:** Always use the highest resolution setting on your digital camera unless you're sure that you'll never use the image for anything other than on-screen display. Even then, you may want to capture the image at the highest setting to give yourself the most flexibility when you size the image. You can always go back and get rid of extra pixels if needed, but you can't add them after the fact with any degree of success.

- **Opening a Photo CD image:** Commercial collections of images on CD-ROM are usually stored in the Kodak Photo CD format, which provides you with the same image at several different pixel dimensions. A standard Photo CD includes an image at 128 x 192 pixels, 256 x 384 pixels, 512 x 768 pixels, 1,024 x 1,536 pixels, and 2,048 x 3,072 pixels. Again, select the image size that's appropriate for the printer or monitor you're going to use to print or display your image.

From smallest to largest, the five sizing options are known in techie terms as Base/16, Base/4, Base, 4 Base, and 16 Base. This kind of information can be helpful when you want to get away from someone at a party. Launch into a heartfelt discourse on the merits of the various Base options, and you can bore almost anyone into a hasty retreat. (Chapter 1 includes a table listing the dimensions for each of the Base options in case you want a handy reference source to stick in your pocket protector.)

However you plan to input images into your computer, use these two formulas to determine how many pixels you need for printed images:

Number of pixels across = output resolution × desired output width

Number of pixels down = output resolution × desired output height

Suppose that you want to create a print that's 3 inches wide and 5 inches tall. You have a 600-dpi printer, and after checking the manual (radical notion!), you discover that the optimum image resolution for your printer is 300 ppi. You multiply 3×300 and 5×300, which tells you that you need an image that's 900 pixels wide by 1,500 pixels tall.

So if you're opening a Photo CD image, you choose the 4 Base option, which gives you 1,024 x 1,536 pixels. (After you edit the image, you can delete the extra pixels, if necessary.) If you're scanning an image, set the output dimensions to 3 inches by 5 inches and set the image resolution to 300 ppi. And if you're taking the shot with an entry-level digital camera . . . well, you probably need to get a loaner from someone with a more expensive model. You can't get blood out of a turnip, and neither can you get a 900-x-1,500-pixel image out of a $200 digital camera that offers a maximum image capture of 640 x 480 pixels.

If you're inputting an image for on-screen use, simply choose the pixel dimensions to match the amount of screen space that you want the image to occupy. For further instructions, see "Sizing images for the screen," earlier in this chapter. If your scanner software doesn't offer pixels as a unit of measurement, use the formulas shown a few paragraphs ago to determine the right scanner settings.

How deep are your bits?

You may occasionally hear people referring to something called *bit depth*. Well, not if you keep company with sane, normal people, of course. But if you lurk in the Internet image-editing newsgroups or hang around the coffee shops where all the out-of-work digital artists gather, you'll definitely catch wind of the term.

Just so that you don't feel like a total outsider, bit depth is a measure of how many colors an image can contain. Bit depth is sometimes also called *pixel depth* or *color depth*.

Common bit-depth values range from 1-bit to 24-bit. Each bit can represent two colors. So a 1-bit image puts two colors at your disposal (black and white). A bit depth of 8 translates to 256 colors (2^8 =256); 16 bits gives you about 32,000 colors; and 24 bits delivers a whopping 16 million colors.

A higher bit depth translates to a more vibrant, natural-looking image. (See Color Plate 3-1 for a look at the difference between an 8-bit color image and a 24-bit color image.) But higher bit depth also means a larger image file, because all those extra bits mean more data for your computer to store.

Chapter 4
Saving Your Masterpiece

• •

• •

*I*n the old days — you know, before Bill Gates and Co. owned the world — saving a piece of artwork was an easy proposition. Your kid came home from school toting a masterful rendition of a rainbow. You hung the picture on the refrigerator for a while, and then you stashed it in a memory box in the closet. No major effort required. At least, not until 20 years later, when you needed to remember where you put the memory box and which kid painted which rainbow.

Saving digital artwork is a bit more complex. You need to deal with technical issues such as choosing a file format, and you also need to think about what storage medium is appropriate for your images. Incredibly geeky terms such as *JPEG, lossy compression,* and *GIF89A* rear their ugly heads.

This chapter helps you sort out all the mumbo-jumbo so that you can glide smoothly through the process of saving your images. In addition to explaining what file format to use when, this chapter offers some suggestions about buying removable storage devices, such as Zip drives. And to ensure that you'll be able to find an image after you save it to disk, I show you how to catalog your images using the EasyPhoto program that comes with PhotoDeluxe.

Saving Rules!

One painfully important lesson that new computer users learn — usually the hard way — is that any edits to an open document are completely unprotected until the file is saved to disk, whether to your computer's hard drive or to a removable storage device such as a floppy disk. This harsh rule of life applies to images as well. If PhotoDeluxe freezes or your computer shuts itself down in a fit of anger, any unsaved changes to your image are history.

Saving an image is about the least exciting thing you can do in PhotoDeluxe. But unless you want all your hard work to go up in digital smoke, you absolutely, positively, need to get in the habit of saving early and saving often. The following sections tell you everything you need to know.

The PhotoDeluxe approach to saving

When you ask PhotoDeluxe to open an image, the program determines the image's file format. Discussed ad nauseam later in this chapter, *file format* simply refers to the method used to store image data. Different formats store data differently inside the image file.

Like many programs, PhotoDeluxe has its own unique method of saving images, known as the *native format,* or, in some circles, the *proprietary format.* The PhotoDeluxe native format goes by the initials PDD.

If the file that you want to open is a PDD file, PhotoDeluxe opens the original image file, just as you would expect. But if the image was stored in any other file format, PhotoDeluxe creates a working copy of the image, opens the copy, and converts the copy to the PDD format. Your edits are applied to the PDD copy, not to your original image.

Why would PhotoDeluxe go to the trouble of converting the image to PDD? Because PDD is designed to enable PhotoDeluxe to apply your edits more efficiently, thereby speeding up your editing work. In addition, the PDD format *supports* (can save) any image layers that you create, as discussed in Chapter 10. With the exception of the Adobe Photoshop native format, PDD is the only format available for use in PhotoDeluxe that can save layers.

I bring up all this native format stuff because it comes into play when you save a file. Because of the PhotoDeluxe approach to file formats, you need to remember the following rules:

✔ Always save in the PDD format until you're completely finished with your image. Only then should you save the image in one of the other formats discussed in "Format Fever," later in this chapter.

✔ To assist you in adhering to this rule, PhotoDeluxe doesn't offer you the option of saving in any format *but* PDD when you choose the Save command. To save in another format, you have to choose the File⇨Send To command in Version 2, File⇨Save As in the Business Edition, and File⇨Export in Version 3. (Do you think maybe Adobe is having a hard time deciding what name to give this option?)

✔ All three commands just mentioned save a *copy* of the open image in the new file format. The PDD version remains on-screen. If you make further edits, PhotoDeluxe applies the changes to the PDD version, *not* to the version you saved in the other file format. If you want to update that other version, you need to choose the Send To, Save As, or Export command again, depending on which version of the program you use.

✔ If you're editing an image that has never been saved in the PDD format, the PDD version you see on-screen is temporary. When you close the image, PhotoDeluxe asks whether you want to save the PDD version, even if you already saved the image in another format. If you say thanks but no thanks, the PDD version is erased.

✔ After you save the image in another file format, you may want to delete the PDD version of the image to free up some disk space. On the other hand, you may want to retain the PDD version if you saved the image in JPEG, GIF, or some other file format that throws away some image data in the saving process. (For more on that intriguing subject, see "Format Fever," later in this chapter.) You may also want to keep a PDD version of an image that contains layers so that you can manipulate the layers at a later date, if necessary.

Everyday saves

As discussed mere paragraphs ago, you should save in the native PhotoDeluxe format, PDD, until your image is completely finished. At that point, you can create a copy of the image in another file format if you like. But for working in PhotoDeluxe, PDD is the way to go.

To save an image in the PDD format for the first time, jog down the following path:

1. **Choose File⇨Save.**

   Or press Ctrl+S on a PC (⌘+S on a Mac). Either way, the dialog box shown in Figure 4-1 appears.

2. **Give your image a name.**

   Type the name into the File Name box (or, on a Mac, into the Save This Document As box, shown in Figure 4-2).

Up One Level

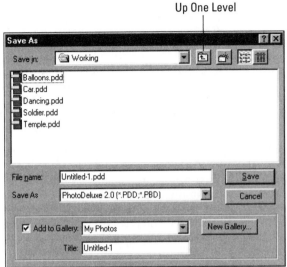

Figure 4-1:
The Save
As dialog
box is key
to making
sure your
hard work
doesn't
vanish in a
poof of
electronic
smoke.

3. Choose a storage cabinet.

In other words, specify the drive and/or folder where you want to store the document. In Windows, choose a folder or drive from the Save In drop-down list to display its contents in the file list box. Double-click a folder in the file list box to see what that folder contains. To move up a level in the folder/drive structure, click the Up One Level button (labeled in Figure 4-1).

On a Mac, choose your folder or drive from the Folder drop-down list.

Folder drop-down list

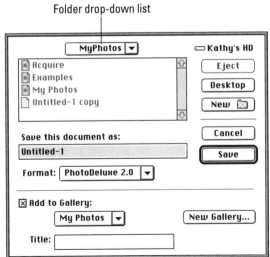

Figure 4-2:
The Save
As dialog
box as it
appears on
a Mac.

4. Create an EasyPhoto thumbnail if you want.

If you check the Add to Gallery option at the bottom of the dialog box, PhotoDeluxe adds a thumbnail preview of your image to EasyPhoto, the image browser that comes with PhotoDeluxe. Select the EasyPhoto gallery where you want to store the thumbnail from the drop-down list next to the Add to Gallery check box and enter a title for the image in the Title option box. This text appears with your thumbnail in the EasyPhoto gallery.

The name that you enter here doesn't have to be the same as your file-name; for example, if your official filename is JK1014.PPD, you can give your thumbnail a title that's a little less obscure, such as *Beerbottle*. Don't make your name too long, or you can't see the entire name in the EasyPhoto browser window.

For more information about saving EasyPhoto thumbnails, read "A Few EasyPhoto Tricks," later in this chapter.

5. Click Save.

PhotoDeluxe does your bidding and saves your image as instructed. Your image remains on-screen, tempting you to do further damage.

One save is never enough

Saving an image protects only those edits that you made before you issued the Save command. If you do any further editing, you must resave the image to retain the new changes.

Unlike some programs, PhotoDeluxe doesn't offer an autosave feature that saves your image every so often without any input from you. That's good, because you can experiment freely with your image. If the program were saving your changes on its own, you might get stuck with some edits that you later decide you don't like.

When you close an image, PhotoDeluxe reminds you to save the image if you haven't already done so. However, you have to assume the responsibility for remembering to save the image during your editing sessions. Whenever you complete a successful edit, save the image. That way, if your computer crashes, you don't lose the whole day's work (gasp).

To resave the image in a flash, just press Ctrl+S (⌘+S on the Mac). Alternatively, you can choose File⇨Save. Either way, PhotoDeluxe resaves the image without bothering you with the Save As dialog box.

Saving in a format other than PDD

If you're familiar with other image editors, you probably expected to be able to select from dozens of file formats when you save your image. And when you encountered the PhotoDeluxe Save As dialog box, you no doubt said something like, "What the?" or, if you're more wordy, "Hey, how come I can't save this image in any format other than the PhotoDeluxe format? Boy, they just don't make 'em like they used to!" Or something like that.

Either way, calm down. PhotoDeluxe can save your image in about any file format that you want. The command you need just happens to be located in an out-of-the-way spot. My guess is that the folks at Adobe tucked the option away to ensure that users relied on the PDD format for everyday saving. Using the PDD format, after all, makes the program run more efficiently, which is why you should save to another format only if absolutely necessary and only after you're done applying all your edits to the image.

But enough about the why. Here's the how-to for saving in another format if you're using Version 2 or Version 3:

1. **Choose File⇨Send To⇨File Format.**

   In Version 3, choose File⇨Export⇨File Format instead.

   PhotoDeluxe displays the Export dialog box, which is a virtual twin of the Save As dialog box that you get when you choose the standard Save command (refer to Figures 4-1 and 4-2). But this time, formats other than PDD are available to you.

   One format, GIF, is absent from the list of format options. Skip through this chapter to "GIF: Another Web favorite" for instructions on saving to GIF.

2. **Select your format.**

   In Windows, choose the format from the Save As pop-up menu. On a Mac, make your selection from the Format pop-up menu. Check out "Format Fever," later in this chapter, for a thorough review of the mainstream format options.

3. **Do all the other standard saving stuff.**

   In other words, follow Steps 2 through 5 in the preceding set of steps. Note that you can't create an EasyPhoto thumbnail when using some file formats. If the EasyPhoto options become dimmed and unavailable after you select a file format, the program can't add a thumbnail to the gallery.

   For some file formats, PhotoDeluxe may offer you dialog boxes that contain additional saving options. In "Format Fever" later in this chapter, I explain the available options for each individual file format.

In the Business Edition, choose File⇨Save As to save your image in a format other than PDD. The Save As submenu offers several format choices, including JPEG. Choose the Other option to access format choices not found on the submenu. Depending on which option you select, PhotoDeluxe opens either the Save, Save As, or Export dialog box — all three work essentially the same way. Give your image a name, select a location on disk, and so on, just as described in the preceding steps.

In some cases, the dialog box that appears when you save the image includes two additional options that don't show up when you choose the regular Save command: Flatten Image and Save Alpha Channels (or Don't Include Alpha Channels). If your image contains layers, as discussed in Chapter 10, choosing any file format except the PhotoDeluxe format (PDD) and the Adobe Photoshop format (PSD) flattens all your layers into one. The Flatten Image option becomes selected automatically for you.

You can ignore the alpha channels thing altogether. This option is one of several that seems to have been lifted from Photoshop when Adobe created PhotoDeluxe. The option has no purpose whatsoever in PhotoDeluxe.

When you save an image as prescribed in these steps, you're merely making a copy of the PDD version that you see on-screen. If you make further edits, pressing Ctrl+S (⌘+S on the Mac) or choosing the Save command saves the PDD version of the image, *not* the one you saved in the new file format. To resave that image, you must choose File⇨Send To⇨File Format (or Export, or Save As, in Version 3 and the Business Edition, respectively) and repeat the entire saving process — entering a filename, choosing the file format, and so on. After you click Save, PhotoDeluxe tells you that the file already exists and asks whether you want to replace the file with the new image. Click Yes to do so. Click No if you think better of the whole idea.

Saving an image with a new name or location

At times, you may want to keep several versions of the same image. For example, say that you need to create a high-resolution image for a print piece but want a low-resolution version for a Web page. You can save the image once at the high resolution, and then reduce the resolution for the Web page and save that low-res image under a different name.

Additionally, you may want to save a copy of your image to a different location on your hard drive or to a removable storage device, such as a floppy disk or a Zip disk.

To save an image with a different name or to another location on disk, choose File⇨Save As in Version 2 and 3. PhotoDeluxe displays the regular Save As dialog box, described earlier. Enter a new filename or choose a storage location — or both — and click Save. Like the Save command, the Save As command enables you to save in the PDD (native PhotoDeluxe) format only. To save the image in some other format, use the process described in the preceding section.

If you're using the Business Edition, choose File⇨Save As and then make a selection from the resulting submenu. To save in the PDD format, choose PhotoDeluxe. To save in another format, select the format from the submenu or select the Other option at the bottom of the submenu. Whichever decision you make, you're taken to the Save As dialog box, where things work as described earlier in this section.

Format Fever

In the computer world, everyone is trying to outdo everyone else. Somebody comes up with a clever way to do something, and right away, other folks look for an even better way to do the exact same thing. This competition is great for consumers, because we have more options. But a wide range of choices can also lead to frustration, because figuring out which option is best often requires an advanced degree in science or math or computer programming — or all three.

Such is the case with image file formats. Computer wizards have developed dozens of different formats (methods of storing image data). And dozens of additional formats are in the works, heaven help us all.

Each format has its own unique advantages and disadvantages, and, unfortunately, no particular format is right for all purposes. The good news is that many formats are either too obscure or too inefficient to be worth your attention, leaving just a handful of choices to consider. The following sections explain the best formats for your images, and Table 4-1 offers a quick-glance guide to which format you should use when.

Just to make mere mortals like us feel silly, most file format names consist of acronyms — JPEG, GIF, and the like. (Developers earn extra points if they can invent an acronym that tells you absolutely nothing about the format.) In some cases, you say the acronym as if it were a real word: PICT is pronounced *pict,* for example. Other times, you pronounce each letter in the acronym: EPS is *E-P-S.* Be sure to pay attention to the pronunciation guidelines in the upcoming format discussions so that you aren't marked as easy prey by roving gangs of computer geeks.

Table 4-1	What Format Do I Use?
For This Purpose	**Use This Format**
Everyday editing in PhotoDeluxe	PDD
Saving an image for use on a Web page	JPEG or GIF
Creating a Web image with a transparent background	GIF
Sending an image as an e-mail attachment	JPEG
Exporting an image to a drawing or page layout program	TIFF or EPS
Exchanging image files with other users, Mac or Windows	TIFF or JPEG
Creating a Windows resource file (screen saver, help file image, and so on)	BMP
Creating Macintosh resource file	PICT

PDD: The everyday editing format

I believe that I droned on sufficiently about the native PhotoDeluxe format, PDD, earlier in this chapter (see "The PhotoDeluxe approach to saving"). But to recap:

- ✔ PDD is optimized to enable PhotoDeluxe to carry out your commands as efficiently as possible.

- ✔ PDD is one of only two formats available to you in PhotoDeluxe that saves any individual layers that you create in PhotoDeluxe. (Image layers are discussed in Chapter 10.) The other format that supports layers is the Adobe Photoshop native format, PSD. Other formats that you can save to in PhotoDeluxe merge all layers into one.

- ✔ Use PDD exclusively while you're in the process of working with an image in PhotoDeluxe. You may want to set up a special folder to store your works-in-progress PDD images. Convert images to another format only after you're finished with all your editing. And if you save the image in a data-destructive format such as JPEG or GIF, retain the PDD version in case you ever need the original image data back.

PDD, by the way, is pronounced *puh-duh-duh*. Say it really fast, so that you sound like a sputtering lawn mower.

Oh, heck, I can't do that to you, no matter how entertaining it would be to hear a bunch of PhotoDeluxe users walking around making sputtering lawn mower sounds. The truth is that you should say *P-D-D.* Forgive me — sometimes spending long, lonely hours shackled to a computer brings out the worst in me.

TIFF: The file exchange format

TIFF, pronounced *tiff,* as in *petty little spat,* stands for Tagged Image File Format. (Extra points to the format-naming committee on that one!) You have my permission to forget what TIFF means. But do remember the following:

✔ TIFF is one of the more widely used formats today. TIFF images can be opened by many programs on both the Mac and Windows platforms. If you need to share images across platforms or open the image in a program other than PhotoDeluxe, TIFF is a good option.

✔ Some formats, including JPEG and GIF, sacrifice some image data in order to shrink the size of the image file. TIFF, however, retains all the image data, which makes the format a good choice for images where the highest picture quality is important.

✔ The downside is that TIFF files are usually larger than JPEG or GIF files, which is why TIFF isn't used for images on Web pages, where small file size is necessary.

✔ When you save to TIFF, PhotoDeluxe displays the dialog box shown in Figure 4-3 after you click the Save button in the Export dialog box. If you're saving the image for use on a Mac system, click the Macintosh option. For an image that you intend to use on a PC, click PC instead.

Figure 4-3:
The saving
options for
a TIFF file.

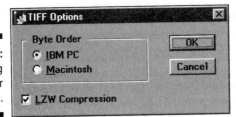

✔ The TIFF Options dialog box offers one additional choice: LZW Compression. *Compression* is a method of removing some image data from a file in order to make the file smaller. LZW stands for Lempel-Ziv-Welch, the three guys who invented the compression scheme.

Several forms of compression exist. Some types of compression, such as LZW, remove only redundant image data and so do no visible harm to your image quality. This type of compression is called *lossless compression*. Other types of compression, including JPEG compression, are called *lossy* because they throw away more important image data and can reduce image quality.

The trade-off is file size. With lossless compression, you retain more image data, which usually results in better image quality, but the image file takes up more room on disk. With lossy compression, you get significantly smaller files but sometimes sacrifice more image quality than is acceptable. Ultimately, you have to be the judge about which is more important, file size or image quality.

✔ Applying LZW compression is generally a good idea — we all need to conserve our file storage space, after all. How much the compression reduces your file size varies from image to image because different images contain different amounts of redundant data.

However, some programs can't open LZW-compressed images. If you're trying to import a TIFF image into some other program and the program refuses to open the file, try resaving the image with LZW compression turned off.

JPEG: The incredible shrinking format

JPEG (say it *jay-peg*) was developed by a committee of gurus called the Joint Photographic Experts Group — hence the name. JPEG offers distinct advantages and disadvantages:

✔ JPEG is widely supported on both the Macintosh and Windows platforms. Translated into English, that means that you can open a JPEG image in just about any program that accepts images — Mac or Windows. This, as Martha Stewart would say, is a Good Thing.

✔ JPEG enables you to compress the image data so that the size of the file is significantly reduced. For this reason, JPEG is one of the more popular formats on the World Wide Web. Smaller file sizes means that visitors to your Web site spend less time downloading your images. Also a good thing.

✔ The drawback is that JPEG compression is *lossy*, which means that some valuable image data may be dumped in the interest of reducing the file size. When you save a file to JPEG, you can specify how much compression you want to apply. The more compression, the more data is sacrificed, and the more your image quality is at risk.

With some images, you may not notice a great deal of damage. But if you compress an image too much, your image can become decidedly jagged and suffer from a loss of detail, as illustrated in Figure 4-4. The top image is the original TIFF image. The bottom example shows what happened to the image after I resaved the image using the maximum amount of JPEG compression. The quality loss grows more noticeable as you increase the image size or zoom in on the image, as I did to create the inset areas for each example.

Figure 4-4: The difference in image quality between a TIFF version of an image (top) and a JPEG version saved with maximum compression (bottom) becomes more noticeable when you enlarge the image (inset areas).

Just how much damage is done by JPEG compression depends on the image, however. Some images look okay even with a high degree of compression, whereas others turn incredibly ugly. You simply need to experiment to see how much compression is too much.

✔ Each time you open, edit, and resave to JPEG, you do more damage to your image. Merely opening and closing the image is fine, but if you make any changes and resave the image, the file is recompressed during the saving process, which means more data loss.

Now that you know the pros and cons of JPEG, you can save to the format as follows:

1. **Make a backup copy of your original image.**

   Saving to JPEG destroys some of your image data, so *always* make a backup copy in some other format (PDD or TIFF).

2. **Save the image to JPEG using the appropriate command on the File menu.**

   In Version 2, choose File➪Send To➪File Format; in Version 3, choose File➪Export➪File Format. In the Business Edition, choose File➪Save As➪ JPEG File. Whew, I sure do wish somebody would come up with a command name and stick with it!

   Give your image a name, location on disk, and so on. (See "Saving in a format other than PDD," earlier in this chapter, if you need more information.) After you click Save, PhotoDeluxe displays the JPEG Options dialog box, shown in Figure 4-5. (In the Business Edition, the dialog box looks slightly different; you get an Advanced button instead of an Options button.)

Figure 4-5: The JPEG Options dialog box in Version 2.

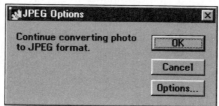

3. **Click the Options button (or the Advanced button in the Business Edition).**

   A second JPEG Options dialog box, shown in Figure 4-6, appears.

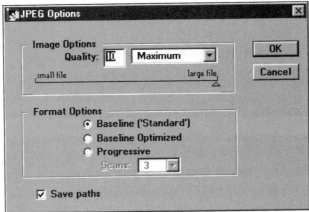

Figure 4-6:
Choose
Maximum
to retain
more
original
image data,
which
results in
better
image
quality.

4. **Choose a compression level.**

The controls in the Image Options portion of the dialog box enable you to choose the image quality you need. The lower the Quality setting, the higher the compression amount and the smaller the file size. Of course, a lower Quality setting also means that more image data is dumped, increasing the chances that your image will suffer.

Not one to limit your options, PhotoDeluxe gives you three different ways to set the Quality value. You can choose an option from the drop-down list, which offers four general settings: Maximum, High, Medium, and Low. Or if you want slightly more control, you can enter a value from 0 through 10 in the Quality option box. Lower values translate to lower image quality and a higher degree of compression.

Finally, you can drag the triangle on the slider bar. Drag to the left to apply lots of compression and create a smaller image file. Drag to the right to apply minimum compression, which results in a larger file.

For Web images, a middle-of-the-road setting is generally acceptable. For print images, apply a smaller amount of compression, keeping in mind that the damage done by compression tends to be more noticeable as you increase the print size of your image.

5. **Choose a Format Options radio button.**

You have three choices:

- Select Baseline ("Standard") for print images.

- Select Baseline Optimized if you're creating a Web image and you don't want any portion of your image to appear on-screen until all the image data is downloaded to the viewer's computer.

- Select Progressive if you want your image to appear gradually on the Web page as image data is downloaded. When the initial image data is received, a low-quality version of the image is displayed.

As more and more data makes its way to the viewer's computer, the image quality improves.

The Scans value determines how many intermediate images the viewer sees before the total image is displayed. You can specify 3, 4, or 5 intermediate images; the default setting of 3 is fine.

The Progressive option is my choice because it gives viewers something to look at while they wait for the picture to download. Additionally, viewers can usually determine whether the picture is of interest to them before the download process finishes. So they can click away to something else if they want without wasting time downloading the entire picture.

However, progressive JPEG images require more RAM to view. In addition, some older Web browsers gag on them. So if visitors to your Web site complain that they're having trouble viewing your images, the Progressive option may be the problem.

6. Click OK.

You can ignore that Save Paths check box in the JPEG Options dialog box. The option enables you to take advantage of an editing feature available in Adobe Photoshop, but not in PhotoDeluxe. (Like other dialog boxes, this one was taken directly from Photoshop and not fully customized for PhotoDeluxe.)

Image-editing wonks use the term *jpegged* to refer to images that have been through the JPEG compression factory.

Determining exactly how much JPEG compression you can get away with is a matter of trial and error. If you don't like what you see after you save the image, reopen the backup copy and save it to JPEG again, this time choosing a higher Quality setting.

GIF: Another Web favorite

The Graphics Interchange Format, better known as GIF, is another popular format for Web images. GIF was developed to enable CompuServe members to share images online, which is why the format is sometimes called CompuServe GIF.

Like JPEG, GIF has some valuable advantages as well as some important drawbacks. Here's what you need to know:

✔ First, your image can contain a maximum of 256 colors. Put another way, GIF can save 8-bit images or smaller. (See Chapter 3 for a discussion of bit depth.) When you save to GIF, PhotoDeluxe converts the image to an 8-bit image and reduces the number of colors to 256.

- GIF is best suited for images that feature large expanses of flat color. With this type of image, you may not notice a huge difference after PhotoDeluxe strips your image down to 256 colors. But for images with a broad spectrum of colors, your image can turn blotchy, as illustrated in Color Plate 3-1. The top image is a 24-bit image, which translates to 16 million colors, whereas the bottom image is an 8-bit image. With only 256 colors, the 8-bit image just doesn't have enough shades to represent subtle color differences.

- Reducing an image to 256 colors is sometimes called *indexing* because the image-editing program consults a color index to determine what color to assign to pixels whose original colors aren't included in the 256-color palette.

- The advantage of limiting the image to 256 colors is a greatly reduced file size, which is why GIF is a great Web format. For example, the 16-million-color image in Color Plate 3-1 consumes roughly three times as much space on disk as the 256-color version.

- Another feature that makes GIF popular with Web designers is the ability to make portions of the image transparent, so that the Web page background shows through. Figure 4-7 shows an example.

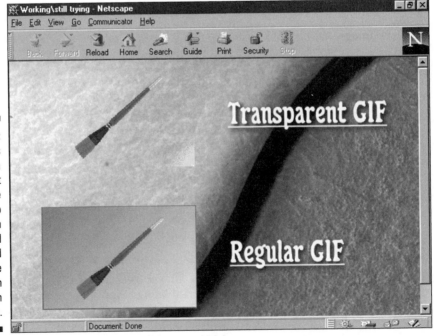

Figure 4-7: Examples of a transparent GIF image (top paintbrush image) and a standard GIF image (bottom paintbrush image).

The paintbrush image at the bottom portion of the window in Figure 4-7 (the one labeled Regular GIF) was saved as a standard GIF, without the transparency feature. You see the paintbrush, the image background (which I filled with a blend of colors), and an outline that I applied around the border.

To create the paintbrush at the top of the window (labeled Transparent GIF), I saved the image using the GIF transparency option. I made everything but the paintbrush transparent, so that the brush appears to float over the Web page. All the image pixels are still there — they're just invisible. Note that I missed some of the pixels in the lower right corner of the image when I was applying the transparency. (Actually, I missed them on purpose to make a point later on.)

✔ Although GIF is good for Web images, don't use GIF for images that you want to attach to e-mail messages. Some e-mail programs can't handle GIF, so use JPEG instead.

The following sections give you the step-by-step instructions for creating both a standard GIF image and one that takes advantage of the transparency option.

Creating a standard GIF image

When you save to GIF, PhotoDeluxe makes a copy of your image, reduces the copy to 256 colors, converts it to GIF, and stores the GIF file on disk. The PDD version of the image that you see on-screen isn't affected in any way. If you haven't yet saved the PDD version of the image, be sure to do so before you close the image. That way, if you ever need the image at its original color depth, you have it.

Now that you've been adequately briefed, here's how to save your image to GIF:

1. **Choose the GIF89a Export command.**

   In Version 2, the command is found on the File⇨Send to submenu; in Version 3, the command is housed on the File⇨Export submenu; and in the Business Edition, the command lives on the File⇨Save As submenu.

   I do believe the folks who invented this format take the prize for the least user-friendly name, don't you? At any rate, when you choose the command, the GIF89a Export Options dialog box shown in Figure 4-8 appears.

2. **Click OK.**

   PhotoDeluxe displays the Export GIF89a dialog box, which is a clone of the standard Export dialog box, which is itself an offshoot of the Save As dialog box.

3. **Assign your image a name and location on disk.**

   If you need help, read "Everyday saves," earlier in this chapter.

Figure 4-8:
The
gateway
to GIF.

4. **Click Save.**

PhotoDeluxe saves a copy of your image in the GIF format as in-structed. To see what effect the color indexing had on the image, you need to open the GIF file; as explained earlier, the on-screen image is the original PDD version and doesn't reflect the reduction in colors.

Keep in mind that when you open the GIF file, PhotoDeluxe makes a copy of the file, converts it to the native PDD format, and displays that PDD copy on-screen, as discussed earlier in "The PhotoDeluxe approach to saving." Because PDD images are 24-bit images, you once again have a full spectrum of colors available if you want to make further edits to the image. You don't, however, get back the color data you lost when you saved to GIF. And if you resave to GIF, the image is once again stripped down to the 256-color limit.

If you don't like what you see when you open the GIF version of your image, close the PDD copy, delete the GIF file on disk, and reopen the *original* image — the one you started with before you saved to GIF for the first time. Now you're back to square one.

When you follow the preceding steps, you create an *interlaced* GIF image. An interlaced GIF image is like a progressive JPEG image. The image appears gradually on the viewer's screen as the image data is downloaded. A noninterlaced image appears all at once after the entire image file is received.

If you want to create a noninterlaced image, click the Advanced button in the GIF89a Export Options dialog box that appears in Step 1. You get a second dialog box of options (peek ahead at Figure 4-9 for a look). Click the Interlaced check box to deselect the option, click OK to return to the first dialog box, and then follow the remaining steps.

Creating a transparent GIF image

As illustrated by the top paintbrush image in Figure 4-7, GIF offers a transparency feature. Using this option, you can make some of your image pixels transparent, so that the background Web page can be seen within the image border. GIF transparency doesn't actually remove any pixels from the image; it simply makes them invisible to the viewer.

Keep in mind that GIF transparency works on a pixel-color basis. You specify what colors you want to make transparent, and *any* pixels of that color become invisible. For example, if you have a multicolor vase set against a blue background and you tell PhotoDeluxe to make blue pixels transparent, the background disappears. But any blue areas of the vase also become transparent. To prevent portions of your vase from disappearing, you need to change the image background to some color that doesn't show up on the vase, too. Note that when you look at the original image in Figure 4-7 (the one labeled Regular GIF), you're looking at a grayscale version of the color original. In the original image, the background is vivid blue; the paintbrush handle is red, white, and black; and the bristles are yellow. So making the blue pixels transparent didn't affect any of the paintbrush pixels.

The steps for creating a transparent GIF seem complicated at first glance, but they're actually pretty simple:

1. Choose the GIF89a Export Command.

   Choose File➪Send To➪GIF89a in Version 2. Or if you use the Business Edition, choose File➪Save As➪GIF89a Export. In Version 3, choose File➪Export➪GIF89a, yada yada yada.

   The GIF89a Export Options dialog box shown in Figure 4-8 appears, just as when you create a standard GIF image.

2. Click Advanced.

   In the Business Edition, click Options instead.

   Either way, PhotoDeluxe offers up a second GIF options dialog box, shown in Figure 4-9. Don't freak out — the options in the dialog box aren't as complex as they appear.

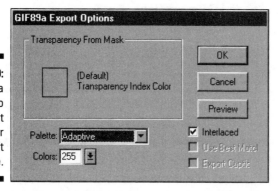

Figure 4-9: Choose a color to represent your transparent pixels here.

3. Set the transparency preview color.

Okay, once more in English: When you view your image in PhotoDeluxe, the program uses a particular color, called the *preview color,* to represent transparent pixels. This coloring of transparent pixels happens only in PhotoDeluxe; when you view the image on the Web page, the pixels are invisible.

By default, the preview color is the same gray that was once commonly used as a background color for Web pages. If your image contains many *non*transparent pixels that are a similar shade of gray, change the preview color to some other shade so that you can more easily distinguish transparent pixels from opaque pixels when you view the image in PhotoDeluxe. To change the color, click the Transparency Index Color box and select a color from the Color Picker, as explained in Chapter 9.

4. Decide whether you want an interlaced image.

GIF, like JPEG, enables you to decide how you want your image to be displayed on the viewer's screen. If you turn on the Interlaced option, the image is displayed bit by bit as the image data makes its way to the viewer's modem. The viewer sees a faint rendition of the image when the image data first arrives. As more and more data is received, the image is filled in. If you turn off the Interlaced option, the viewer sees nothing until all the image data is received. Then the image is displayed in its entirety.

There is no right or wrong choice here; just pick the one that makes you happy. As a viewer, I prefer Interlaced images because I get bored looking at a blank screen while waiting for the image to download (and the process doesn't take long enough to allow me to eat lunch or do anything else important before the image pops on the screen).

5. Ignore the Palette and Colors options.

Unless your client or Web site administrator tells you otherwise, set the Palette option to Adaptive and the Colors option to 255.

6. Click Preview.

The dialog box shown in Figure 4-10 appears. Here's where you have the opportunity to tell PhotoDeluxe which colors you want to make invisible.

7. Click the Eyedropper button and then click the colors that you want to make transparent.

You can either click the color in the image preview at the top of the dialog box or click a color swatch at the bottom of the dialog box. After you click a color, its swatch becomes surrounded by a heavy black outline. All pixels of that color turn the color that you selected as your preview color in Step 4. In Figure 4-10, I set the transparency preview color to white.

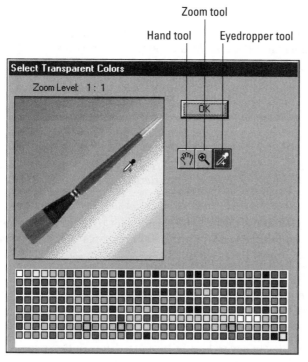

Zoom tool

Hand tool   Eyedropper tool

Figure 4-10:
Click the
colors that
you want
to be
transparent.

If you change your mind about making a color transparent, Ctrl+click the swatch (⌘+click on a Mac) to make the color opaque again. You can tell that the color is deselected because the heavy black outline disappears from around the color swatch.

Click the Zoom button and then click in the image preview to zoom in for a closer look at your image. Alt+click (Option+click on a Mac) to zoom out. Click the Hand button and drag in the image preview to display hidden portions of the image.

After you select a broad array of colors with the Eyedropper, be sure to zoom way in on your image and scroll around the entire image. Make sure that you didn't leave any stray pixels behind, as I did in Figure 4-7 (you can see the offending pixels in the bottom right corner of the image). When you're zoomed out on the image, stray pixels can be difficult to see. Also inspect the portions of the image that you *don't* want to make transparent to make sure that you haven't selected any colors that are in those areas.

8. Click OK.

PhotoDeluxe takes you to the Export GIF89 dialog box, which looks
suspiciously like the standard Export dialog box discussed earlier in
this chapter — and it works the same way, too. (See "Saving in a format
other rthan PDD" earlier in this chapter.) Choose a filename and a file
location and click Save. PhotoDeluxe saves a copy of your image in the
GIF format. The original PDD version of the image remains on-screen.

To see how well you did at making the right pixels transparent, you must
open the GIF version of your image. The PDD version on-screen looks the
same as it did before you saved to GIF. If you don't already have a copy of
your image saved at the original color depth, be sure to save the PDD
version before you close it.

If you, in fact, left some pixels behind and want to make them transparent —
or you went too far and want to restore some pixels to their original
opacity — just repeat the preceding steps.

Special-use formats

In addition to the mainstream formats TIFF, JPEG, and GIF, PhotoDeluxe can
save and open files in several other formats. A few of those formats are so
obscure or limited in their applications that I won't bore you by discussing
them here. The following list discusses other formats that may come in
handy on occasion, as well as one format, FlashPix, that you may hear more
about in the future.

✔ **PICT:** Pronounced *pict,* as in *picture,* this format is the native graphics
format for Macintosh computers. Use PICT only if you want to share
your images with a Mac user who doesn't have any way to open TIFF or
JPEG files. You can open PICT files inside SimpleText and other basic
Mac programs. You can also use PICT to save images that are to be
used as so-called *system resources* — images for an online Help system,
for example.

✔ **BMP:** BMP is short for *Windows Bitmap,* the native format for Windows
graphics. Some people refer to BMP files as *bimp* files. But other folks
use the less goofy-sounding *bitmap,* which leads to confusion over
whether they're using the term in the generic sense, as in a pixel-based
picture, or in the specific file format sense. I prefer to say *B-M-P* to avoid
this problem, but you can use your discretion.

BMP today is pretty much limited to saving images that will be used as Windows system resources. You can use BMP when creating images for online Help systems, for example, or for an image that you want to use as Windows wallpaper (the picture behind all the icons on your desktop). For instructions on how to create wallpaper, check out Chapter 13.

✔ **PDF:** Pronounced *P-D-F,* this format is the native format used by Adobe Acrobat. Acrobat is a program used to view electronic documents, such as the online manuals that are often included on the CDs you use to install new software.

The Acrobat document viewer is provided free of charge (it's included on your PhotoDeluxe CD-ROM and is also available at Adobe's Web site, `www.adobe.com`). Acrobat is available for Windows, Mac, UNIX, and DOS. So if you want to send your image to someone without any other means of viewing the picture, Acrobat is a convenient solution.

To save in the PDF format, choose File⇨Send To⇨Acrobat File in Version 2, File⇨Export⇨Acrobat File in Version 3, and File⇨Save As⇨ Acrobat PDF File in the Business Edition. PhotoDeluxe displays the standard Save dialog box and selects PDF as the file format. Give the file a name and specify where you want to store the file on disk. Then click Save. PhotoDeluxe makes a copy of your image in the PDF format.

Unfortunately, PhotoDeluxe is limited in its ability to open PDF files. Version 3 and the Business Edition can't open any PDF files, even those you save to the PDF format in PhotoDeluxe. Version 2 can open PDF files that were created in either Version 2 or Version 1 of PhotoDeluxe, but not those created in other programs.

✔ **EPS:** EPS (*E-P-S*) stands for Encapsulated PostScript, which is a computer language used by most drawing and page-layout programs as well as by higher-end printers. EPS files are much larger than TIFF or JPEG files, so save to EPS only if your layout or drawing program can't work with anything else or if your commercial printer requests the file in EPS format. You can find out more about the various EPS options available to you by reading the PhotoDeluxe Help system information.

✔ **PSD:** Say *P-S-D,* not *pssst.* This format is the native format for Adobe Photoshop, big brother of Adobe PhotoDeluxe. Version 4 and higher of Photoshop can open PhotoDeluxe PDD files, but Version 3 can't. Save to PSD if you need to open your PhotoDeluxe file in Photoshop 3.

✔ **FlashPix:** FlashPix is a new format being developed by an organization known as the Digital Imaging Group, or DIG for short. DIG includes representatives from Kodak, Microsoft, Hewlett-Packard, Live Picture, and other major players in the digital imaging industry.

The main intent of FlashPix is to enable users to view and edit images more efficiently. Because of the way FlashPix stores images, you don't need a mondo-expensive, high-powered computer system to process large images, say the format's developers.

FlashPix is fairly complicated to explain, but here's the general idea: Your image is stored at several different sizes — for example, 640 x 480 pixels, 320 x 240 pixels, and 160 x 120 pixels — all in the same file. The different versions of the image are stacked in a pyramid structure, with the largest version on the bottom. When you edit or view the image, the program you're using works with the smallest possible version that enables you to do what you want to do. The program digs down to the bottom, largest version of the image only when necessary — when you zoom in for a closer look at the image, for example. Because most operations can be done using the smaller version of the image, your computer needs less time and system resources to do your bidding. The DIG estimates that a FlashPix image requires about 20 percent less RAM to view than a TIFF image, for example.

If FlashPix lives up to its promise, I expect that the format will become very popular for Web imagery and for creating images for games and other virtual reality programs, two uses where small file size and processing speed are critical. Certainly FlashPix is backed by enough industry muscle to push it into the mainstream sooner or later. But at this time, I don't recommend saving to the format unless a client or Web site administrator requests it.

Older Web browsers can't open FlashPix images, so you'll disappoint some of your Web site viewers if you use FlashPix. In addition, you can't import FlashPix images into most word processors, page layout programs, and other programs that you may be using to create documents containing images. A final drawback to FlashPix is that a FlashPix file consumes about 33 percent more disk storage space than a TIFF file. You can apply JPEG compression to a FlashPix image to reduce the file size, but then you sacrifice some of your image quality just as you do when you save a standard JPEG image.

If, despite all these cautions, you save in the FlashPix format, PhotoDeluxe gives you the option of applying JPEG compression after you click the Save button in the Save As dialog box. If you don't want to compress the image, choose the No Compression option in Version 2. In the Business Edition and Version 3, select the None option from the Encoding drop-down list. If you want to compress the image, select the

Use JPEG Compression option in Version 2; in the Business Edition and Version 3, select JPEG from the Encoding drop-down list. You're then asked to specify the amount of compression, just as when you save a standard JPEG image (see the JPEG section earlier in this chapter for details).

A Few EasyPhoto Tricks

When you install PhotoDeluxe, you automatically install a program called EasyPhoto as well. With EasyPhoto, you can

✔ Scroll through your image files and see thumbnail previews of each image. So if you're not sure exactly what name you gave an image when you saved it to disk, you can track it down using EasyPhoto.

✔ Organize your thumbnails into *galleries,* or categories of images. For example, you can set things up so that thumbnails of all your animal images are in one gallery, and the thumbnails of all your people images are in another gallery. Note that sorting your thumbnails in EasyPhoto *does not* organize your actual image files — only the previews that you see in EasyPhoto.

As image browsers and catalog programs go, EasyPhoto is in the middle of the road in terms of features. If you store hundreds of images, you may want to invest in something more powerful, such as ThumbsPlus by Cerious Software, Inc., or Portfolio from Extensis. You can find trial versions of both programs, as well as a few others, on the CD at the back of this book.

But if you're just starting to build your inventory of images, EasyPhoto may work just fine for you. And EasyPhoto has the advantage of being incorporated into PhotoDeluxe, which means that you can open and use the EasyPhoto browser without switching programs.

You can also run EasyPhoto on its own, if you prefer. In Windows, just work your way up from the Start button to the Programs menu to the Adobe menu and finally to the PhotoDeluxe menu. Then click the EasyPhoto program item. On a Mac, locate the EasyPhoto folder, which is stored inside the main PhotoDeluxe folder. Double-click the EasyPhoto icon to start the program.

Usually, you're better off running EasyPhoto from within PhotoDeluxe. In the PhotoDeluxe program window, you can enlarge the EasyPhoto browser so that you can see two, three, or even more rows of thumbnails at a time. When you run EasyPhoto outside PhotoDeluxe, you can display only one row at a time. For a look at how the browser appears inside PhotoDeluxe, flip to Figure 1-5 in Chapter 1; to see how the browser looks outside PhotoDeluxe, check out Figure 4-11.

Add Photos

Figure 4-11:
The
EasyPhoto
browser
window as
it appears
outside
PhotoDeluxe.

The only reason that you may want to launch EasyPhoto outside PhotoDeluxe is to add several images to a gallery at a time. Inside PhotoDeluxe, you can add only one image at a time, and you have to open and save the image in order to do so.

The following sections explain how to create thumbnails, organize them into EasyPhoto galleries, add captions to your thumbnails, and view the captions and other image information inside the browser window. You also find out how to dump a batch of images into a gallery in one quick process and how to delete images from a gallery.

After you create and organize your thumbnails, check out "Opening the sample images" and "Opening images in an EasyPhoto gallery" in Chapter 1 to find out more about viewing your thumbnails and working with the browser window. And if you want to find out more about other EasyPhoto features not discussed in this book, start EasyPhoto outside of PhotoDeluxe and choose Help⇨Easy Photo Help.

Creating an image gallery

As mentioned a few paragraphs ago, you can organize your image thumbnails into categories or, in EasyPhoto lingo, *galleries*. When you run EasyPhoto outside PhotoDeluxe, each gallery is contained in its own window. The different galleries appear on different panels in the browser window when you open EasyPhoto in PhotoDeluxe. (Choose File⊅Open Special⊅My Photos to open the browser window in Version 2; choose File⊅My Photos⊅Show My Photos in the Business Edition and Version 3.)

The following list offers a few factoids about EasyPhoto galleries:

- EasyPhoto automatically creates an Examples gallery, which contains thumbnails of the clip art images on the PhotoDeluxe CD, as well as a My Photos gallery, which contains thumbnails for images that you create. In Version 2, an Acquire gallery is created if you scan directly into PhotoDeluxe or download from a digital camera. (See the section on scanning in Chapter 1 for more information.)

- You can create additional galleries if you like. Choose File⊅My Photos⊅ Create New Gallery inside PhotoDeluxe. A dialog box appears, showing a list of all your current galleries. Type the name of the new gallery in the New Gallery Name box and click Create. If you want to create a second gallery, type another name and click Create again. Click Done when you have all the galleries that you can possibly stand.

- If you're in the process of saving an image to disk and you decide that you want to create a new gallery for it, click the New Gallery button at the bottom of the Save As dialog box and proceed as just described. (For more about the Save As dialog box, read "Everyday saves," earlier in this chapter.)

- To get rid of a gallery and all thumbnails in the gallery, choose File⊅My Photos⊅Delete Gallery. Select the name of the gallery that you want to trash and click Delete. After you finish your gallery-destroying mission, click Done.

- When you close PhotoDeluxe or close the EasyPhoto browser, you're prompted to save any new galleries that you create. If you don't save the gallery, only the thumbnails are deleted. Your original image files remain intact.

Adding and deleting photos from a gallery

As discussed earlier in this chapter, you can create a thumbnail during the process of saving an image by checking the Add to Gallery option at the bottom of the Save As dialog box. Choose the gallery where you want to store the thumbnail from the drop-down list next to the Add to Gallery check box, and type a title in the Title box. The title appears with the thumbnail in the EasyPhoto browser. You don't have to use the same name that you gave to the actual image file, although you can if you so desire. Keep in mind that if your name is too long, the entire name isn't displayed in the browser. Your image name can contain as many as 32 characters, but only about 12 characters are displayed in the browser.

To add several images to a gallery at the same time, use the following steps to get the job done quickly:

1. **Start EasyPhoto outside of PhotoDeluxe.**

   For best results, shut down PhotoDeluxe before you start EasyPhoto. Running the two programs at the same time in this fashion can cause some system hang-ups.

   The program launches, and each gallery you have created appears in its own browser window.

   If you're already running EasyPhoto and want to open a gallery that you closed, press Ctrl+O (⌘+O on a Mac) or choose File➪Create or Open Photo Gallery to open the dialog box shown in Figure 4-12. You can then double-click the name of the gallery that you want to open. Alternatively, you can click the Create New Gallery button to start a new gallery for your images.

2. **Click the Add Photos to Gallery button or choose File➪Add Photos to Gallery.**

   The button is labeled in Figure 4-11. In the Mac version of EasyPhoto, the button appears on a separate, floating toolbar rather than at the top of the browser window.

   After you click the button, the dialog box shown in Figure 4-13 appears. To add thumbnails for images stored on a CD, click the CD button. To add thumbnails for images stored on either your hard drive or a removable storage disk (floppy, Zip, and so on), click the Hard Disk or Diskette button. On a Mac, click OK after you choose the icon.

   The third button, Photo Reader or Camera, enables you to scan images or download images from a camera directly into EasyPhoto. The process works just as described in Chapter 1, in "Scanning directly into PhotoDeluxe."

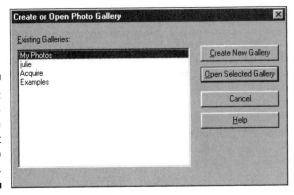

Figure 4-12:
Double-click the gallery that you want to open.

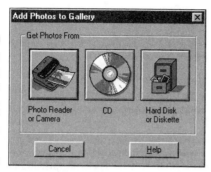

Figure 4-13:
The first
step in
adding a
batch of
thumbnails
to a gallery.

3. **Choose the photos that you want to add to the gallery.**

After you click a button in Step 2, you see a dialog box similar to the
one shown in Figure 4-14, assuming that you chose the Hard Disk or
Diskette option earlier. (The Mac version is arranged differently, but
contains mostly the same elements.) Choose the folder or drive that
contains the photos you want to add to the browser from the scrolling
list on the left side of the dialog box. The Select Photos list box displays
all the image files in the selected folder or drive. If you chose the CD
option, your dialog box contains a list of all images on the CD.

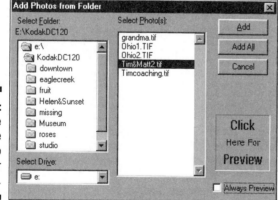

Figure 4-14:
Select one
or more
images to
add to your
gallery.

After you find the image you want to add to the gallery, click its name. In Windows, you can Ctrl+click on additional images to add several pictures to the gallery. If you want to create thumbnails for all the images, don't do a thing — yet.

If you're using a Mac, a preview of the image appears in the dialog box. In Windows, you may need to click the Click Here For Preview area in the bottom right corner of the dialog box to see a thumbnail of the image. If you select the Always Preview option, EasyPhoto automatically displays a thumbnail for every image that you select in the Select Photos list. Displaying the thumbnails eats up some time, so I turn this option off unless I really need it. Note that if you're adding images from a CD, EasyPhoto automatically displays the thumbnails without any input from you.

4. Click the Add button.

Or, if you want to add all the images to the gallery, click the Add All button. EasyPhoto adds the thumbnails as you request.

If you're adding images from a CD, EasyPhoto may prompt you for the name of the CD before it adds the thumbnails. Go ahead and enter an identifying name for the CD. The next time you add images from the same CD, you shouldn't have to take this step.

To delete a thumbnail from a gallery, click the thumbnail in the browser window and press Delete. You can do this whether you're running EasyPhoto inside or outside of PhotoDeluxe. The thumbnail is removed from EasyPhoto, but the actual image file (on disk, on CD, or whatever) remains.

To remove a bunch of thumbnails at once, click the first one, Shift+click the rest and then press Delete. Be sure to Shift+click on the thumbnail image rather than the thumbnail title.

Adding captions and viewing image information

If you press and hold down your mouse button on a thumbnail title, you display a box containing some vital image information: the image filename and the location where the file is stored on disk. Flip back to Figure 1-5, in Chapter 1, for a peek at how the box looks. Or better yet, try displaying the box yourself.

The top of the information box includes room for an image caption or other notes that you want to record, such as the date you captured the photograph. To add a caption or notes to a thumbnail while you're running EasyPhoto inside PhotoDeluxe, choose File⇨My Photos⇨Show Photo Info or, in Windows, right-click the thumbnail and choose Edit Photo. If you're running EasyPhoto on its own, outside of PhotoDeluxe, choose Edit⇨Edit

Photo Information. Either approach displays the dialog box shown in Figure 4-15. Here you can add or change the title of the thumbnail as well as enter a caption or image information.

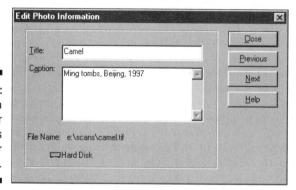

Figure 4-15:
Add a
caption or
other notes
to your
thumbnail.

 You can annotate (add captions and notes) to several images with one trip to the dialog box. After you add the information for the first image, click Next to add information for the next thumbnail in the current gallery. Click Previous to enter information for the previous image. Click Close after you finish annotating all your images.

Tracking down a lost image

Adding captions and titles to your thumbnails can come in handy down the road when you need to track down a particular image. EasyPhoto has a command that you can use to search for all images that contain a particular word or phrase in the title or caption.

To go on your image hunt, Start EasyPhoto outside of PhotoDeluxe and choose Edit➪Find Photos to display the dialog box shown in Figure 4-16. Enter the phrase or word that you want to search for in the option box and

Figure 4-16:
You can
search for
images
according
to caption
or title
information.

specify whether you want to dig through just the currently open gallery or all galleries. Then click Find. EasyPhoto displays thumbnails of all images that match your search criteria inside a new gallery.

Press and hold on the thumbnail title to see the image's filename and location on disk. Then close down EasyPhoto; you can save or destroy the new gallery as you see fit. Finally, switch back to PhotoDeluxe and use the File⇨Open File command to open the image. (Remember, you shouldn't run EasyPhoto and PhotoDeluxe separately because doing so can cause system crashes.) If you click the By Example tab in the dialog box shown in Figure 4-16, you can search for images that resemble the selected image. Well, at least, you're supposed to be able to do so. I didn't have much success getting this feature to work because EasyPhoto wasn't terribly discriminating. Searching the Examples gallery for images that look like a black comb image turned up everything from a picture of a black Halloween mask to a bird's nest. Hmmm. I can personally do without this feature, but if you want to give it a try, click the thumbnail that you want to use as a basis for your search and then choose Edit⇨Find Photos. (You must run EasyPhoto outside of PhotoDeluxe to access this command.) When the dialog box shown in Figure 4-16 appears, click the By Example tab and click Find.

Yikes! Where Do I Put All This Stuff?

If you create and save many large images, you can quickly run out of storage space on your computer's hard drive. You can purge existing files to make room for new ones, or you can invest in some sort of removable storage device, such as those Iomega Zip drives that everyone is talking about these days.

What about that floppy disk drive that came with your computer, you ask? Can't you just store images on floppies? Well, yes, if the images are small. But remember that a floppy can hold less than 1.5MB of data, and many of your images may be larger than that.

Shopping for additional image closet space can be a daunting task because so many different types of removable storage exist. I don't have room for a thorough discussion of all the options, but here's a quick overview:

✔ At the bottom end of the price spectrum are so-called "super floppies," which are basically floppy disks on steroids. Super floppies can store 100MB or more of data on disks that are just a little larger than a standard floppy disk. The Iomega Zip disk is the most popular product in this category. Of course, you need a Zip drive to store data on Zip disks. A Zip drive now costs between $100 and $200, depending on whether you get the plain vanilla version that's been on the market for a while or the new Zip Plus, which offers some additional user features and technical options. Whichever version of the drive you buy, a Zip disk sets you back about $13.

Zip drives are now provided as standard or optional equipment on many new computers. Because the Zip drive is now in such widespread use, it's a good option if you need to share large image files with other users or transport images to a professional printer.

A newcomer to the marketplace in this category is the Imation SuperDisk LS-120, which can store data on both 120MB disks as well as old-fashioned floppies. The SuperDisk has been getting a lot of attention lately and is offered as an option in some new computer systems. However, a standard floppy drive can't read the SuperDisk disks, so if you need to swap files with other people, compatibility may be an issue with the SuperDisk. The drive itself comes in at around $150, and each 120MB disk costs about $13.

✔ For additional cash, you can get more storage capacity. You can find removable drives that store anywhere from 200MB or data up to a whopping 4GB. One popular option, the Iomega Jaz, comes in both 1GB and 2GB versions, for $299 and $350, respectively. Jaz data cartridges make you wince at $75 for a 1GB cartridge and $125 for the 2GB option.

Drives such as the Jaz are popular with some graphics professionals who routinely create and store enormous image files. But if you're in the habit of sharing images with everyday folks, remember that they won't be able to open your images unless they have the same expensive taste in data storage.

✔ Another option is to have your images transferred to CD-ROM at a digital imaging lab (check your Yellow Pages for a lab in your area). You can put about 650MB of data on a CD. In my city (Indianapolis), the cost is just under $40 for the first 150MB of data transferred. You can keep taking the CD back to the lab until you fill it up. The benefit of storing your images on CD is that most computers these days have CD-ROM drives, which makes sharing your images with others easy. If you want a duplicate CD made, the cost is about $25.

In the back of this book, you can find a coupon from Firehouse Image Center, an Indianapolis digital imaging company that offers CD-transfer services as well as printing and scanning services. You can visit the company's Web site at www.Fire-house.net for more information on available services and prices.

If you're a cutting-edge kind of person, you may want to check out the new CD-ROM recorders that enable you to burn your own images onto CD. Before you get into this can of worms, however, do plenty of research. Many different forms of consumer-level CD hardware exist, and not all are as reliable or easy to use as others. In addition, not every CD-ROM drive can read all types of CDs made by every CD unit, so be especially cautious if sharing images with others is a big concern.

✔ If you don't plan to do much file-swapping, you can also consider adding a second hard drive to your computer to increase your file-storage space. But if you ever need to transfer those images to another system or share an image file with another user, you may need to invest in a removable storage device as well.

✔ Finally, for those folks who want to archive lots of files but don't necessarily need to access those files on a regular basis, tape drives are an option. Tape drives offer large-capacity storage at relatively low prices, but saving and accessing files with these babies is slow. One option in this category is the Seagate TapeStor Travan, which sells for about $350 and uses 4GB tape cartridges at $35 each.

To sum up, the best choice for everyday mortals at present is either investing in a Zip drive or having images professionally stored on a CD-ROM. Graphics professionals may need higher-end options, such as a Jaz. Before you choose any storage device, be sure to consider the cost of the storage media — how many MB can you store per $1? — as well as whether the people with whom you share files will be able to access data stored on that media.

Image data, like any computer data, can degrade over time. With storage devices that use magnetic media, which includes floppy disks and Zip disks among others, data loss can start to become noticeable after ten years. Devices that use magneto-optical media, another kind of storage technology, give your data a longer life span — about 30 years. However, magneto-optical devices are more expensive than regular magnetic media devices, which puts them beyond the reach of the general image-editing public.

Writing your images to Photo CD is the best option for long-term archival storage of images. Professional labs use CDs that have a special coating, such as Kodak's InfoGuard, that is designed to prevent data loss. Images stored on these CDs have a life expectancy of about 100 years — roughly the same as a print photograph. Without this coating, data loss can occur in just a few years.

Chapter 5
Putting Pixels on Paper

• •

In This Chapter

▶ Sending an image to the printer

▶ Choosing the paper size and image orientation

▶ Getting printed colors to match on-screen colors

▶ Choosing the right printer for your home or office

▶ Preparing an image for professional printing

▶ Improving the appearance of your prints

• •

*G*etting a digital image from your computer onto paper isn't a difficult proposition. You choose File⇨Print, and a minute or so later, your image comes creeping out of the printer.

Getting a *good* print of a digital image is another matter entirely. Any number of factors can hamper your efforts to reproduce your images on paper, from choosing the wrong image resolution to buying the wrong paper. For a process that seems, on the surface, like such a simple one, printing can often lead you into a complex maze of problems.

This chapter helps you understand the mechanics of putting pixels on paper so that you can get the best possible prints of your images. In addition to covering the basics of sending an image to your printer, I offer some guidance on choosing a printer for your home or office, sending your images to a professional for printing, and getting your printed colors to match your on-screen colors.

Printing Basics

Sending an image from PhotoDeluxe to the printer is a simple matter of choosing the File⇨Print command. But before you get to that command, you need to move through a few preparatory steps. The following sections outline the printing process.

Basic printing procedures

If you have more than one printer attached to your system and you're using a Macintosh, use the Chooser to select the printer that you want to access before taking the following steps. In Windows, you can choose the printer from inside the first dialog box referenced in the steps, so you can dive right in.

1. **Open the image you want to print.**

2. **Select the area to be printed.**

You can print just a portion of the image by selecting that area before initiating the print process. See Chapter 8 for information on how to draw a selection outline. If you want to print the entire image, press Ctrl+D (⌘+D on the Mac) to get rid of any existing selection outlines.

Alternatively, you can choose to print only certain layers in a multilay- ered image. Any layers that are visible print; layers that are hidden don't get to go to the dance. You hide and reveal layers by clicking the little eyeball icons in the Layers palette, as explained in Chapter 10.

3. **Select a printer, page size, and print orientation.**

To do this, choose File⇨Page Setup to enter the Page Setup dialog box, shown in Figure 5-1. This dialog box varies depending on your printer and operating system, but usually includes options that enable you to select a printer, page size, and a page orientation.

If you're new to the printing game, the Landscape orientation setting prints your image sideways on the page, with the top of your image running parallel to the long edge of the paper. The Portrait option prints your image normally, with the top of the image parallel to the short edge of the paper. The two settings were so named because landscape paintings usually have a horizontal orientation, and portrait paintings typically have a vertical orientation.

On a Mac, some page setup dialog boxes offer a Reduce or Enlarge option. You can use this option to scale your image for printing only. If you want to permanently resize the image, you must do so in the Photo Size dialog box, as described in the next step.

After you specify the printer, page size, and orientation you want, click OK.

4. **Set the image size and resolution.**

You accomplish both chores in the Photo Size dialog box (choose Size⇨Photo Size).

The settings you choose in the Photo Size dialog box are critical to the printed appearance of your image, so take the time to read and under- stand "Sizing an image for printing" and "The right ppi for printing" in Chapter 3.

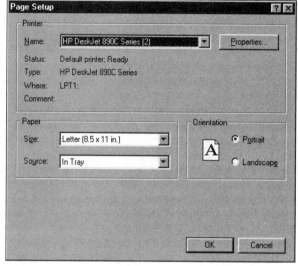

Figure 5-1:
Set the
paper size,
printer,
and page
orientation
here.

5. **Preview the image.**

Choose File⇨Print Preview or press Ctrl+/ (forward slash) on a PC or
⌘+/ on a Mac to display a preview of your printed image. PhotoDeluxe
presents a window showing how your image will appear on the page
according to the choices you made in Steps 2 and 3. If the image
doesn't fit on the page, you need to rethink either your paper size or
your image size.

6. **Give the print command.**

Choose File⇨Print or, better yet, get acquainted with the universal
keyboard shortcut for printing: Ctrl+P in Windows and ⌘+P on a Mac.

The Print dialog box, shown in Figure 5-2, bounds onto the playing field.
The dialog box may look slightly different, depending on your printer
and operating system.

In Version 3, the Print dialog box contains a button not shown in Figure 5-2: the ColorApp button. Clicking this button takes you to the
Adjust Color Printing dialog box, discussed later in this chapter, in the
section "Calibrating Printer and Monitor." This feature is designed to
help you correct discrepancies between your on-screen colors and
your printed colors.

7. **Set your printer options.**

In Windows, click Setup, which returns you to the Page Setup dialog
box, and then click the Properties button.

On a Mac, click the Options button to access any available printer
options not available through the first print dialog box.

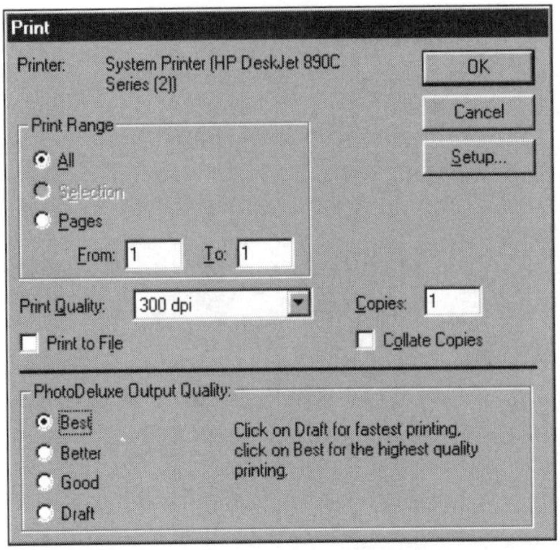

Figure 5-2:
The Print
dialog box
contains all
your
printing
options.

You're chauffeured to a dialog box that contains all the various settings available for your particular model of printer. I'm afraid that I can't help you determine which settings to use; printers simply vary too much from model to model. So consult your printer manual to see what settings are appropriate for your printing project.

After you choose your printer options, click OK to return to the Print dialog box on a Mac. In Windows, click OK to return to the Page Setup dialog box and then click OK again to return to the Print dialog box.

8. Specify the number of copies, the print range, and the print quality.

If you selected a portion of your image before you choose the Print command, you can print just the selection by choosing Selection as your Print Range option in Windows. On a Mac, choose the Print Selected Area option. (Note that the specific option names may vary slightly depending on your printer.) If you don't choose the Selection option as the print range, the entire image prints.

As for the Print Quality settings, they don't override any printer-specific settings that you choose — that is, those that you access via the Properties or Options button. But they do control how much image data is sent to the printer.

In order to keep your system from blowing its memory and storage-space stack, PhotoDeluxe limits the amount of data that you can send to the printer. The amount of data that PhotoDeluxe passes along to the printer depends on the capabilities of the printer you selected. The cap is proportionate to the printer's maximum dpi (the number of dots of ink the printer can apply to represent each inch of the image). For most printers, the image data is capped at 300 ppi (image pixels per inch); but for some printers, such as the Epson inkjets that can print at 1,440 dpi (printer ink dots per inch), the image resolution limit is just a tad higher.

If you choose the Best option in the Print dialog box, you send the maximum amount of data to the printer, within the allowable cap. In other words, if you set your image resolution to 300 ppi, all the image data goes to the printer. If you choose a lesser print quality, PhotoDeluxe sends a lower-resolution file to the printer to speed up printing time.

Bottom line: To achieve the best possible print quality, select the Best option. Use the other options for printing drafts of your image.

9. Send that image to the printer.

To close the Print dialog box and send the image information to the printer, click OK (Windows) or Print (Mac). Assuming that your printer and your computer are correctly connected and on speaking terms, the printer does its thing and then spits out your printed image.

You usually don't have to go through all this rigmarole every time you print. If you know that the default settings in the Page Setup dialog box are okay for your print project, you can skip Step 3. And if the default settings for your specific printer are acceptable, you can skip Step 7. Just press Ctrl+P (or ⌘+P), choose the number of copies, print range, and print quality, and then click OK.

Printing multiple copies on the same page

The Business Edition offers a special printing option, called the Print Multiple command, that makes it easy for you to print multiple copies of an image on the same page. You can use this feature to print your face on a sheet of business cards, for example. This option is specially designed to facilitate printing on labels, business card stock, and other special print media produced by Avery. (You can, however, substitute products from another manufacturer as long as the stock sizes are the same as those from Avery.)

Version 3 offers this same print option, with an extra feature. In addition to helping you print images on Avery stock, the Version 3 Print Multiple command enables you to set up your image for printing in standard photo-graph sizes: $3^1/_2$ x 5 inches, 5 x 7 inches, 8 x 10 inches, and so on.

To take advantage of the multiple-copy option, follow these steps:

1. Choose File⇨Print Multiple.

The Print Multiple dialog box, shown in Figure 5-3, appears.

2. Select a paper type.

The Paper Type option shows the currently selected paper. By default, the paper size you chose in the Page Setup dialog box is selected. (See the preceding section for more information.) To select one of the stock media products produced by Avery — or, in Version 3, a photographic print size — instead, click Change to display the Choose Paper Type

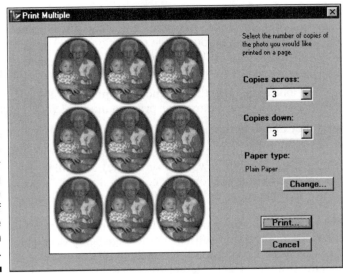

Figure 5-3:
Version 3
and the
Business
Edition have
a tool for
printing
multiple
copies of
the same
image on
one page.

dialog box, shown in Figure 5-4. For printing on Avery products (or similar products from other vendors), select Avery from the top drop-down list and then select the specific Avery product from the scroll-down list. To choose a photographic print size in Version 3, choose Standard Photo Print Size from the top drop-down list and then choose the print size from the list below.

Select Plain Paper from the top drop-down list to use the page size defined in the Page Setup dialog box instead of the Avery or photo size options.

Click OK to return to the Print Multiple dialog box.

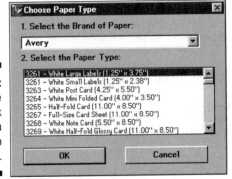

Figure 5-4:
Select the
paper stock
that you
want to
use.

3. Specify the number of copies that you want to print on each page.

Use the Copies Across and Copies Down drop-down lists to specify how many rows and columns of images you want to print. The choices that are available in the drop-down list are based on the paper size you selected in Step 2 and the size of your image. (PhotoDeluxe looks at the paper size and figures out the maximum number of copies that can fit on the page.)

4. Click Print.

Calibrating Printer and Monitor

One of the pitfalls of printing digital images is that the on-screen colors and the printed colors rarely match. Sometimes you get close, but many times printed and on-screen hues aren't even in the same ballpark. The reasons for this color discrepancy are explained in the sidebar "Why what you see isn't what you get," later in this chapter.

Version 3 includes a tool that may help resolve some of the differences. Before you print for the first time from PhotoDeluxe, take these steps to calibrate your printer and monitor. Also repeat the process anytime you change printers or print media (paper stock). Before you begin, make sure that your monitor is set to display more than 256 colors.

1. Choose File⇨Adjust Color Printing.

The dialog box shown in Figure 5-5 appears. Actually, only the top half of the dialog box appears, and the Less button shown in the figure is instead a More button. (This arrangement becomes clear in the next few steps.)

2. Select your printer type from the drop-down menu at the top of the dialog box.

If you don't see your printer type listed, choose Other or Generic Color Printer.

3. Click the More button.

Now your dialog box looks just like the one in Figure 5-5.

4. Click the Print button.

In order to get the printer and monitor in sync, PhotoDeluxe displays a sample image on-screen and then asks you to print the image so that you can compare the two versions.

After you click the Print button, the standard Print dialog box appears, just as when you print any other image. Choose your printer settings and send that image off to the printer.

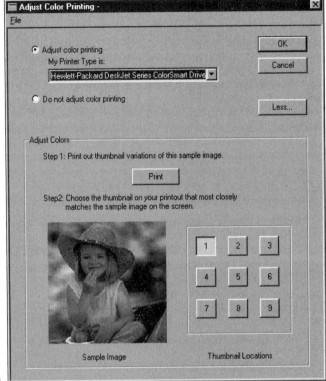

Figure 5-5:
PhotoDeluxe
includes a
tool that
aims to
calibrate
your
monitor
colors with
your printed
colors.

5. Compare the printout with the on-screen image.

Nine different versions of the image appear on your printout. Find the
one that most closely matches the image you see on-screen. Then click
the corresponding thumbnail button in the Adjust Color Printing dialog
box. For example, if the image in the middle of the page looks like the
closest match, click the center thumbnail button (number 5).

6. Click OK to close the dialog box.

Now do a test print on your own image to compare the on-screen colors
with printed colors. If you don't get close color matching, try selecting
a different thumbnail in the Adjust Color Printing dialog box and do
another test print. If none of the thumbnail selections improve color
matching, select the Do Not Adjust Color Printing option and give that
setting a whirl.

Keep in mind that even the most expensive color matching systems on
the planet can't achieve perfect color synchronization between monitor
and printer. So don't expect a total correction of color matching
problems from the Adjust Color Printing command — consider yourself
fortunate if your printer colors and monitor colors appear to be in the
same ballpark.

Why what you see isn't what you get

When you print your first color image, you may be dismayed at how much the colors on the printed page differ from those on your monitor. This color shift happens for a good reason: Monitors and printers create colors in two different ways.

Your monitor uses the *RGB color model* — which is a techie way of saying that it mixes red, green, and blue light to create all the colors that you see on-screen. Full-intensity red, green, and blue together make white, whereas a complete absence of red, green, and blue makes black. If this concept seems foreign to you, imagine aiming red, green, and blue lights at the same spot on the wall. You get a white spotlight on your wall. Conversely, if you turn off all three lights, you get . . . well, welcome to a black room.

Printers, on the other hand, create colors by mixing cyan, magenta, yellow, and black inks — otherwise known as the *CMYK color model.* If you mix full-strength cyan, magenta, yellow, and black ink, you get black, which is directly opposite of what you get if you mix full-intensity red, green, and blue light.

The mismatch between on-screen colors and printer colors arises not just because one device uses light and another uses ink, but because the CMYK and RGB *color space,* or *gamut,* are different. Put in plain English,

that means that CMYK can't create as many different colors as RGB. Your printer just isn't capable of reproducing the most vivid colors that you see on-screen, so it substitutes the nearest matching color. Usually, this results in prints that appear duller than the on-screen version of the image. (Colors that can't be created by a particular color model are said to be *out of gamut,* by the way.)

Some printers do a better job of color matching than others. Most printer software enables you to tweak the printer's color settings if the printed output varies too greatly from the on-screen image. But if you can't get acceptable results by using the printer software, you may want to adjust the actual image colors, using the commands discussed in Chapter 6. Play with the Color Balance and Saturation controls in PhotoDeluxe to compensate for the color shift that occurs with your printer.

Also keep in mind that the brightness of the paper you use as well as the print quality you choose can affect the colors that you see on the printed page. Experiment with different settings and different papers, and also consult your printer manual for suggestions on improving color matching. And if you're using Version 3 of PhotoDeluxe, give the Adjust Color Printing feature a whirl, as discussed in the section, "Calibrating Printer and Monitor."

Shopper's Guide to Printers

I know that when you read that headline, you hoped that I was going to share privileged information about the best buys in printers. Sorry, but I have to disappoint you. Printer manufacturers are turning out new models at breakneck speed, with everyone trying to capture the growing digital imaging market. If I were to recommend a printer, a better model at a better price would surely be on the market before this book made it from the printer to the bookseller. And you'd just end up hating me for steering you toward an outdated product. I can, however, offer you some general buying advice, which I do in the next two sections.

What type of printer is right for me?

The printers available to the average home or small-business buyer fall into a few distinct categories. These different types of printers each cater to a special market niche, so you need to carefully consider your printing needs before you go shopping. Here's a quick look at the advantages and disadvantages of each of the main categories of machines:

✔ **Inkjet:** Inkjet printers spray droplets of ink onto the page. Inkjets deliver a reasonable facsimile of a photograph at an economical price, which makes them the most popular choice among home and small-office users. You can get a good inkjet for less than $400, and the ink cost per print ranges from about 8 to 20 cents, assuming that your photo covers about 15 percent of an $8^1/_2$-x-11-inch page. Within this category, several important features vary from printer to printer:

- Some inkjets have four ink cartridges, one each for the cyan, yellow, magenta, and black ink. Others have just two cartridges — one for the black and one for the cyan, magenta, and yellow — and yet other models combine all four inks into one cartridge. The different colors of ink are consumed at different rates, however, which means that if you have all your inks in one or two cartridges, you usually end up throwing away some ink when one color is gone.

- Lower-priced models sometimes omit the black ink, which means that black areas of your images tend to look muddy brown, not black. Steer clear of these models if you can afford better.

- Certain inkjet models are geared toward people whose primary concern is output that comes as close to a traditional photograph as possible. These printers, sometimes called *photocentric printers,* print your image on glossy photo stock and may or may not be able to print on regular paper. They typically consume a lot of ink per print, and the glossy photo stock is about $1 per $8^1/_2$ x 11 sheet. So your cost per print is relatively high.

- Other models are geared more toward folks who want their printers to do dual duty as a text printer and a graphics printer. These models can handle plain as well as glossy paper, but they may not match the glossy-print quality of the models designed expressly for photo printing. On the other hand, the photo printers don't do a good job on text because they're not engineered to do so.

- Output from inkjet printers varies widely, so be sure to compare sample printouts before you buy. Some printers deliver wonderful results, but others are downright stinky. Ink smearing and page warping (from too-wet ink) is a problem with some models, the clarity of the printed image varies widely from machine to machine. As a rule, the newest models on the market tend to do the best job of reproducing images.

✔ **Dye-sub:** Dye-sub is short for *dye-sublimation*. Dye-sub printers transfer colored dye to the paper using a heat process, which is why they are sometimes known as *thermal dye* printers. The Fargo FotoFUN! is one popular model in this category.

Dye-sub printers do the best job at creating prints that look and feel like traditional photographs. However, they can print only on special coated stock; you can't print plain-paper drafts of your images. Most dye-subs for the consumer market can't print anything larger than snapshot size images, either.

A dye-sub printer is ideal if you want a second printer just for printing top-quality images. The printer cost is about the same as for a good-quality inkjet — FotoFUN!, for example, runs about $500. The cost per each snapshot-size print is roughly $1. But if you need to print text documents or drafts on plain paper, the dye-sub option isn't for you.

✔ **Thermo-autochrome:** These machines print on light-sensitive paper instead of applying ink, toner, or dye to the page. The process is similar to the one used in older-model fax machines (the ones that print on thermal paper rather than plain paper). You can take home a thermo-autochrome printer for about $400; a printout costs about 75 cents.

Like dye-sub printers, these printers can't print on plain paper, and they create snapshot-size printouts only. So they're not suitable in situations where you need one printer for images and text documents. More importantly, thermo-autochrome printers don't do such a hot job on images, either, which is why these printers miss my vote. However, some newer models offer a feature that enables you to print stickers — for kid's scrapbooks, employee badges, and the like — which make them attractive to some users with special needs.

✔ **Micro-dry:** A few printers, most notably those made by Alps Electric, use ribbon cartridges that are coated with dry, resin-based ink. (The cartridges look like the ones you used to put in a typewriter — remember those?) The ink is heated and transferred to the paper during the printing process.

Micro-dry printers can print on plain and glossy stock, and because the ink is dry, you don't get the smearing and page-warping that sometimes happens with inkjet printing. And, micro-dry prints don't fade with exposure to light, a problem with prints from inkjets, dye-subs, and lasers. However, these printers have had a problem with slight *color banding.* On light areas of the image, you can sometimes see tiny strokes of individual ink colors rather than a nice, smooth blend of color. The cost of the printer and cost per print are roughly equivalent to that of a good inkjet.

One Alps model, the MD-1300, offers dual printing modes: You can print with the standard micro-dry inks or put in special ink cartridges for dye-sub printing on glossy stock. Expect to see more of these hybrid-style printers in the future, as manufacturers work to satisfy users who need to print on plain paper for text and everyday image work but also want to generate dye-sub quality prints of really special images.

✔ **Laser:** Laser printers transfer toner to paper using a heat process that's more complex than I care to explain here and doesn't really matter to you anyway. Color lasers cost far more than inkjets — expect to pay a minimum of about $1,000. Lasers can produce good output on plain paper, although a high-quality laser paper usually delivers better results. Toner cost per image runs about 3 to 16 cents, assuming 15 percent coverage of a letter-size page.

Some laser printers do a better job than inkjets at printing photos, while others do not. But where laser printers really shine is in quantity printing situations. If you need to print large numbers of images on a daily basis, you're wise to consider a laser printer; inkjet printers just aren't geared for that type of demanding performance. In other words, laser printers are suitable for office settings, but typically not for casual users.

Shopping tips

After you determine what category is appropriate for your needs, the following tips can help you narrow down your choices:

✔ **Don't worry too much about dpi.** Printer vendors make a big deal about their printers' *dpi* — the number of *d*ots of color that the printer can create *p*er linear *i*nch. But dpi is not as critical as the manufacturers would have you believe; the real story is in the technology the printer uses to create your printouts. A dye-sub printer that has a resolution of 300 dpi creates far superior prints to an inkjet that has double the resolution, for example. Even among similar types of printers, dpi can be misleading. Different brands of inkjet printers spray ink onto the page differently, for example, so the model with the highest dpi doesn't necessarily create the best prints. When comparing output, trust your eyes, not the dpi marketing hype.

✔ **Get opinions from other users.** Check out the current issues of computer magazines for reviews on the specific model you're considering. And if you're on the Internet, point your newsgroup reader toward `comp.periphs.printers` to see what other users have to say about various printers. I've found that the people who are using the printers every day often have better information about what's good and what's not than the experts who review hardware for a living. After all, the reviewer evaluates a printer only for a limited time period, whereas the real user is working with the thing on an ongoing basis.

✔ **Consider the consumables, not just the printer.** Factor in the cost of paper and ink into your pricing decision, not just the initial cost of the printer. Find out whether the printer you're considering does a good job on plain paper or just expensive coated stock, too. I chose a printer based on its ability to create good-quality plain-paper prints, for example, because I mostly print drafts of images that are later professionally printed. Make sure that the model you choose fits your daily printing needs.

Tips for Better Prints

Choosing a good printer has a major impact on the quality of your images. But you also can improve your output by keeping these tips in mind:

✔ **Use the right printer cable:** I know, it sounds like a silly thing to worry about. But newer printers require a special cable known as a *bi-directional IEEE 1284 compliant cable* in order to operate correctly. For whatever reason, these cables aren't included with most printers; you have to buy them separately. Because the special cables are more expensive than the garden-variety cable, many people opt for the cheaper type. But those cheaper cables can interfere with the communication between your printer and computer and can actually affect your printer's performance.

✔ **Use a high-enough resolution:** Face facts: You're not going to get a decent print with a puny image resolution, no matter how good your printer. By the same token, setting the image resolution too high can also lead to poor-quality printouts.

Most consumer-model printers do their best work with an image resolution of 200 to 300 ppi. Check your printer manual for specific recommendations about image resolution, because each model is geared to accept a certain optimum resolution.

And don't mix up printer resolution — dpi — and image resolution — ppi. For more on sorting out the two terms, read "Dpi ≠ ppi" in Chapter 3.

✔ **Buy good paper:** For everyday drafts of images, plain paper is fine. But when you really want the best printouts, upgrade to premium stock or glossy photo stock. You will be amazed at the difference in the look of your printed images. (Of course, dye-sub and thermal-autochrome printers use only one kind of stock, so you don't have to worry about this issue with those types of printers.)

> ✔ **Get creative:** Most printers sold for the home and small-office consumer offer accessories that enable you to reproduce your images on a variety of media, from T-shirts to coffee mugs to greeting cards. Explore these special printing options when you want to preserve a special image. A picture on paper is nice, but the same scene on a coffee mug or T-shirt is a true keepsake.

Professional Printing Options

On those occasions when you have special printing needs, you may want to consider turning your image over to a professional. An increasing number of businesses are jumping on the digital printing bandwagon, offering a variety of printing services to those who can't afford to put a high-end printing press in their back bedrooms.

If you need high-end output for a four-color brochure or magazine, plan to take your image to a professional service bureau or a commercial printer. The price varies according to the size and scope of the job, naturally. Be sure to consult with the customer service representative to find out the appropriate image resolution, what file format to use when saving the image, and what type of removable storage media the printer can accept (Zip disk, floppy, SyQuest, and so on). Also, because this kind of printing typically requires that images be converted to the CMYK color model, be sure to tell the service rep that you're submitting an RGB file and need to have it converted. Unfortunately, PhotoDeluxe can't do the conversion for you.

What if you want just one really good print of an image? You may want to locate a printer or digital imaging lab that can print your picture on a professional photographic printer. In my neck of the woods — Central Indiana — a dye-sub print costs about $50. The price is steep, but the results are terrific. Again, be sure to find out what type of file you need to submit and what image resolution is appropriate for optimum output.

If you're interested in getting a professional print of a special image, flip to the back of this book, where you can find a coupon for printing from Firehouse Image Center, a Central Indiana digital imaging lab. Or check out the company's Web site, www.Fire-house.net, for more information.

Alternatively, many retail photo-processing labs now can print digital images on regular photographic paper. The price is quite reasonable — around $2 for a 4-x-6-inch snapshot and $10 for an 8-x-10 print. If you can't find an outlet in your area that can do the job, many online companies provide this service via mail order. In many cases, you can e-mail your image file to the print lab if you prefer. Check out Chapter 17 for information on two online photo printing services, Fujifilm.net and Kodak PhotoNet, or search for "digital printing services" or something similar with your Web browser.

Part II
Editing Boot Camp

The 5th Wave   By Rich Tennant

"THAT'S A LOVELY SCANNED IMAGE OF YOUR SISTER'S PORTRAIT. NOW TAKE IT OFF THE BODY OF THAT PIT VIPER BEFORE SHE COMES IN THE ROOM."

In this part . . .

In the early days of computing, people often used the phrase, "Garbage in, garbage out." The saying referred to the fact that the output you generated from a computer depended on the quality of the data that you fed *into* the computer.

With image editing, the "garbage in, garbage out" motto gets turned on its ear, spun around the room, and flung against the wall. Using PhotoDeluxe, you can turn a stinky, rotten image into a compelling digital masterpiece — or, at least, a much improved version of its former self.

This part presents the basic techniques for enhancing your images. You find out how to apply color corrections, fix soft focus, move or copy a portion of your image from one spot to another, and perform all manner of other essential editing tasks. I even show you how to cover up unsightly image blemishes using some top-secret patching techniques.

Capable as PhotoDeluxe is at making something out of nothing, though, you still need to be wary of PEBKAC* errors. These image-killing mistakes occur when users apply edits willy-nilly, using no restraint at all and *certainly* without taking the time to read the insightful and always entertaining instructions found in this book. So consider yourself reminded — unless you want to ruin perfectly good images and make awful images worse, you have to actually *read* the sentences, paragraphs, and pages in this part.

*PEBKAC (pronounced *pebb-kaaaaaack!*): Problem Exists Between Keyboard and Chair

Chapter 6

Everyday Edits

• •

In This Chapter

▶ Approaching your edits from the right perspective

▶ Undoing mistakes

▶ Cropping out unwanted image elements

▶ Adjusting image brightness and contrast

▶ Making your colors more vivid

▶ Correcting out-of-whack colors

▶ Modifying the image canvas area

▶ Adding borders and drop shadows

• •

*B*ack in the '50s, my grandmother bought a state-of-the-art sewing machine capable of producing about a zillion different stitches. That machine is still alive and kicking, having sewn up everything from a dress for my first high school dance to curtains for my first house. But in all the years of use and abuse that machine received, only a handful of its features were ever used. The truth is that 99 percent of all sewing projects can be accomplished with a few basic stitches and tools.

In case you're wondering where this "Sewing with Julie" introduction is going, let me jump right to the analogy: The tools discussed in this chapter are like the basic features on my vintage sewing machine. They're not the fanciest tools in the PhotoDeluxe collection, but they're the ones you rely on day in and day out to give your images a more professional, finished look.

You find out how to crop an image; adjust color balance, contrast, and brightness; and apply a simple border around an image or selected area. You also get a primer on image-editing safety — that is, how to approach your editing so that you don't wind up hurting your image in the process of trying to improve it. With the information gleaned from this chapter, you can stitch up any frayed edges in your image in no time.

Touching Up Like a Pro

PhotoDeluxe gives you several powerful tools for cleaning up images. But if you don't use the editing tools carefully, you can do more damage than good.

To keep yourself out of harm's way, keep the following rules in mind as you go about your editing business, whether you're using the tools described in this or any other chapter:

✔ PhotoDeluxe offers several commands that promise to correct common image problems automatically, with little effort on your part. These commands include filters that are supposed to remove the dreaded "red eye" problem that crops up in so many snapshots, get rid of dust and scratches that tend to make their way into scanned images, and correct image brightness.

On some images, the automatic commands do an acceptable job. But just as often, they either do no good or cause a new problem while fixing another. In this chapter and Chapter 7, I introduce you to the PhotoDeluxe quick-fix filters, explain the best way to use them, and suggest alternative methods for solving your image problems when a quick fix doesn't fix.

✔ As explained in Chapter 8, you can use the PhotoDeluxe selection tools to rope off a portion of the image so that your edits affect only that area. So stop and consider whether you want to apply the edit to the entire image or to a specific troublesome area. In most cases, selective correction is the way to go.

For example, suppose that the foreground of your image is too dark, and the background is too light. If you raise the brightness of the whole image, your foreground may look better, but your background can appear even more overexposed. For better results, select the foreground before you lighten the image. Then invert the selection so that the background is selected rather than the foreground and reduce the brightness of the background only. Again, you can find out how to make this type of image selection in Chapter 8.

✔ To give yourself an editing safety net, copy the layer that you want to edit (usually the background layer) to a new layer. Then do your editing on the new layer. That way, you can simply delete the new layer and start over if you muck things up. Your original layer remains untouched.

Layers are explored fully in Chapter 10. But just to save you the trouble of flipping to that chapter, here's a quick how-to: To duplicate a layer, display the Layers palette by choosing View➪Show Layers. Then drag the layer name to the New Layer icon, as illustrated in Figure 6-1. PhotoDeluxe creates a new layer, named Layer Copy, and makes that layer active — so your edits affect the new layer only. If you screw up and want to delete the new layer, drag it to the Trash icon in the Layers palette.

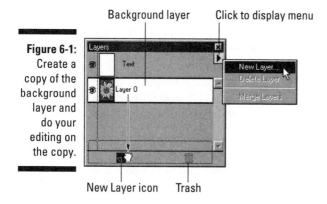

Background layer · Click to display menu

Figure 6-1:
Create a
copy of the
background
layer and
do your
editing on
the copy.

New Layer icon · Trash

When you're done editing, mush the new layer and the original layer together by choosing Merge Layers from the palette menu, unfurled in Figure 6-1. (Click the little triangle to make the menu appear.) As long as you keep the opacity of the new layer at 100 percent, your edited layer blots out everything in the underlying layer.

✔ Be sure to save a backup copy of your original image before you begin editing. If you happen to totally destroy an image, you can choose the File⇨Revert to Last Saved command (discussed later in this chapter) to go back to square one.

✔ Finally, use a light hand when applying image correction commands. Otherwise, your edits become obvious, and your images look amateurish.

✔ Speaking of looking amateurish, if you want to avoid sounding like a beginner, refer to image correction commands (those adjust brightness, sharpness, and so on) as *filters,* not commands. Please don't ask me why — this is just one of those lingo things that the digital imaging crowd started, and you have to go along if you want to fit in.

Undoing Editing Goofs

Before you leap off the image-editing cliff, become familiar with a few safety nets that have been thoughtfully provided for you. If you make an edit that you regret, you have several ways to fix things:

✔ **Edit⇨Undo:** This command undoes your most recent editing action. Choose Undo immediately after you mess up, or your opportunity to correct your mistake vanishes.

Don't go to all the trouble of choosing the Undo command from the Edit menu, however. Instead, press Ctrl+Z (⌘+Z on a Mac). Or just click the Undo button in the image-editing window.

PhotoDeluxe even gives you a way to correct a mistaken Undo. If you choose Undo and then think better of it, simply choose the command again. But do so before you make any other editing move, or you can't undo your undo.

✔ **File⇨Revert to Last Saved:** This command restores your image to the way it appeared the last time you saved it (using the Save command, discussed in Chapter 4). Use this option when you want to undo a whole series of blunders. But remember, you don't have access to the Revert to Last Saved command unless you actually saved your image in the first place. Also, Revert to Last Saved works only for images saved in the PDD file format. So, as recommended in Chapter 4, save early, save often, and use that PDD format until you're completely finished editing your image.

✔ **Delete Layer:** As explained in the preceding section, performing your edits on a duplicate image layer affords you an extra, er, layer of protection. If you're not happy with your edits, you simply trash the editing layer, create a new editing layer, and start over. To delete a layer, choose Delete Layer from the Layers palette menu or drag the layer name to the Trash icon in the palette. You can find out more about all this intriguing layers stuff in Chapter 10.

Snipping Away Parts of Your Image

To trim away unwanted portions of your image, press Ctrl+7 to pick up the PhotoDeluxe Crop tool. (Press ⌘+7 on a Mac.) Or, if you can't remember that keyboard shortcut, choose Size⇨Trim.

Drag with the Crop tool to enclose the portion of the image that you want to *retain* in a dotted outline, known hither and yon as a *marquee* and shown in the left side of Figure 6-2. After you release the mouse button, the marquee appears as a solid outline with four square handles at each corner. You can use these handles to adjust the crop marquee, as discussed in the upcoming bulleted list. But if the crop marquee is okay, click to crop the image. PhotoDeluxe snips off the unwanted portions of the image, leaving just the area inside the marquee, as shown in the right side of Figure 6-2.

In Version 3, you must click outside the marquee boundary to complete the crop. In other versions, clicking anywhere does the job.

If you don't get the crop marquee just right the first time, you can press Escape any time before you click to execute the crop. After you press Escape, the crop marquee vanishes, as does the crop tool. To try again, you must reselect the tool. But unless your crop marquee is really out of whack, adjust the existing marquee instead of starting over from scratch. Place your cursor over one of the marquee handles until it becomes a double-headed arrow. You can then adjust the crop marquee as follows:

✔ Drag any of the four handles to enlarge or shrink the marquee.

✔ To move the marquee so that a different portion of the image is enclosed, press Ctrl as you drag a marquee handle in Version 2 and the Business Edition. On a Mac, press Command as you drag the handle.

In Version 3, just drag anywhere inside the marquee outline to move the marquee into place.

✔ You can rotate the marquee to rotate your image and crop it at the same time. For example, take a look at the example on the left in Figure 6-3. Some say that shot, taken from a sailboat in St. Maarten, was the result of too many island cocktails. I say that our sailboat was rocked by waves just as I pressed the shutter button. Either way, I managed to crop the image and save the ship from sliding off the earth with one deft application of the Crop tool.

Crop marquee

Figure 6-2: Drag to enclose the area you want to retain, then click to crop.

Crop cursor

To rotate and crop at the same time, place your mouse over a marquee handle until the double-headed arrow cursor appears and then press and hold the Alt key (Windows) or Option key (Mac) as you drag in a clockwise or counterclockwise direction, as shown in the left image of Figure 6-3. When you have the marquee just so, let up on the mouse button and then click to crop the image. PhotoDeluxe rotates and trims the picture at the same time, as illustrated in the right image of the figure.

Marquee handle   Double-arrow cursor

Figure 6-3:
You can
rotate and
crop in one
easy move.

To make sure that you rotate the image to the right degree, line up one side of the crop marquee with an image element that should be perfectly vertical or horizontal. For example, I aligned the bottom edge of my crop marquee in Figure 6-3 with the horizon line — where sea and sky meet. Then I enlarged the marquee to the size that you see in the figure.

Don't apply the rotating crop too many times to the same image. Each time you rotate the image, PhotoDeluxe reorganizes the pixels in the image to come up with the rotated version; the process can cause some image degradation.

Fixing Brightness and Contrast

If you're into instant gratification — and who isn't? — the Instant Fix command, found on the Quality menu in Version 2, has surely caught your attention. Ditto for the Extensis IntelliFix command that replaces the Instant Fix command in the Business Edition, and for the entire menu of Extensis Instant Fix Tools that shows up on the Effects menu in Version 3. All these commands imply that they can make dull, tired images look bright and shiny new with a single click of the mouse.

On some images, these commands work as promised. But on other images, they either don't result in any noticeable improvement or, worse, alter the colors in your image in unwanted ways.

For an example, take a look at Color Plate 6-1. The left image is my original daisy, which I scanned from a print photograph. The print darkened and faded in the ten years or so since I shot the picture, giving the flower a dim, gloomy face. Nobody likes a depressed daisy, so I put the image through the Instant Fix machine in Version 2. The result, shown in the middle image of Color Plate 6-1, is a much brighter daisy. But the filter shifted the image colors dramatically, and although the new flower is lovely, it has nothing to do with my original picture.

As instant-fix machines go, the Extensis IntelliFix filter — a PhotoDeluxe plug-in created by Extensis and included with the Business Edition as well as Version 3 — is much more capable than the Instant Fix filter. Whereas the Instant Fix command adjusts brightness and contrast, the IntelliFix command adjusts brightness, contrast, saturation, and sharpness. Applying the IntelliFix filter to my original daisy image did brighten up the image somewhat and didn't result in the dramatic color shift that I got with Instant Fix. On the downside, IntelliFix sharpened background areas, which I wanted to leave at their original blurry state (see Chapter 7 for more information about this sharpness stuff).

In Version 3, you get a broader range of Extensis correction filters, which you can explore by choosing Effects⇨Extensis Instant Fix Tools. On the resulting menu are automatic filters to adjust brightness and contrast individually, sharpen the image, and remove unwanted color casts that often appear in images shot in fluorescent light. You also get the IntelliFix filter discussed in the preceding paragraph, along with the original Instant Fix command on the Quality menu.

Don't ignore these instant correction tools altogether — by all means, give them a whirl before you go to the trouble of making manual corrections. You may find that a particular instant correction tool is just the ticket for correcting a recurring problem with images from your digital camera or scanner, for example.

But my guess is that you aren't going to be satisfied with the results of the automatic filters very often, especially if you're really concerned with image quality. If you don't like the results you get, press Ctrl+Z (⌘+Z) or click the Undo button in the image window. Then, to adjust image brightness and contrast manually, choose Quality⇨Brightness/Contrast and shake hands with the dialog box shown in Figure 6-4.

I'm guessing that you can figure out what's what in this dialog box all by your lonesome, but a few hints may help:

✔ For a quick way to display the Brightness/Contrast dialog box, press Ctrl+B (⌘+B on a Mac).

✔ Drag the slider triangle under each slider bar to raise or lower the brightness and contrast. Or type new values in the Brightness or Contrast option boxes. If you want to lower the value, enter a minus sign before the value you type. Otherwise, PhotoDeluxe assumes you want to enter a positive value.

✔ You can also raise or lower the value in the active option box (the one that's highlighted) by using the arrow keys on your keyboard. Press the up arrow to raise the value by one, press the down arrow to lower the value by one. Press Shift+up arrow to raise the value by ten; press Shift+down arrow to lower the value by ten. (To make an option box active, double-click it.)

✔ Select the Preview check box to preview the results of your changes in the image window.

✔ Raising the brightness value sometimes washes out the colors in your image. You may be able to strengthen the colors somewhat by raising the saturation, as explained in "Making Your Colors More Vivid," later in this chapter.

Figure 6-4:
Adjust brightness and contrast here.

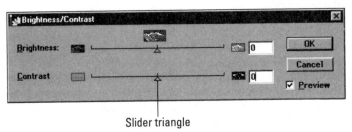

Slider triangle

To create the final image in Color Plate 6-1, I first selected just the daisy so that my adjustments wouldn't affect the image background, which looked pretty decent in its original state. (Check out Chapter 8 for information on how to create this kind of selection.) I raised the Brightness value to about +20 and the Contrast value to +15. Then, because the image was still a bit dingy, I made a small adjustment to the daisy's colors with the Color Balance filter (explored later in this chapter, in "Balancing Out-of-Kilter Colors"). I boosted the cyan and yellow and reduced the red and blue. Finally, I inverted my selection and brightened up the background just a tad. The result: a daisy that looks as fresh and bright as the day it burst into bloom.

When you're adjusting the brightness of an image, keep in mind that pictures tend to darken when printed. So you usually want your images to look a little too light on-screen if you plan to print them.

If you're preparing images for on-screen display, on the other hand, be aware that Mac screens and PC screens differ a little in brightness. If you're using an Apple-brand monitor, images on your screen probably look brighter than they do on the average PC monitor. (Other brands of monitors are sometimes calibrated to PC standards even when they're sold for use with a Mac.) So you may want to boost the brightness beyond what looks good on your

Mac screen if most of your expected audience will view the image on a PC. The opposite holds true if you're a PC user who's preparing images for display on a Macintosh monitor.

Making Your Colors More Vivid

If you watch much TV, you're probably aware of a current trend among commercials: the digital manipulation of colors. One popular trick is boosting the *saturation,* or intensity, of some or all colors in a scene. Skies are eye-popping blue, not just the ordinary blue that you see when you wander outside and look up. Grass is astoundingly green, unlike anything you could grow even if you dumped a boatload of chemicals on your lawn.

You can create the same kind of vivid colors in PhotoDeluxe, although I encourage you to keep the saturation in the realm of the believable. Pump up the saturation too much, and your image looks unnatural — you can fool some of the people some of the time, but most folks notice right away that you've digitally altered the picture.

With that caution in mind, if you find yourself with an image that looks a little washed out, like the one in the left half of Color Plate 6-2, the Hue/Saturation command can work wonders. By tweaking the saturation, you can bring dull colors back to life, as I did in the right image in the color plate.

To crank up your colors, choose Quality⇨Hue/Saturation. Or better yet, press Ctrl+U (⌘+U on a Mac). PhotoDeluxe responds by dragging out the Hue/Saturation dialog box, shown in Figure 6-5.

Figure 6-5:
Strengthen
your colors
with the
Saturation
control.

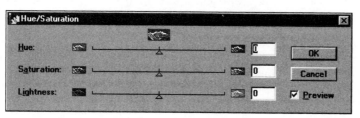

To make your colors more intense, drag the Saturation slider triangle to the right. Or double-click the corresponding option box and enter a value from the keyboard. Higher numbers increase the color intensity; lower values fade colors back. To reduce the saturation from the original level, enter a negative number (you must type the minus sign before your value).

Keep the Preview check box selected so that you can preview the results of your changes in the image window. To return to the original saturation values, Alt+click the Cancel button (Option+click on a Mac). When you click, the Cancel button becomes the Reset button. Click the Reset button to restore the original values.

Don't confuse the Lightness control in the Hue/Saturation dialog box with the Brightness control in the Brightness/Contrast dialog box. Increasing the Lightness value has a negative effect on image contrast, so don't use this control to make your images lighter unless you want to create a faded-out look. Instead, use the Brightness/Contrast command, discussed earlier in "Fixing Brightness and Contrast." To see the difference between the Brightness control and the Lightness control, open up an image and apply one command to the top half of your image and the other to the bottom. (Use the selection techniques discussed in Chapter 8 to select one part of the image, apply one of the commands, and then select the other part of the image and try the other command.)

The Hue control shifts your image pixels around the color wheel, an effect discussed in Chapter 9.

Balancing Out-of-Kilter Colors

Old photographs, images from digital cameras, and scanned pictures often have problems with *color balance.* The image in Color Plate 6-3 is a perfect example. I shot this picture in Lake Tahoe after I made the mistake of buying some outdated film from a souvenir shop. Unfortunately, I didn't notice the expiration date until after I shot the entire roll of film. As a result, my snowman is bending over backward to figure out why pink snow is blanketing the California/Nevada border.

Well, live and learn — and in the meantime, fix problems like this in PhotoDeluxe. You have two color-correction tools at your disposal: the Color Balance command and the Variations command. Both commands do the same thing but go about it in different ways, as described in the next two sections. Choose the approach that you find easier.

You can sometimes use the Color Balance command to compensate for discrepancies between what you see on-screen and what your printer prints. For more on this problem, read the sidebar "Why what you see isn't what you get" in Chapter 5.

The Color Balance command

Using the Color Balance command, you can adjust the colors in your image while previewing your changes in the image window. You also can make more-subtle adjustments than with the Variations command.

To open the Color Balance dialog box, shown in Figure 6-6, choose Quality⇨ Color Balance or press Ctrl+Y (⌘+Y on a Mac). You know, *Y,* as in "Y are my colors so out of whack?"

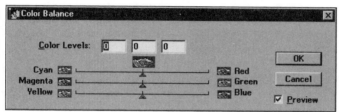

The controls in the dialog box work as follows:

- ✔ Drag the slider triangles to shift the color balance. If you want to remove a red cast from an image, for example, drag the slider toward the Cyan end of the top slider bar. PhotoDeluxe decreases the amount of red in your image and increases the amount of cyan, which lives opposite red on the color wheel. In Color Plate 6-3, I reduced the red, increased the green, and added just a bit more blue to get rid of the pink snowfall effect.

- ✔ As you drag the sliders, the values in the Color Levels option boxes change to reflect your decisions. The first option box corresponds to the top slider bar, the middle box to the middle slider bar, and the third box to the bottom slider bar.

- ✔ If you have a batch of images that all suffer from the same color balance problem, you may want to note the values you enter in the Color Levels option boxes. That way, you can enter the same values for all the images to achieve a consistent color balance.

- ✔ Values in the Color Levels boxes can range from +100 to –100. (If you're entering a negative value, you must type in the minus sign before the value, but if you're entering a positive number, you don't need to type the plus sign — just the value.) Values higher or lower than +30 or –30 tend to create blotchy, unnatural results, so use moderation.

✔ To reset the color balance to the values that were in place when you opened the dialog box, Alt+click the Cancel button, which turns into a Reset button, and click the Reset button. On a Mac, Option+click the Cancel button to fetch the Reset button.

The Variations command

To try another approach to color correction, choose Quality⇨Variations or Effects⇨Adjust⇨Variations. Both commands display the Variations dialog box, shown in Figure 6-7.

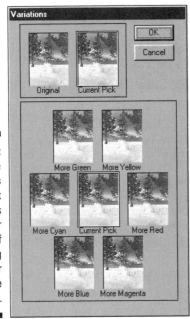

Figure 6-7: The Variations dialog box offers another method of correcting color balance problems.

The dialog box contains thumbnail views of your image. To raise the amount of one color, click on the corresponding thumbnail. For example, to add green to the image, click the More Green thumbnail. To reduce the amount of a color, click the *opposite* thumbnail. If you want your image to contain less green, for example, click the More Magenta thumbnail.

As you click the More thumbnails, the two Current Pick thumbnails show you the effect of your changes. The Original thumbnail shows how your image looked when you opened the dialog box. If you decide that you want to return to the original color balance, either click Cancel to close the dialog box without applying your changes or Alt+click the Cancel button (Option+click on a Mac). Then click the Reset button, which takes the place of the Cancel button when you Alt+click or Option+click.

Unfortunately, you can't preview your changes in the image window as you can when using the Color Balance command; you have to rely on the thumbnails. Also, you're limited to adding and subtracting colors in preset increments. You can't make small adjustments as you can in the Color Balance dialog box. For this reason, I usually rely on Color Balance when I want to make subtle color changes.

Changing the Canvas Size

As explained in Chapter 2, every PhotoDeluxe image rests on a transparent canvas. On occasion, you may want to change the canvas size, which you accomplish inside the Canvas Size dialog box, shown in Figure 6-8. To open the dialog box, choose Size⇨Canvas Size.

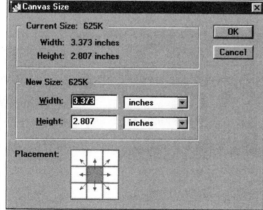

Figure 6-8:
Reduce or enlarge the image canvas here.

The most common reason for enlarging the canvas is to join two images together. Suppose that you have two 640-x-480-pixel images. One image shows your kitchen as it appeared 30 years ago, when you thought you couldn't live without an avocado green stove and dishwasher. Another image shows your kitchen after you came to your senses and replaced those green monstrosities with sleek almond-colored appliances. Now, for whatever reason, you decide that you want to place the two kitchen images side-by-side in the same image — a before-and-after illustration of your decorating project, perhaps. You open the first image, double the width of the canvas, and copy and paste the second image onto the new canvas area. If you enlarge the canvas too much, you can use the Canvas Size command to trim away the excess. Always cut away unused canvas, because those extra canvas pixels add to your image file size.

The Canvas Size dialog box is a little baffling at first, but easy enough to use when you understand how it works. Here's what you need to know:

- ✔ Select the unit of measure that you want to use from the pop-up menus next to the Width and Height option boxes.

- ✔ Enter the new dimensions of your desired canvas in the Width and Height option boxes.

- ✔ If you choose Percent as your unit of measurement, you can enlarge or reduce the canvas a percentage of the original size as opposed to entering specific dimensions.

- ✔ Click on a square in the Placement grid to specify where you want your image positioned on the new canvas. If you click the center square, PhotoDeluxe positions your image smack dab in the middle of the new canvas.

- ✔ Click OK to close the dialog box and create your new canvas.

If you enter a canvas size that's smaller than your original canvas, PhotoDeluxe warns you that some of your existing image is destined for the cutting room floor. Click Proceed if you want to go ahead.

The Canvas Size command can come in handy when you want to trim just a few pixels off your image — a precision maneuver that can be difficult using the Crop tool. Just choose Pixels as your unit of measurement, enter the new image dimensions, and click OK to trim away the unwanted pixels.

Adding a Border

If you're easily distracted and/or you have a *lot* of time on your hands, you may have noticed that all the images in this book are surrounded by a black border. To surround your images with a similar border — or one of a different color — first select the area that you want to outline. Press Ctrl+A (⌘+A on a Mac) to select the entire image. Then choose Effects⇨Outline. PhotoDeluxe rushes to the closet and drags out the Outline dialog box, shown in Figure 6-9.

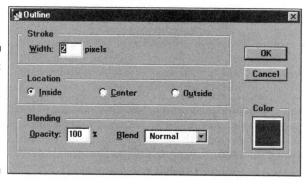

Figure 6-9:
Add a
border to
your image
with the
Outline
command.

Don't apply your border until after you finish any color corrections, resizing, or sharpening. All these commands can result in a blurry or off-color border because they affect the border pixels just like the other pixels in the image.

The Outline dialog box gives you a wealth of options for applying your border, as follows:

✔ The Width option determines the thickness of the border. FYI, I placed a one-pixel border around the screen shot shown in Figure 6-9.

By the way, professional image editors refer to borders as *strokes.* That's because what you're really doing when you apply a border is laying down a stroke of color along the selection outline. Or so they say.

✔ Choose a Location option to specify where you want the border with respect to the selection outline. To put the border inside the selection outline, choose Inside. If you choose Center, the border rides the selection outline like a cowboy straddling a fence. Outside, surprisingly enough, places the border just outside the selection outline.

✔ If you selected the whole image before you chose the Outline command, Inside is your only option. The Outside option calls for the stroke to be placed outside the selection outline, and PhotoDeluxe has no empty canvas area on which to paint the stroke — your image covers the entire thing. You can choose the command, but your image is completely unaffected by it. If you want to apply the Outline command with the Outside option, enlarge the canvas size first. For example, if you want to add a one-pixel border around your image, choose the Size⇨Canvas Size command and raise the Width and Height values by 2, as explained earlier in "Changing the Canvas Size." (You need one pixel's worth of canvas for each side of the image, so you need to make the canvas 2 pixels wider and 2 pixels taller.)

Similarly, Center asks PhotoDeluxe to place one-half of the stroke outside the selection outline, and unless you first enlarge the canvas, the program doesn't have anywhere to put the half that goes outside the outline. So if you choose Center, expect to get only the portion of the border that falls inside the selection — which is exactly one-half the size you specified in the Width option box.

✔ The Blending options enable you to vary the opacity of the border and alter the way that the border pixels blend with the original image pixels. These options work the same as they do for the painting tools, Selection Fill command, and image layers. For more details, check out "Adjusting opacity" and "Blending pixels in cruel and unusual ways" in Chapter 9. For a solid border, leave the Opacity value at 100 and the Blend mode at Normal.

Adding a Drop Shadow

To wrap up this chapter, I want to fill you in on one more common image-editing task: adding a drop shadow behind an object. Figure 6-10 shows examples of two drop shadows created by using the Drop Shadow command.

Here's the process for creating shadows:

Figure 6-10:
A hard-edged drop shadow (left) and a softer version (right).

1. **Select the portion of the image to which you want to apply the shadow.**

   Selection techniques are explored in Chapter 8. To select the entire image, press Ctrl+A (⌘+A on the Mac).

If you want to apply the shadow to the entire image, be sure to increase the canvas size first, using the Canvas Size command discussed earlier in this chapter. Otherwise, your drop shadow is hidden from view by the image.

2. Choose Effects⇨Drop Shadow.

The Drop Shadow dialog box shown in Figure 6-11 appears.

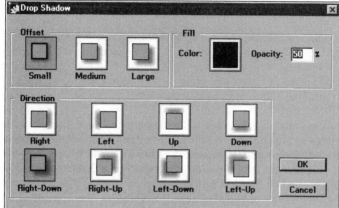

Figure 6-11: Choose the size and direction of your drop shadow here.

3. Choose your shadow size and direction.

Click an icon in the Offset area to specify the size of your shadow — Small, Medium, or Large. Click a direction icon to tell PhotoDeluxe how to orient the shadow with respect to the image.

4. Choose a shadow color.

Click the Color icon and choose a shadow color from the Color Picker dialog box, as discussed in Chapter 9.

5. Set the shadow opacity.

For a solid shadow like the one in the left half of Figure 6-10, set the opacity value to 100 percent. You can always adjust the opacity later, so don't sweat this decision too much now.

6. Click OK.

PhotoDeluxe creates a copy of the original selection and places the copy on a new layer. The program also adds a new layer to hold the shadow.

As explained in Chapter 10, having your shadow on a separate layer from the rest of the image means that you can move the shadow without affecting the rest of the image. Just click the shadow with the

Object Selection tool and drag the shadow into place. Or press Ctrl+G (⌘+G on a Mac) to select the Move tool and then press the arrow keys on your keyboard to nudge the shadow into place. One press of an arrow key moves the shadow one pixel; press Shift along with an arrow key to move the shadow ten pixels.

If you want to change the opacity of the shadow, choose View⇨Show Layers to display the Layers palette. Then double-click the shadow layer in the Layers palette, as discussed in Chapter 10, and change the Opacity value in the dialog box that appears.

After you get the shadow just right, merge the shadow layer and the two image layers together by choosing the Merge Layers command from the Layers palette menu. Or, if you want to retain the right to shift the shadow layer around in the future, leave the layers as they are. And if you want to delete the shadow altogether, just drag the shadow layer to the Trash icon in the Layers palette

If you want a soft, fuzzy shadow like the one in the right half of Figure 6-10, you simply apply the Soften blur filter to the shadow layer. Click the Shadow layer in the Layers palette and then choose Effects⇨Blur⇨Soften. Raise the Radius value in the Soften dialog box until you achieve an effect you like. Be sure to turn on the Preview check box in the dialog box so that you can preview the results of your Radius setting in the image window.

Chapter 7
Turning Garbage into Gold

· ·

In This Chapter

▶ Getting rid of red eyes

▶ Fooling the eye with hocus focus

▶ Mastering the Unsharp Mask filter

▶ Eliminating dust, scratches, speckles, and jaggies

▶ Creating a patch to cover up unwanted image elements and flaws

▶ Hiding moiré patterns and decreasing image noise

· ·

Most weekend mornings, you can find me plopped in front of the TV, watching gardening shows. I don't do much actual gardening myself, mind you, because it requires a zillion times more energy and time than I have to spare. Still, I enjoy watching TV gardeners spin the fantasy that anybody can turn a scraggly plot of land into a blooming oasis in 30 minutes, give or take a few commercial breaks.

This chapter is the digital imaging equivalent of a do-it-yourself gardening show, with one exception. With the techniques I show you in the next few pages, you really *can* turn a rotten image into an acceptable, if not altogether terrific, picture. You can remove scratches and dust from scanned images, get rid of those glowing red eyes that occur in many snapshots, and even use some digital sleight-of-hand to bring blurry images into sharper focus.

Within the same amount of time that those TV gardeners spend rescuing another homeowner from the depths of landscape despair, you can raise a whole crop of prize-winning pictures. And the best part is, no smelly fertilizer is required.

Removing Red Eye

May as well start with a biggie: how to fix the red-eye phenomenon that occurs when you take pictures with most point-and-shoot cameras. Red eye is caused by the camera's flash reflecting in your subjects' eyes, creating a demonic-looking effect. The top image in Color Plate 7-1 shows an example.

PhotoDeluxe offers a special filter that's supposed to replace the unwanted red pixels in the eye with a more natural color. To give this filter a try, do the following:

1. **Select the red portion of the eye.**

   You can draw around the red-eye zone with the Oval tool or click the red pixels with the Color Wand. Both selection tools are explained in Chapter 8. Zoom in on your image so that you limit your selection to the red-eye portion as much as possible.

2. **Choose Effects⇨PhotoDeluxe⇨Remove Red Eye.**

   PhotoDeluxe replaces the red pixels with darkish, blue-black pixels.

Well, that's the way it's supposed to happen, anyway. If the red-eye area is very large, only a small area of red is replaced, as illustrated by the second image in Color Plate 7-1. You have to keep reapplying the filter over and over and over to replace all the red-eye pixels. Alternatively, if the red-eye area is very small, PhotoDeluxe may recolor more pixels than you want. The result can be an unnatural dark blob rather than a proper pupil.

If your red-eye area happens to be just the right size, the filter may work just fine. Go ahead and give the filter a try, and if the results are less than satisfactory, press Ctrl+Z (⌘+Z on the Mac) or click the Undo button in the image window. Then use the following more professional — and more successful — approach.

1. **Select the red-eye areas.**

   Zoom way in on each eye and use the selection tools discussed in Chapter 8 to select the red-eye areas. I find that the Color Wand usually works well for this job.

   Be careful not to select the white pixels usually found in the eye area. The white areas give the eye its natural highlights, so you want to preserve them.

2. **Create a new layer.**

   Choose View⇨Show Layers to display the Layers palette. Then choose New Layer from the pop-up menu in the top-right corner of the palette. (Click the right-pointing arrow to make the menu appear.) When the New Layer dialog box appears, enter a name for the layer (if you want), and choose Normal as the Blend mode. Leave the Opacity value at 100 percent and then click OK.

3. **Choose Effects⇨Selection Fill.**

   PhotoDeluxe displays the Selection Fill dialog box, which is explored fully in Chapter 9.

4. **Choose your new pupil color.**

   Click the Color box inside the Selection Fill dialog box to display the Color Picker, also discussed in Chapter 9. To get a natural-looking eye, move your cursor into the image window and click on the darkest portion of the eyeball. For example, I clicked the dark ring around the outside of the iris in Color Plate 7-1. Absolute black tends to give the eyes a stark, unnatural look.

   Click OK to close the Color Picker after you decide on a color.

5. **Click the Selection option in the Selection Fill dialog box.**

   And set the Opacity value to 100 and the Blend mode to Normal.

6. **Click OK.**

   The new dark-eye pixels are created on the layer you added in Step 1. If you're not happy with the results, double-click the eye layer name in the Layers palette to redisplay the Layer Options dialog box. Fool around with the Opacity value and Blend mode until you get a natural-looking eye. Or, if you want to try filling the eye with another color, drag the eye layer to the Trash icon in the Layers palette. Then create another new layer and try again. Your eyeball selection remains intact, so you can easily experiment with different colors. After you fill the red-eye area, zoom out to view the results of your handiwork; when you're zoomed way in, the eye is likely to look odd no matter how well you've done the job.

   After the eyes look the way you want, choose Merge Layers from the Layers palette menu to flatten your image. (For more on working with layers, read Chapter 10.)

Another variation on this technique is to use the Effects⇔Feather command rather than the Selection Fill command. The Feather command, described in Chapter 8, softens the harsh edges of a selection outline so that the color you use to fill the red-eye area fades in gradually from the edge of the selection. Give this alternative a try, with the Feather value set to 1 to 3 pixels, if the preceding steps don't give you a natural-looking result. As in the Selection Fill dialog box, click the Color box to set the new eye color. Set the Blend mode to Normal and the Opacity to 100 percent. Then click the Fill Selection icon and click OK.

Creating the Illusion of Sharper Focus

Digital images have an annoying tendency to appear a little soft, as if the photographer didn't get the focus quite right when shooting the picture. Aging celebrities appreciate the soft-focus effect because it makes wrinkles and other evidence of long life less noticeable. But unless you're specifically going for that petroleum-jelly-on-the-lens look, you'll want to run most images through one of the PhotoDeluxe sharpening filters. You have several sharpening options, all explained in the upcoming sections.

How sharpening fools the eye

Technically, no image-editing program can restore focus to a soft image. What PhotoDeluxe and other programs with sharpening filters do is create the *illusion* of sharper focus with some clever pixel manipulation.

Sharpening fools the eye by adding small halos along the borders between dark and light areas of the image. (Image-editing gurus refer to those borders as *edges.*) On the dark side of the border, the pixels take on a dark halo. The pixels on the light side of the border get a light halo. The effect is to increase the contrast between the two regions, which makes the eye think that focus has improved. Artists have been using this technique for centuries, as have photographers with advanced darkroom experience.

For a look at this concept in action, see the left column of Figure 7-1 and Color Plate 7-2. The top-left image is the original — four simple bands of color. The bottom-left image was sharpened using the Sharpen More filter. Along the border between each band of color, the filter created a dark halo on one side and a light halo on the other.

Managed with a steady hand — or in this case, a careful mouse — sharpening can dramatically improve an image. But too much sharpening can give your image the jaggies, making the individual pixels more noticeable. Sharpening also emphasizes any pixelization that may be present in your image. Done to an extreme, sharpening can even create unwanted color shifts. So use some discretion when you work with the sharpening filters.

Remember, too, that you can sharpen just one portion of your image by selecting that area before you apply the sharpening filter. I used this approach to sharpen the daisy image shown in Color Plate 6-1 (and discussed in Chapter 6). I wanted to keep the soft, blurry look of the background, so I selected and sharpened just the flower. (Selection techniques are explored in Chapter 8, if you need help.)

A blurry background has the added benefit of making the foreground object appear to be in sharper focus. So if sharpening the foreground subject doesn't do the trick, try selecting the background and applying a slight blur. The PhotoDeluxe blurring filters are hashed out in Chapter 12.

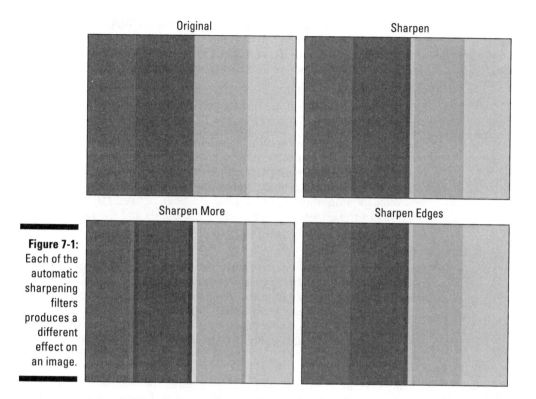

Figure 7-1:
Each of the automatic sharpening filters produces a different effect on an image.

Your sharpening options

PhotoDeluxe offers several sharpening filters, which are all found on the Effects menu. All are one-shot filters, with the exception of the curiously named Unsharp Mask filter. *One-shot* means that PhotoDeluxe applies the sharpening automatically when you choose the filter; you don't have the option of increasing or limiting the amount of sharpening. Unsharp Mask, the best sharpening tool of the bunch, enables you to control different aspects of the sharpening effect.

Each of the sharpening filters works differently, producing a specific effect on your image. Here's what you need to know:

  ✔ Effects⇨Sharpen⇨Sharpen applies subtle light and dark halos along the edges of the image — that is, areas where contrasting pixels come together. For an example of the Sharpen filter in action, look at the top-right image in Figure 7-1 and Color Plate 7-2. This filter, by the way, is also found on the Quality menu. The results are the same no matter which menu you use to access the filter.

✔ Version 3 users get a similar sharpening effect from Effects⇨Extensis Instant Fix Tools⇨Auto Sharpen. In fact, the effects of the two filters are so similar I dare say you won't notice any difference. But please feel free to try. I don't think you've had enough to do lately, anyway.

✔ Sharpen More adds halos that are stronger than those applied by Sharpen, as illustrated in the bottom-left example in Figure 7-1 and Color Plate 7-2.

✔ Sharpen Edges applies the same level of sharpening as Sharpen, but only along borders where there is a significant change in contrast. For example, see the bottom-right image in Figure 7-1 and Color Plate 7-2. The edge between the teal and yellow band is sharpened (in the grayscale version of the figure, look at the edge between the two middle bands). But the edges between the two teal bands and the two yellow bands are ignored (in the grayscale figure, inspect the edges between the outside bands and their interior neighbors).

✔ Unsharp Mask enables you to control how and where you want your halos added. You can specify how intense you want PhotoDeluxe to make the halos, how big to make them, and how different two pixels must be before sharpening is applied. This filter is discussed in detail in the next section, but for now take a peek at Color Plate 7-3, where you can see some of the sharpening variations that are possible with Unsharp Mask.

As with most things in life, the option that requires the most work, Unsharp Mask, typically delivers the best results. Sharpen and Auto Sharpen (Version 3 only) usually don't go far enough, Sharpen More tends to go too far, and Sharpen Edges can create unnatural shifts between sharpened areas and unsharpened areas.

Even so, the one-shot filters may do the trick on some images, and because you can certainly apply them more quickly than Unsharp Mask, you may as well give them a go. If you don't like the results, press Ctrl+Z (⌘+Z on a Mac) or click the Undo button in the image window and head for the Unsharp Mask filter, where you can gain better control over your sharpening.

To see how each of the sharpening filters works on a real-life image, set your sights on Figure 7-2 and Color Plate 7-4. The original feather image, shown in the center of the figure, was perfectly focused in its original print state but came out of my scanner decidedly soft.

Passing the image through the Sharpen filter helped a little, but not enough (top-left image). Sharpen More (top right) made things a little too crisp — the feather looks almost brittle in some areas. Sharpen Edges (bottom left) did a good job in high-contrast areas, but the interior of the feather remains too soft because the filter didn't find any significant edges to sharpen.

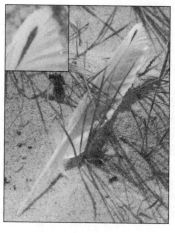

Figure 7-2:
How each of the sharpening filters affected my original image (center). Clockwise, from top left: Sharpen, Sharpen More, Unsharp Mask, and Sharpen Edges.

Using the Unsharp Mask filter, I was able to adjust the sharpening so that both background and feather appear in good focus while retaining the, uh, featheriness of the feather. The inset areas in the upper left of each example give you a closer look at the differences in each sharpening filter's effect. Head for the next section to find out how to successfully sharpen your own images by playing with the Unsharp Mask controls.

Unsharp Mask: The best solution

In case you're wondering where this filter got its odd name, unsharp masking is a technique used in traditional photography to create the illusion of sharper focus. At any rate, choosing Effects⇨Sharpen⇨Unsharp Mask brings to life the Unsharp Mask dialog box, shown in Figure 7-3.

Figure 7-3:
The all-powerful Unsharp Mask dialog box.

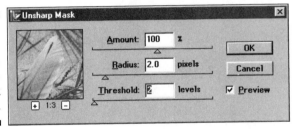

The Amount, Radius, and Threshold settings enable you to tell PhotoDeluxe exactly how you want your image to be sharpened. The controls work as follows:

✔ The Amount value determines the intensity of the halos that are added to the edges in your image. (Read "How sharpening fools the eye," earlier in this section, if you don't know what I'm talking about.) A higher value creates stronger halos, as illustrated by Color Plate 7-2 and Figure 7-4. The left column shows the results of using an Amount value of 100 percent, and the right column shows the effect of doubling the Amount value to 200 percent.

For best results, apply the filter with a lower value — say, in the 50 to 100 percent range. If the sharpening effect is too minimal, apply the filter a second time. You usually get more-natural results applying the filter several times at low Amount values than you do applying it once with a large Amount value.

✔ The Radius value determines the range of pixels that are affected by the sharpening. If you set a low Radius value, the haloing is concentrated in a narrow region, as in the top row of Color Plate 7-3 and Figure 7-4, where I set the Radius value to 1. If you set a high Radius value, the haloing is distributed over a broader area and fades out gradually, as illustrated in the bottom row of Color Plate 7-3 and Figure 7-4. For the bottom-row examples, I set the Radius value to 2.

Amount, 100%   Amount, 200%

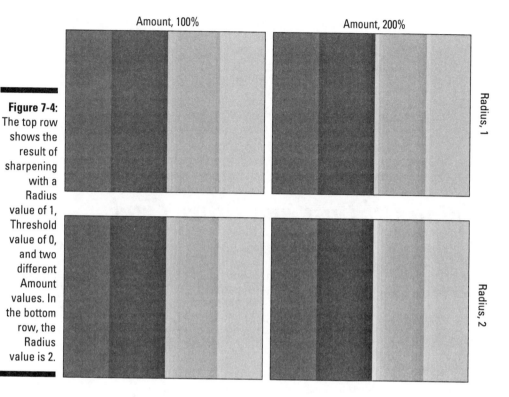

Radius, 1

Radius, 2

Figure 7-4:
The top row shows the result of sharpening with a Radius value of 1, Threshold value of 0, and two different Amount values. In the bottom row, the Radius value is 2.

Usually, a setting of 0.5 to 1 is appropriate for on-screen images. Print images do better with slightly higher Radius values — say, 1 to 2. Anything above 2 tends to create artificial-looking results and can even have the effect of softening your edges, which is the exact opposite of what you're trying to accomplish.

Keep in mind, too, that you may need to adjust the Radius value as well as other sharpening values to accommodate different printers. An image output on a home inkjet printer, for example, usually requires a bit more sharpening than those output on a high-resolution, commercial printer.

✔ The Threshold value tells PhotoDeluxe how much difference in contrast must occur before sharpening is applied. If you leave the Threshold value set at 0, the slightest difference in contrast results in sharpening. If you raise the value, PhotoDeluxe is more selective; it sharpens the edges only in areas of high contrast, similar to what happens when you use the Sharpen Edges command.

Usually, you can leave the Threshold value at 0. But experiment with raising the value slightly if your image contains areas that are soft-looking in real life — such as the feather interior in Figure 7-2 and Color Plate 7-4, or a baby's skin. For those images, a Threshold value in the 2 to 20 range can be a better choice.

Also bear in mind that sharpening tends to exaggerate *noise* — jaggedy areas that sometimes show up in images that have been overly jaypegged (compressed) or that were captured in insufficient lighting. Raising the Threshold value to 1 or 2 can sometimes enable you to sharpen the image without bringing out noise.

For the record, I used an Amount value of 100, a Radius value of 2, and a Threshold value of 1 to create the bottom-right example in Figure 7-2 and Color Plate 7-4. But you need to experiment with the values to determine the appropriate settings for your image.

Wiping Off Dust and Other Crud

If you work with scanned images much, you're probably familiar with the kind of problems illustrated in Figure 7-5. During the scanning process, a bit of dust or some other tiny bit of flotsam got between the photograph and the scanner glass, resulting in the white fleck that is so appropriately labeled *crud* in Figure 7-5. As if that weren't bad enough, the original print (and negative) came back from the processing lab with a big scratch running all the way from one side of the picture to the other — a defect that the scanner faithfully reproduced. Poor Beastie — such a noble creature deserves better.

Faithful family friend   Scratch   Crud

Figure 7-5:
This poor
doggie
suffers from
embarrassing
image
defects.

PhotoDeluxe offers a Dust & Scratches filter that is designed to remove scratches, dust bunnies, and other impurities from your image. But the filter can sometimes do more harm than good, and you often get better results by cleaning up your images manually, using the Clone tool. The next two sections describe both options.

Applying the Dust & Scratches filter

The Dust & Scratches filter works by searching for pixels that are dissimilar in color and then blurring the pixels in the immediate vicinity. For example, if you have a white scratch across a black area, as in the center of the forehead in Figure 7-5, PhotoDeluxe "sees" those white pixels as a defect and blurs the area.

All well and good — except that PhotoDeluxe isn't really capable of determining which contrasting pixels represent image defects and which represent image detail. As you can see in Figure 7-6, the filter did a good job of making the scratch and scanner crud less noticeable. But in the process, it destroyed the focus of the image. Everywhere a light pixel met up with a dark pixel — which happens a lot in this picture — PhotoDeluxe applied the blurring effect, resulting in an unacceptably soft image.

Figure 7-6: Applying the Dust & Scratches filter to the entire image blurred my furry friend too much.

Applying Dust & Scratches to your entire image, as I did in Figure 7-6, rarely yields good results. But you sometimes can remove defects without compromising your image if you follow these steps for using the filter:

1. **Select the defect.**

   Using the tools discussed in Chapter 8, select the defect and a few surrounding pixels. The smaller the selection, the better.

2. **Choose Quality⇨Remove Dust/Scratches.**

   The dialog box shown in Figure 7-7 appears.

Figure 7-7:
Inside the
Dust &
Scratches
dialog box.

3. **Set the Threshold value to 0.**

   The Threshold value determines how different two pixels must be before PhotoDeluxe blurs them. If you drag the Threshold slider all the way to the left or enter 0 in the option box, all pixels inside the selection are fair game. You refine the Threshold value later; for now, set it at 0.

4. **Set the Radius value.**

   The Radius value tells PhotoDeluxe how big an area to scan when it searches for differing pixels. The smaller the Radius value, the less damage to your image. Use the smallest possible Radius value that hides the defects.

   Be sure to select the Preview check box so that you can preview the results of the Dust & Scratches filter in the image window as well as in the preview area inside the dialog box. Remember, you can drag inside the preview area to see a hidden portion of the image. Click the plus and minus buttons beneath the preview area to zoom in and out on your image.

5. **Now raise the Threshold level.**

   Raise the value as much as you can without bringing the defect back into view.

6. **Click OK.**

Keep repeating these steps until you've cleared your image of all unwanted dirt, dust, and other specks. Using the filter in this way takes a bit more time but delivers much better results than trying to clean up your entire image with one pass of the filter.

Each time you select and blur a defect, examine the image closely. If you wind up with an area that's noticeably blurry compared with the rest of the image, press Ctrl+Z (⌘+Z) to undo your work. Then use the technique discussed in the next section to cover up the defect.

Cloning good pixels over bad

One of the more useful tools in the PhotoDeluxe bag of tricks is the Clone tool. Using this tool, you can copy "good" pixels and paint them over the defective pixels in your image. To create Figure 7-8 from the original, scratch-and-dent version in Figure 7-5, I cloned pixels from just below the scratch and used the clones to cover the scratch, thereby removing the defect without the blurring that accompanies the Dust & Scratches filter. I used the same method to cover up the speck of scanner crud on the ear.

Figure 7-8:
Cloning
good pixels
over
defective
pixels
eliminates
defects
without
ruining
focus.

I rely on the Clone tool almost every day to cover up blemishes in images, whether I'm trying to rid a picture of tiny dust flecks or some larger defect, like an ex-boyfriend. Unfortunately, the Clone tool is also one of the more difficult tools for new users to grasp, in part because no real-life equivalent exists. The Brush tool is easy — you drag with it to paint a stroke of color, just like you do with a real paintbrush. But the Clone tool? Only those wacky scientists in that sheep-growing lab seem to have one, and I doubt that their Clone tool works much like the PhotoDeluxe Clone tool.

The best way to explain the Clone tool is to walk you through the steps of using it. As you read, try out the tool for yourself. The Clone tool is one of those things that usually doesn't make much sense until you actually see it operate on-screen.

1. **Zoom in on the defect.**

   You need a close-up view for successful cloning. Figure 7-9 shows a zoom-in on the scratch area from Figure 7-5. You're looking at the forehead area between Beastie's eyes. The row of light gray pixels is the scratch.

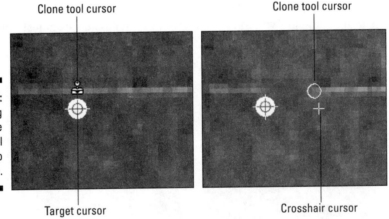

Clone tool cursor   Clone tool cursor

Figure 7-9:
Working
with the
Clone tool
to cover up
a scratch.

Target cursor   Crosshair cursor

2. **Choose Tools⇨Clone.**

   PhotoDeluxe displays two cursors in the image window, as shown in Figure 7-9, and also opens the Clone palette. (One cursor is the mouse cursor, so you have to move your mouse pointer into the image window to see the cursor.)

3. **Position the target cursor over the good pixels that you want to clone.**

   Drag the target cursor (labeled in Figure 7-9) so that it's directly over the pixels that you want to copy onto the bad pixels. In Figure 7-9, I positioned the target cursor just below the scratch.

If you're working on a multilayered image, be sure that the layer that contains the pixels you want to clone is the highlighted (active) layer in the Layers palette. The Clone tool can't "see" through layers to pick up pixels. Nor can it paint cloned pixels from one layer onto another layer. (See Chapter 10 for more Layers information.)

4. **Position the Clone tool cursor over the first bad pixel(s) that you want to cover up.**

   I positioned the Clone tool cursor (also labeled in the figure) on the scratch, just above the target cursor in Figure 7-9.

   By default, the Clone tool cursor looks like a rubber stamp, as in the left image in Figure 7-9. This cursor is a carryover from Photoshop, where the Clone tool is called the Rubber Stamp tool. Whether the rubber stamp icon was a conscious decision or an oversight by the folks at Adobe, I don't know. But I do know that the rubber stamp cursor gets in the way when you're trying to make precise edits. To get a clearer view of what you're doing, press Ctrl+K (⌘+K on the Mac) to open the Cursors dialog box. Select Brush Size in the Painting Options portion of the dialog box and then click OK. Now the Clone tool cursor is a circle that reflects the size of the brush tip you choose, as shown in the right half of Figure 7-9. (You choose the brush tip in the next step.)

5. **Choose a brush size and softness.**

   The Clone palette, like the Brushes palette described in Chapter 9, contains icons representing different brush tips for the Clone tool. You can choose a soft, fuzzy brush or a hard-edged one, and you can vary the size of your brush as well. If you choose a big, soft brush, you clone in big, fuzzy strokes, as if you were painting with a large paintbrush. If you choose a small, hard-edged brush, you clone in small, sharp strokes, as if you were drawing with a hard pencil.

   Click the icon for the size and shape of brush that you want to use. The top six brushes are hard-edged; the rest are fuzzy. The bottom four icons give you a 35-, 45-, 60-, or 100-pixel brush size (the icons would be too big for the palette if they represented the actual brush size).

   In Figure 7-9, I chose a hard brush that was the size of the scratch I wanted to cover up. If you're trying to cover up a larger defect, however, you get better results if you keep the brush size small and clone in small increments instead of trying to clone over the entire problem area with one or two strokes of the Clone tool.

6. **Click or drag to clone.**

   If you click, the pixels underneath the target cursor are cloned onto the pixels underneath the Clone tool cursor. You can click at several different spots on the defect to clone the same target pixels repeatedly if you want.

Alternatively, you can drag the Clone tool cursor to clone pixels along the length and direction of your drag (stay with me here). As soon as you begin dragging, a crosshair cursor emerges from the target cursor, as shown in the right side of Figure 7-9. That crosshair cursor shows you what pixels are being cloned onto the pixels underneath the Clone tool cursor. For example, in the right half of Figure 7-9, I dragged the Clone tool cursor from its original position, just above the target cursor, to the right along the scratch pixels. As I dragged, the Clone tool picked up the pixels underneath the crosshair cursor and painted them onto the scratch.

When you release the mouse button, the crosshair cursor scurries back to the target cursor. If you click or drag, you begin cloning from the original target area again. So you may need to reposition the target cursor before you do more cloning.

Successful cloning takes some practice, but I promise that after you become familiar with this tool, you'll never want to be without it. The following tips provide some additional hints for getting the most from your cloning experiments:

✔ Because the Clone tool is technically a painting tool — you "paint" with existing pixels — all the options available for the Brush tool and other painting tools are also available for the Clone tool. In addition to being able to change the brush size and cursor shape, as discussed in the preceding steps, you can vary the opacity of the tool.

To change the opacity of the pixels you paint with the Clone tool, press a number key. Press 0 to make your pixels fully opaque, so that they cover up the underlying pixels completely. Press any number between 1 and 9 to make the pixels transparent, so that some of the underlying pixels show through the cloned pixels. Lower numbers make the cloned pixels more transparent. Using a medium transparency can sometimes help cloned pixels blend with original pixels more naturally. Experiment to see what opacity works best for your image.

✔ PhotoDeluxe doesn't have a palette or menu item that tells you what opacity value is in force. And the opacity value stays in effect until you change it. So if the Clone tool or any other painting or editing tool doesn't seem to be working, you may have lowered the opacity in a previous editing job. Press 0 to return the tool to full opacity.

✔ Try to avoid cloning repeatedly from the same source (target) pixels. You wind up with too many similar pixels, creating an unnatural, obvious edit. Instead, clone several times from different target areas. If the scratch in Figure 7-9 were a little larger, for example, I would have cloned once from the bottom of the scratch and once from the top.

✔ Before you begin cloning, save your image. Also copy the layer that contains the pixels that you're cloning to a new layer, as described in Chapter 6, and do your cloning work on the new layer. If you screw up, just trash the new layer and start again.

TIP

✔ You can clone pixels from one image to another. Open both image windows side by side, as discussed in Chapter 1, and click the window of the image that contains the pixels that you want to clone. Choose the Clone tool and position the target cursor. Then move your cursor into the other window and click or drag to begin cloning.

Creating a Digital Patch

The Clone tool, discussed in the preceding section, is great for hiding some unwanted image elements or defects. But another option is to create a patch to cover up the offending pixels. For example, consider Figure 7-10. I like the way this statue is set in silhouette against a fair sky. I'd like it a lot more without that ugly construction tower — or whatever it is — and stray tree branches in the bottom-right corner of the image.

You could clone pixels from the surrounding sky over the offending elements, but that technique would require quite a bit of clicking and dragging with the Clone tool. A more efficient option is to select a large area of sky, copy the selection, and then use the copy as a patch to hide the crane and branches.

Figure 7-10: That ugly metal construction thingy has to go.

The one fly in the ointment is that all the selection tools in Version 2 and Version 3 draw hard-edged selections. So simply copying and moving surrounding pixels can give you an obvious patch, as in the left image of Figure 7-11. To create a seamless patch like the one in the right image of Figure 7-11, you have to do a little fancy footwork involving the Feather command and the Layers palette.

Figure 7-11: A standard patch is noticeable (left), but a feathered patch is invisible (right).

Here's the secret formula for creating top-notch patches in Version 2 and Version 3. If you're using the Business edition, check out the steps at the end of this section for a more efficient patching option.

1. **Choose View⇨Show Layers and View⇨Show Selections.**

    PhotoDeluxe displays the Layers and Selections palettes, which are essential to this job. You can find out all about the Layers palette in Chapter 10. The Selections palette and all the selection tools are covered in Chapter 8.

2. **Drag the background layer name to the New Layer icon.**

    Flip ahead to Figure 10-4 to see this concept in action. I'm assuming that your background layer contains your original image and that the area you want to use as the basis of your patch is on that layer. If you're working on a multilayered image, drag the layer that contains the patch pixels to the New Layer icon.

    Your new layer is added directly above the original layer in the Layers palette. The new layer is active, which means that your edits affect pixels on that layer only.

3. **Select the pixels that you want to use as a patch.**

Use the selection tools discussed in Chapter 8 to enclose the patch pixels in a selection outline. Try to grab pixels that are as close as possible in color and brightness to the ones that now surround the area you want to cover. To create the patch for Figure 7-10, for example, I used the Oval tool to select a patch of sky just to the left of the tower. The patch is slightly reduced in area in the next step, so select a patch area that's just a little larger than the object you want to hide.

When patching an area like that in Figure 7-10, you get more-natural results if you create several small patches, taken from different areas surrounding the unwanted pixels, rather than creating one large patch. In my case, I covered the tower and tree branches with four or five patches created from different areas of sky.

If you're patching an irregularly shaped area, select the pixels that you want to cover up, plus a few pixels around all sides of the unwanted pixels. Then click the Move or New icon in the Selections palette (discussed in Chapter 8) and Ctrl+Alt+drag the selection outline onto the area that you plan to use as a patch (⌘+Option+drag on a Mac).

4. **Choose Effects⇨Feather to display the Feather dialog box.**

In this dialog box, shown in Figure 7-12, you can *feather* a selection — that is, make its edges soft and fuzzy, so that it appears to fade in gradually from the background.

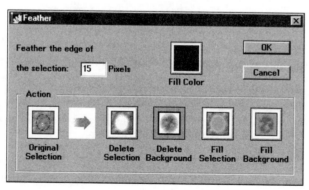

Figure 7-12:
The Feather command is key to creating a natural-looking patch.

5. **Enter a Feather value.**

The Feather value adjusts the fuzziness of your selection. Higher values make your selection edges fuzzier. I used a value of 15 to create my patch. If your patch is very small, you may need a smaller Feather value. (You can find out more about other uses of the Feather command in Chapter 8, by the way.)

6. **Click the Delete Background icon and click OK.**

   Now your new layer contains a nicely feathered patch. To see the patch without the underlying background, Alt+click the Eyeball icon to the left of the layer name in the Layers palette (Option+click on a Mac). Alt+click/Option+click again to make all your image layers visible again.

7. **Click the None icon in the Selections palette or press Ctrl+D (⌘+D on a Mac).**

   Either approach deactivates the selection outline, which is critical to the patching process. If you don't lose the selection outline, you wind up copying a hard-edged patch. The patch itself is feathered, but your selection outline isn't.

8. **Select the Move tool.**

   Click the Move icon in the Selections palette or press Ctrl+G (⌘+G on a Mac).

9. **Drag or nudge the patch into place.**

   To nudge the patch in small increments, press the arrow keys on your keyboard. One press of an arrow key moves the patch one pixel; Shift+arrow moves the patch ten pixels.

   If your patch isn't quite large enough to cover the image blemish, drag the patch layer to the New Layer icon to create a second patch on another layer. Then use the second patch to hide more of the unwanted element.

10. **Choose Merge Layers from the Layers palette menu.**

    PhotoDeluxe merges your patch layer and background layer into one.

    After you choose this command, your patch layer is firmly adhered to your background image layer, and you can no longer adjust the patch. So be sure that the patch is good before you merge your layers. You may want to print your image first to get a good look at your patching job. If you don't like the results, drag the patch layer or layers to the Trash icon in the Layers palette and start over.

The steps for creating a patch seem long and involved, but after you work through them a few times, you'll see how easy it is to erase reality from your images.

Folks who invested the extra bucks in the Business Edition bought an easier path to creating image patches. In the Business Edition, one of the selection tools — the Smart Select tool — is capable of drawing feathered selection outlines. So to create a feathered patch, you can take this approach to your patching work:

1. **Follow Steps 1 and 2 in the preceding set of steps.**

2. **Activate the SmartSelect tool.**

Choose the tool from the Selections palette. When you do, the SmartSelect Options palette appears. In the palette, you can adjust the sensitivity of the tool and the brush size, as explained in Chapter 8. More importantly, you can choose to feather the selection by using a Feather value other than 0.

The Feather value makes your selection outline fuzzy, just like the Feather command described earlier. For a patch, try a Feather value in the 5 to 15 pixel range. The higher the value, the fuzzier the edges of your selection. For more information about the Sensitivity and Brush Width options, review the section on the SmartSelect tool in Chapter 8.

3. **Draw your selection outline.**

   Again, check out Chapter 8 for the specifics.

4. **Alt+drag the selection over the area you want to patch (Option+drag on a Mac).**

   If the patch covers the entire blemish, you're done. If not, you can Alt+ or Option+drag the patch over more of the damaged pixels. Or, if you want to create a patch from another area of the image, press Ctrl+D (⌘+D) to get rid of the current selection outline. Then draw another selection outline and Alt+ or Option+drag that patch into place.

After you finish patching, you can fuse the patch layer together with the underlying image layer by choosing Merge Layers from the Layers palette menu. Or you can simply delete the underlying image layer, which leaves you with just the patched, corrected image.

Note that you can do all your patching on the original image layer, but by working on a copy of the original image layer, you give yourself the option of deleting the patching layer if you screw up.

Fading Away Noise, Jaggies, and Moiré Patterns

When digital imaging gurus turn up their noses at an image, you can often hear them dissing the photo because it suffers from one of three problems: noise, jaggies, or moiré patterns. For those of you who don't have your official digital-imaging decoder rings handy, the three terms mean the following:

✔ *Noise* refers to speckles that give the image a grainy look. Noise often occurs in images that were shot in low light.

✔ *Jaggies* refers to a blocky, pixelated effect caused by oversharpening, applying too much JPEG compression, or overenlarging an image.

> ✔ *Moiré* patterns are tiny, diagonal lines that appear ingrained in an image. Moiré patterns often occur when you scan old photographs or pictures from newspaper or magazine articles. (You pronounce the problem *mor-ay,* in case you were wondering.)

The following sections offer some tips for fixing all three unsightly blemishes.

Quieting noise

If your image suffers from *noise* — speckles that give the image a grainy look — you can sometimes correct the problem by applying the Despeckle filter. The filter searches for edges (areas of high contrast) in the image. Then it applies a slight blur to everything *but* the edge areas to make the noise less pronounced.

Unfortunately, Despeckle is a one-shot filter — you don't have any control over how much blurring is applied. Sometimes the filter works great, but other times it blurs the image too much. To give Despeckle a try, choose Effects⇨Noise⇨Despeckle.

The Business Edition and Version 3 offer a noise-reducing filter that enables you to control the extent of the softening. Choose Effects⇨Noise⇨Reduce Graininess. A dialog box appears with a single Smoothness slider bar. Use the lowest possible Smoothness value that rids your image of noise. Unfortunately, you can't preview the effects of this filter in the image window; you have to rely on the preview inside the dialog box.

In Version 2, you can try applying the Soften filter if your image gets too soft with Despeckle. Choose Effects⇨Blur⇨Soften to display the Soften dialog box, and then adjust the Radius value to increase or decrease the extent of the blur. The disadvantage of the Soften filter is that it softens both edges and non-edges.

For best results with any of these filters, select the noisy areas of the image and apply the filter only to the selection. If you have to apply the filter to the whole image — that is, if the entire image is noisy — you can sometimes firm up the focus after you blur by applying the Unsharp Mask filter. Raise the Threshold level as necessary to prevent the noise from reappearing.

Softening jaggies

The Business Edition and Version 3 also come with a special filter designed to correct pixelization, more commonly known as jaggies. Like the Despeckle and Reduce Graininess filters from the "Quieting noise" discussion, the filter works by applying a subtle blur to the image. Choose Effects⇨Noise⇨JPEG Cleanup to experiment with the filter.

PhotoDeluxe presents you with a dialog box containing a Smoothness value. Raise the value to intensify the blurring effect. You can preview the effects of the filter in the dialog box, but not in the image window.

If you're using Version 2, try applying the Effects➪Blur➪Soften filter to blur jagged edges. With either filter, following up with the Unsharp Mask filter can help to restore lost detail in some cases. Raise the Threshold value in the Unsharp Mask dialog box so that you don't bring back the jagged edges you're trying to hide.

No more moiré

When you scan old photographs or pictures from newspapers or magazines, you can often see tiny diagonal lines in the image. You can see what I mean by looking at the image preview area in Figure 7-13.

Both Version 3 and the Business Edition include a special plug-in filter designed to make moiré patterns disappear. Choose Effects➪Noise➪Remove Moire Pattern to display the dialog box shown in Figure 7-13. To use the filter, first try to align the blinking line in the image preview portion of the dialog box as closely as possible with the lines in the moiré pattern. Drag around the perimeter of the Angle circle, as shown in the figure, or enter a value in the Angle option box to change the angle of the blinking line. Because adjusting the Angle value precisely is difficult using the drag method, you may want to drag to get close to the value you want and then use the type-in-the-number approach to fine-tune the value.

Drag to change Angle value

Figure 7-13:
Align the
blinking line
with the
lines in
the moiré
pattern.

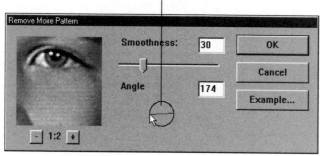

As with the other filters discussed in this section, this filter does its magic by blurring the image. The Softness value determines how much blurring is applied. Use the lowest possible value that makes the moiré pattern disappear. Note that the results of the filter are previewed in the dialog box only, not in the image window as with other PhotoDeluxe filters, which usually provide both previews.

If you're using Version 2, you may be able to achieve similar results by using the Effects⇨Blur⇨Soften filter. Raise the Radius value in the Soften dialog box until the moiré patterns become less noticeable.

After softening your image, try to firm up the image detail by applying the Unsharp Mask filter, as discussed earlier in this chapter. You may need to raise the Threshold value slightly to avoid bringing those unsightly moiré patterns back into focus.

Some scanners provide a moiré-removal filter inside their scanning software. If yours does, try using that feature to reduce or eliminate the moiré pattern in the scanning stage, rather than trying to do after-the-fact correction in PhotoDeluxe.

Chapter 8

Selective Editing

In This Chapter

▶ Telling PhotoDeluxe what part of the picture you want to edit

▶ Uncovering the Selections palette

▶ Drawing round, oval, and irregular selections

▶ Selecting by color

▶ Tracing the edges of an object with the SmartSelect tool

▶ Refining a selection outline

▶ Moving and copying selections

▶ Feathering selections before filling or deleting

*B*efore you paint a room, you cover up the baseboards, windowsills, and other areas with masking tape so that you don't get any paint on them. If you're smart, you also lay down old sheets or plastic on the floor so that if you dribble paint from your brush — or kick an entire paint can over — your carpet doesn't suffer the consequences.

In PhotoDeluxe, the selection tools serve as the digital equivalent of masking tape and old sheets. Using these tools, you can protect portions of your image from being altered when you apply filters, special effects, and other edits. For example, if you want to sharpen the main subject of your image but leave the background blurry, you select the subject before applying a sharpening filter. Any pixels not selected are unaffected by your edit.

Selecting is one of the more important aspects of image editing, which is why this entire chapter is devoted to the subject. You find out how to maneuver the various PhotoDeluxe selection tools, how to refine a selection outline after you initially create it, and how to use some special tricks to select intricate image elements easily. In addition, this chapter explains how to move and copy selected elements from one area of an image to another — and even from one image to another. As if all that weren't tantalizing enough, you also find out how to create a special type of selection that enables you to fade your image into the background.

Knowing When to Select Before You Edit

Selections come into play in several editing scenarios. Pick up the selection tools if you want to do any of the following:

- ✔ **Limit the effects of your edits** to certain areas of the image. Any paint tools, special effects, or image-correction commands affect only the selected areas. You can brighten up one portion of your image while leaving the rest alone, for example. You can even print just the selected area if you want. About the only command that doesn't respect selections is the Photo Size command — you can't alter the resolution of just one area of the image. You can use other commands to resize the area inside a selection, however.

- ✔ **Apply certain commands,** including the Outline command, which creates a border around your selection, and the Feather command, which fuzzes up the edges of your selection so that it appears to fade in gradually from the background. When you choose commands that require a selection, PhotoDeluxe displays an alert box asking you to make the selection if you haven't already done so.

- ✔ **Give yourself some extra editing protection** when using the paint and edit tools. If you have a steady hand, you may be able to apply paint precisely to the pixels that you want to color, for example. But most folks, including me, don't have that kind of hand-to-eye coordination, especially when a mouse is involved. By selecting the areas you want to paint, you make sure that any errant swipes of a painting tool don't affect pixels that you didn't intend to change.

In other words, selections are an everyday part of editing life. Thankfully, most selection jobs are fairly easy, and PhotoDeluxe gives you some sophisticated tools for tackling the more complex selection challenges you may face.

Learning the Lingo

Image-editing gurus routinely make up complicated names for simple things just to keep the rest of us looking like rubes. So that you can toss around selection slang with the best of 'em, here's a quick primer on selection terminology:

- ✔ When you select an area in PhotoDeluxe (and in almost every other image editor), the selected area is surrounded by a dotted line on-screen. (Flip ahead to Figure 8-2 if you want to see the dotted line for yourself.) Common folk refer to the dotted line as the *selection outline,* but snooty sorts call it a *marquee.*

Either way, that dotted line indicates the boundaries of your selection. Any pixels inside the dotted line are selected; pixels outside the dotted line don't get to join in any reindeer games.

✔ Some people are so enamored of the word *marquee* that they use it both as a noun, referring to the selection outline, and as a verb, referring to the act of creating a selection outline. For example, whereas you and I might say, "Select the purple cow," they would say, "Marquee that violet bovine creature for me, won't you darling?"

✔ Folks who have a graphics or printing background often refer to selections as *masks*. The deselected area is said to be *masked,* and the act of selecting pixels is called *masking.*

Using the Selections Palette

You can access the PhotoDeluxe selection tools by choosing them from the Select⇨Selection Tools submenu. But a more convenient option is to display the Selections palette, shown in Figure 8-1. The Selections palette offers you quicker access to different selection tools and also provides some selection options not available on the Select menu.

Figure 8-1: Keep the Selections palette handy when editing.

Packing a huge wallop in a small package, the Selections palette is full of options for creating and refining selection outlines. Here's a guide to the palette controls:

✔ Select the tool that you want to use from the drop-down list at the top of the palette.

✔ The four icons beneath the drop-down list enable you to move, refine, or trash your selection outline. (These icons don't appear when the Object Selection tool is active because this tool doesn't draw selection outlines; rather, it enables you to select and manipulate an entire image or layer.)

✔ Click the Add icon to add more pixels to your existing selection outline; click the Reduce icon to deselect pixels that you previously selected. For more on adjusting your selection outline, march on over to "Fine-Tuning Your Selection Outline," later in this chapter.

✔ Click the New icon and then click the image to cancel the current selection outline and begin a new one. If you click by mistake, click Undo to get your selection outline back.

✔ Click the Move icon to move your selection or the selection outline. For more on the former subject, read "Moving and Copying Selected Pixels," later in this chapter. For details on moving a selection outline, check out "Fine-Tuning Your Selection Outline," also later in this chapter.

✔ The three buttons at the bottom of the palette provide still more selection opportunities. Click All to select the entire image; click None to cancel the current selection outline, so that no pixels are selected. Click Invert to reverse the marquee, so that the areas that are currently deselected become selected, and areas that are currently selected fall outside the selection outline. Got that? If not, read "Inverting a Selection," later in this chapter.

✔ If the Selections palette isn't open, you can use these keyboard shortcuts to invoke the All, None, and Invert options. Press Ctrl+A to select all pixels, Ctrl+D to deselect all pixels, and Ctrl+I to invert the selection. On a Mac, press ⌘+A, ⌘+D, and ⌘+I instead.

✔ You can relocate the Selections palette on-screen by dragging its title bar. (In case you're new to computing, the title bar is the area that contains the name — title — of the palette or window.) To put the palette away, click the Close button in the title bar or choose View⇨Hide Selections.

Choosing the Right Tool for the Job

Each of the PhotoDeluxe selection tools has its own role in your image editing. To choose the right tool for the job, follow these suggestions:

✔ Use the Rectangle, Oval, Circle, or Square tool to select regularly shaped areas. These tools draw — drum roll, please — rectangular, oval, circular, or perfectly square selection outlines.

✔ Pick up the Color Wand if you want to select an area that's dissimilar in color from its surroundings — for example, if you want to select a red rose that's set against a blue background.

✔ You can use the Polygon and Trace tools to draw freehand selection outlines around irregularly shaped image elements. I don't find these tools terribly easy to use for drawing precise selection outlines, but you may have better control of your mouse than I.

✔ The SmartSelect tool is usually a better option for tracing around irregularly-shaped elements. But it works by finding the borders between contrasting pixels, so if the object that you want to select is very similar in color to surrounding pixels, you may want to use another selection tool to carve out your selection outline.

In the Business Edition, the SmartSelect tool is capable of creating feathered selections — selections with fuzzy edges. This feature makes the SmartSelect tool the perfect choice when creating patches to cover up image blemishes, as explained in "Creating a Digital Patch" in Chapter 7.

✔ The Object Selection tool is a breed apart from the other selection tools. You use this tool to select and manipulate layers or entire images — for example, if you want to distort the entire image with the Perspective command discussed in Chapter 12. You also need the Object Selection tool for sizing and moving text, as discussed in Chapter 11, and for relocating selections that you paste into an image, explained in "Moving and Copying Selected Pixels," later in this chapter.

The basic shape tools

The Rectangle, Oval, Square, and Circle tools create selection outlines that are, er, rectangular, oval, square, and circular. Gosh, you'd think that with all the computer expertise under my belt, I could come up with a more compli-cated-sounding description than that, wouldn't you? Hope they don't take away my geek card or anything.

Anyway, to select an area with any of these tools, just drag from one side of the area to another, as illustrated in Figure 8-2. Or, if you prefer, Alt+drag to draw the selection outline from the center of the area outward (Option+drag on the Mac). As you drag, a dotted selection outline — otherwise known as a *marquee* — appears, showing you what you selected.

Here's a secret: You don't really need to ever use the Square or Circle tools. To draw a square selection outline, just press Shift while you drag with the Rectangle tool. To create a perfect circle, Shift+drag with the Oval tool. PhotoDeluxe constrains your drag so that you automatically achieve the perfect circular or square selection outline.

And here's another tip: You can press Ctrl+M (⌘+M on the Mac) to grab the Rectangle tool quickly.

Some people who are new to image editing expect these basic selection tools to perform like similarly named tools in drawing programs such as CorelDraw — where drawing with a rectangle or oval tool creates a filled or outlined shape. In PhotoDeluxe, if you want to create a colored shape — a blue square, for example — you must first draw the selection outline and then use the Selection Fill command to turn all the pixels inside the outline blue. Keep in mind that if you want to create a logo or other simple drawing based on geometric shapes, PhotoDeluxe really isn't the best program for the job. See "Can I edit drawings in PhotoDeluxe?" in Chapter 3, for an explanation.

Figure 8-2:
Drag from one corner to another with the Rectangle tool.

Selection marquee   Rectangle cursor

The Color Wand

The Color Wand, as its name implies — sorta — bases the selection outline on pixel color. When you click with this tool, PhotoDeluxe analyzes the color of the pixel you click. Then it selects a continuous area of pixels that are similar in color.

Suppose that you have a skyline image like the one in Color Plate 8-1. Clicking to the right of the main tower selects an expanse of similarly colored sky pixels, as indicated by the dotted outline. The color wand cursor in the left images in the figure and color plate shows the location of my click. The similar sky pixels on the left of the tower aren't selected because the tower pixels come between those sky pixels and the pixel I originally clicked. That's what I mean by a continuous area of color — the selection outline stops at the point where PhotoDeluxe encounters pixels that are differently colored from the original pixel you click.

Before using the Color Wand, tell PhotoDeluxe how similar color pixels must be in order to become part of the selection. Press Ctrl+K (⌘+K on the Mac) or choose File⇨Preferences⇨Cursors to display the Cursors dialog box, shown in Figure 8-3. Lower the Tolerance value to make the Color Wand more discriminating, so that when you click a pixel with the wand, only pixels that are very similar are selected.

Figure 8-3:
Adjust the
Tolerance
value to
make the
Color Wand
more or
less
discrim-
inating.

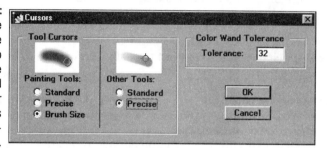

The top-left image in Color Plate 8-1 shows the results of using the default Tolerance value, 32. The bottom-left image shows the selection outline created by doubling the Tolerance value. In the right half of the figure and color plate, I deleted the selected pixels to give you a better idea of the extent of the selections.

With the Tolerance value set at 64, nearly all the sky pixels on the right side of the tower were selected. Adding the remaining sky areas to the selection is a simple matter of clicking the Add button in the Selections palette and clicking again in each remaining sky area with the Color wand. (See "Fine-Tuning a Selection Outline," coming up soon, for more about adding to an existing selection.)

The Color Wand is especially useful for selecting complex objects set against solid-color backgrounds, like the buildings in my example. If you tried to select the buildings with any of the other selection tools, you'd spend all day trying to adjust the outline so that every building was properly selected. But with a few clicks of the Color Wand, you can select the sky and then click the Invert button in the Selections palette so that the deselected areas — the buildings — become selected rather than the sky. The right images in Color Plate 8-1 give you a good idea of just how precisely I was able to create the selection outline by using this method.

The SmartSelect tool

An alternative to the Color Wand, the SmartSelect tool also can be helpful in selecting an area that's surrounded by contrasting pixels. As you drag along the edge of the element that you want to select, the SmartSelect tool automatically places the selection outline along the border between the element and the contrasting pixels that surround it.

Make sense? Didn't to me, either, until I tried out the tool for myself. So grab an image and test out the following steps:

1. **Choose the SmartSelect tool from the Selections palette.**

   When you select this tool, the SmartSelect options palette appears. More on that later.

2. **Click at the spot where you want the selection outline to begin.**

3. **Move the mouse along the edge of the area that you want to select.**

   Don't press the mouse button — just move your mouse so that the cursor follows the edge of the area. As you move the mouse, PhotoDeluxe searches for pixels that contrast those underneath your cursor. Then it lays down a selection outline to separate those contrasting pixels from the ones under your cursor. In Figure 8-4, you can see me in the act of drawing a selection outline along the edge between a portion of the pie and the plate from Figure 8-2.

Selection point

Figure 8-4:
The
SmartSelect
tool in
action.

4. **Add or delete selection points, if necessary.**

   Along the selection outline, notice the little squares that appear every so often. These squares, labeled in Figure 8-4, are called *selection points.* If you want to change the placement of the selection outline, move your cursor over the most recent selection point and press Delete. Keep backing up over selection points and deleting them until you reach the spot where the selection outline went bad.

Now move the mouse again to redraw the selection outline. If the SmartSelect tool doesn't do a good job of finding the edge of the element, you can click to create your own selection points, which anchor the selection outline everywhere you click. Keep moving the mouse and adding and deleting selection points until you reach the spot where you began the selection outline.

5. **When you see the OK cursor, click to complete the selection outline.**

The OK cursor appears when you place the SmartSelect tool cursor over the first selection point in your outline.

If you had trouble making the SmartSelect tool find the edges in your image — the border between the contrasting pixels — you can adjust the sensitivity of the tool to alter its performance. You do this by changing the values in the SmartSelect Options palette, shown in Figure 8-5. The palette on the left is the Version 2 and Version 3 palette; the one on the right is the Business Edition palette.

Figure 8-5:
The SmartSelect Options palette in Version 2 and 3 (left) and the Business Edition (right).

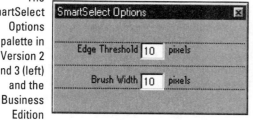

If the area that you're trying to select contrasts only slightly from the background, raise the Edge Threshold value in Version 2 and Version 3; raise the Sensitivity value in the Business Edition. You can enter any value from 1 to 100; higher values make the tool more sensitive to color shifts.

Change the Brush Width value if the SmartSelect tool starts roaming too far from your cursor in its search for contrasting pixels or doesn't go far enough — in other words, if the selection outline starts straying too far from where you want it to be. Lower the value to restrict the tool to a narrower area; raise the value to give the tool more freedom. You can enter a value from 1 to 20.

You can adjust the Business Edition SmartSelect tool in one more way. If you raise the Feather value from 0, you create a soft, fuzzy selection outline instead of a hard-edged one. The result is a gradual transition between the selection and the surrounding area. You can see an example of how a feathered selection looks by flipping ahead to Figure 8-10. This image features a horse image that fades gradually into the white background. I created a feathered selection around the horse's head, inverted the selection so that the background was selected instead of the head, and then deleted the background. I used the Effects⇨Feather command, discussed later in this chapter, to create the image in the figure. But you can achieve the same effect if you set a high feather value and draw the selection with the SmartSelect tool. Granted, if you wanted to create the same effect in this particular horse image, you would have to set all your own custom selection points — clicking your way around the horse in an oval pattern. I use the horse example just to give you an idea of what a feathered selection looks like.

Feathered selections come in especially handy when you want to copy a good portion of your image onto damaged image areas. For more about this concept, see "Creating a Digital Patch" in Chapter 7.

Drag-and-draw tools

With the Polygon and Trace tools, you can draw freehand selection outlines around the object you want to select. The two tools work a little differently, but both require some degree of mouse coordination — a quality that I don't seem to have. If you're good at drawing, though, you may prefer these tools. Otherwise, you can use them to create a general selection outline and then use the techniques discussed later in this chapter to refine the outline.

The Trace tool

To create a selection outline with the Trace tool, just drag around the area that you want to select. If you let up on the mouse button before you come back to the spot where you began the selection outline, PhotoDeluxe automatically completes the selection outline by placing a straight line between the start and end points of your drag.

Press Ctrl+L to switch to the Trace tool quickly (⌘+L on a Mac).

The Polygon tool

The Polygon tool is like the Trace tool with an added feature. To draw a curved segment of your selection outline, just drag with the Polygon tool as you do with the Trace tool. But if you want to draw a straight segment, let up on the mouse button at the spot where you want that straight segment to start. Then click at the spot where you want the segment to end.

PhotoDeluxe creates the straight segment for you, which is a good thing, because drawing a perfectly straight line with a mouse can be a challenge for the steadiest hand.

To complete the selection outline, double-click. If you double-click anywhere but at the beginning of the selection outline, PhotoDeluxe automatically closes the selection outline with a straight segment.

After your first click with the Polygon tool, you can't cancel out of the selection-drawing process. If you change your mind about that selection outline or want to start over, double-click to close the selection outline and then press Ctrl+D (⌘+D) or click the None icon in the Selections palette to lose the selection outline.

The Object Selection tool

The Object Selection tool works differently from all the other selection tools. Instead of drawing a selection outline, this tool selects an entire image or a single layer in the image.

If you're working on a single-layer image — that is, you haven't created any text or additional image layers — clicking the image with the Object Selection tool selects your entire image. On a multiple-layer image, click on any element on the layer that you want to select. You can't select more than one layer at a time, unfortunately.

After you click, PhotoDeluxe surrounds the image or layer with a solid outline and displays a series of resize and rotate handles, as shown in Figure 8-6. This image is a two-layer image: one containing the white background pixels and another containing the text. I clicked the text to select it in the figure.

Resize handle   Rotate handle

Figure 8-6:
Drag the resize and rotate handles to manipulate a layer or image.

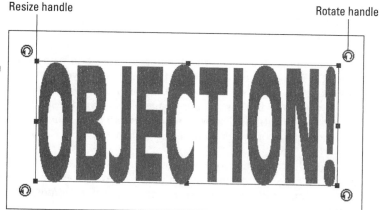

After you display the selection box and handles, you can rotate, move, resize, or distort the image or layer as follows:

- ✔ Drag inside the selection box to move the layer. If you do this when an entire image is selected, you move a portion of the image off the image canvas. The hidden portion of the image is still there, however. To bring it back onto the canvas, just drag it with the Object Selection tool. Or enlarge the canvas size using the Size➪Canvas Size command, covered in Chapter 6.

    As long as you save the image in the PDD (native PhotoDeluxe) format, you retain the hidden portion of the image. But if you save in any other format, the hidden portion is cropped away. The same applies if you move a layer partially off the image canvas.

- ✔ Drag a top or side handle to stretch the image or layer in one direction, creating a distorted effect. To stretch the image both horizontally and vertically (but not necessarily proportionally), Shift+drag a corner handle.

- ✔ Drag a corner handle — no Shift this time — to resize the selection proportionally, so that no distortion takes place.

- ✔ Drag the center side handle past the opposite side handle to flip the selection horizontally. Drag the center top handle past the bottom handle to flip the selection vertically.

- ✔ Drag any rotate handle to spin the selection.

- ✔ Press Alt as you drag to resize or distort a layer without moving the center of the layer. (On a Mac, Option+drag to accomplish the same thing.) This technique enables you to create fun-house-mirror-type effects.

- ✔ When you're done wreaking havoc on your selection, press Enter on a PC or Return on a Mac. Or click outside the selection box.

- ✔ To cancel a transformation in progress, press Esc. If you simply want to undo the last drag of a handle, click the Undo button or press Ctrl+Z (⌘+Z on a Mac).

Resizing an image or layer in this fashion can degrade your image, as can rotating the image. The exception is text on a Text layer; PhotoDeluxe creates text in a way that enables you to safely resize and rotate text as much as you want. But for regular image pixels, avoid resizing if possible and limit your rotations. For best results, try to rotate the layer only once, because multiple rotations do increasing damage.

Of course, when you distort an image, degradation is sort of the point, so if you want to make your image look a mess, distort away. And for even more distortion fun, check out the Distort and Perspective commands, covered in Chapter 14.

Fine-Tuning a Selection Outline

Getting a selection just right the first time is a rare occurrence, especially if you're trying to select a complex subject. The good news is that you can easily adjust the selection outline by using the tricks in the following list.

These techniques work with any of the selection tools except the Object Selection tool.

✔ Didn't grab enough pixels? To select more, click the Add button in the Selections palette. Then use any of the selection tools to start a second selection outline or expand the existing one. You can mix and match selection tools — draw a rectangular selection to select part of your image and then use the Color Wand to select another region, for example.

✔ Does your selection outline encompass elements that you don't want selected? Click the Reduce button in the Selections palette. When the Reduce button is turned on, the selection tools work in reverse. If you drag with the Oval tool, for example, PhotoDeluxe deselects any pixels that you enclose with your drag. If you click with the Color Wand, pixels similar in color to the one that you click are deselected.

✔ You can move the selection outline to another part of your image by clicking the Move icon in the Selections palette. Then Ctrl+Alt+drag inside the selection outline with any tool (except the Object Selection tool). On a Mac, press ⌘ and Option as you drag. This technique comes in handy when you're creating a patch to cover up an unwanted image element, as discussed in Chapter 7. Select the element that you want to hide and then drag the selection outline onto the pixels that you want to use as a patch.

Be sure that you press Ctrl + Alt (or ⌘ + Option) as you drag! Otherwise, you move the pixels inside the selection outline, not just the outline.

To move the selection outline in small increments, press Ctrl+Alt along with the arrow keys on your keyboard (⌘+Option if you're using a Mac). Each press of an arrow key moves the outline one pixel. Ctrl+Alt+Shift+arrow key moves the outline ten pixels.

✔ Keep adding and subtracting pixels from the selection outline until you get things just so. Remember that if a selection tool slips in your hand and you make a mistake, you can click Undo or press Ctrl+Z (⌘+Z on a Mac) to undo your last action.

Inverting a Selection

Sometimes you can get quicker selection results by selecting everything but the element that you want to edit and then inverting the selection. Inverting the selection swaps the selection outline so that pixels that were formerly selected are deselected, and vice versa.

If you haven't already feasted your eyes on Color Plate 8-1, take a look now. Can you imagine trying to select all those buildings and ornamental shapes with any of the selection tools? You'd surely go mad. But with the Color Wand, you can easily select the sky with just a few clicks. (I didn't completely select the sky in this Color Plate, but you get the idea.) You can then invert the selection by clicking the Invert button in the Selections palette, which deselects the sky and selects everything else.

An even quicker way to invert a selection is to press Ctrl+I (⌘+I on a Mac).

Moving and Copying Selected Pixels

Selecting is a neat trick, but it's just the precursor to the main excitement. I mean, those blinking selection marquee lines — which some people refer to as *marching ants* — are fun and all, but they get a little boring after a few minutes. The real action comes when you copy or move selected elements from one place to another. You can put your head on someone else's body, put the 10-carat necklace from some starlet's neck around your own throat, and otherwise push and shove pixels around until even the photographer who snapped the picture wouldn't recognize the image.

The following sections explain how to move and copy a selection within the same image; how to move and copy selections from one image to another; and even how to paste one selection inside another.

The drag-and-drop approach

The easiest way to relocate a selection from one spot in an image to another is to drag it and drop it:

1. **Press Ctrl+G (⌘+G on a Mac).**

   This shortcut selects the Move tool. You can also activate the Move tool by clicking on the Move icon in the Selections palette when any tool but the Object Selection tool is in use. However you pick up the Move tool, your cursor turns into a double-headed arrow.

2. **Drag or Alt+drag inside the selection outline to reposition the selection.**

   Drag or Option+drag on a Mac.

   If you drag without the Alt or Option key, PhotoDeluxe removes the selection from its current home, leaving a hole where the selection used to live. If you're working on the bottom layer of the image, the image canvas shows through the hole. If you move a selection on an upper layer of an image, pixels from the underlying layer become visible through the hole.

   If you Alt+drag or Option+drag, PhotoDeluxe makes a copy of the selection and moves the copy only. The original pixels stay put.

   I used this technique to create the image on the left in Figure 8-7. The original image contained only the rose on the left side of the image. I added the second rose by copying the original rose and then rotating the copied posy with the Object Selection tool, explained earlier in this chapter.

   To nudge the selection into place, press the arrow keys. One press of an arrow key nudges the selection one pixel; Shift+arrow key nudges the selection in ten-pixel increments. Don't worry about the placement of your mouse cursor; PhotoDeluxe completely ignores your mouse and concentrates on the keyboard input when you nudge.

3. **Send the selection to a new layer or merge it with the underlying layer.**

   Your selection currently exists on a *floating layer.* If you display the Layers palette (View⇨Show Layers), you see a layer called "Floating Selection." This is a temporary layer, however. If you click the None icon or click with any selection tool except the Move tool, you fuse the floating selection with the underlying layer. After the floating selection and underlying layer are merged, the selection outline disappears and you can no longer move the selection around to reposition it.

Figure 8-7:
I copied the rose and rotated the copy (left). Then I cut the copy to the Clipboard, leaving a hole in the image (right).

If you want to keep the floating selection independent of the rest of the image, drag the Floating Selection item in the Layers palette to the New Layer icon (the little double-square in the bottom-left corner of the palette). You create a new layer just to hold your selection. For more about layers, see Chapter 10.

You can use this same method to drag and drop a selection from one image to another. Just open both images, place them side-by-side on-screen, and then drag your selection from one image window to the other.

If you're using Windows 95, you can also try this trick for a quick way to copy a selection from PhotoDeluxe to a document in another program: Open both PhotoDeluxe and the program into which you want to copy the selection. Make the PhotoDeluxe window active and drag the selection to the Windows 95 taskbar button for the other program. Don't let up on the mouse button yet! When the other program window appears on-screen, drag from the taskbar up into the program window and release the mouse button. You don't need to Alt+drag to copy in this scenario: A simple drag will do. Note that you can't move a selection (deleting the selection from the original) with this method.

When you select the Move tool (by pressing Ctrl+G or ⌘+G or clicking the Move icon in the Selections palette), the Selections palette indicates that the Object Selection tool is active. For some reason, the palette drop-down menu doesn't include a separate entry for the Move tool. This setup may lead you to believe that the Move tool and the Object Selection tool are one and the same. They're not. If you choose the Object Selection tool from the Selections palette drop-down list or the Select menu, you can nudge a selection using the arrow keys, but you can't drag it using the mouse. As soon as you press your mouse button to begin the drag, the entire layer or image becomes selected, not just the selection. At that point, you can drag the entire layer or image, but you can't nudge using the arrow keys (go figure).

So always use the Move tool to relocated selections, and always press Ctrl+G or ⌘+G or click the Move icon before you try to shift things around, just to make sure that the Move tool is active.

The Edit⇨Duplicate command

If all you want to do is create a copy of your selection, you can choose Edit⇨Duplicate. PhotoDeluxe copies your selection and places it on a new layer. The copy is selected automatically so that you can reposition or resize it by using the Object Selection tool.

The Duplicate command copies your entire image if you don't select a part of the image before you choose the command. The duplicate is offset just a little from the original image so that you can distinguish the copy from the original image.

To choose the Duplicate command quickly, press Ctrl+; — that's a semicolon (⌘+; on a Mac).

For some reason, PhotoDeluxe doesn't enable you to undo the Duplicate command. To get rid of an unwanted duplicate, just press the Delete key. Or drag the duplicate layer to the Trash icon in the Layers palette.

The old Cut/Copy/Paste routine

If you know that you want to retain your selection on its own layer, or if you just have trouble dragging the selection — which can happen when you have a very small selection — you can use the Cut, Copy, and Paste commands to do the job.

You can often use the Cut/Copy/Paste routine to place an image or selection in a document that you're creating in another program, too. For example, you can paste an image into a spreadsheet you're building in Microsoft Excel. Alternatively, you can save the image and import it into the other program. Check the Help system for the program you're using to find out the best procedure to follow.

The following steps walk you through the process of moving or copying a selection from one image to another image. You can use these same steps to move or copy a selection inside the same image as well — just skip Step 3.

1. **Select the pixels that you want to move or copy.**

2. **Choose Edit⇨Copy or Edit⇨Cut.**

   The Copy command duplicates the selection and places the copy in a temporary data holding tank known as the Clipboard. The original selected pixels remain intact.

   The Cut command moves the selection out of the image and onto the Clipboard. A hole appears where the selection once resided, as in the right example of Figure 8-7. In the figure, I selected the rose on the right and cut it to the Clipboard. If you're working on the bottom layer of an image, the image canvas peeks through the hole, as in the figure (I had the canvas background set to white). If you cut a selection from any layer but the bottom layer, the pixels on the underlying layer poke their heads through the hole.

   Press Ctrl+C to choose the Copy command, Ctrl+X to choose Cut. On a Mac, press ⌘+C and ⌘+X instead.

3. **Open the image that you want to copy or move the selection to.**

   If your computer memory is short, you may need to close the first image. Go ahead and do so — the contents of the Clipboard aren't affected.

4. **Choose Edit⇨Paste.**

   Or press Ctrl+V (⌘+V on a Mac). PhotoDeluxe creates a new layer to hold the pasted pixels, positioning the selection smack-dab in the center of the layer.

5. **Manipulate the layer as you will.**

   When you paste the selection, PhotoDeluxe activates the Object Selection tool and displays the layer selection border, resize handles, and rotate handles. These handles are shown in Figure 8-6. You can rotate, move, resize, and distort the selection as described in "The Object Selection tool," earlier in this chapter.

   Alternatively, you can press Ctrl+G to activate the Move tool (⌘+G on a Mac). You can then press the arrow keys to move the selection in small increments. Press an arrow key alone to move the selection one pixel; press Shift+arrow to move it ten pixels. To redisplay the resize and rotate handles, choose the Object Selection tool from the Selections palette. (You need to reselect the tool even though its name already appears in the palette.)

6. **Merge the new layer or keep it separate.**

   You can merge the new layer with the underlying layer by choosing Merge Layers from the Layers palette menu. (Choose View⇨Show Layers and click the right-pointing triangle to display the menu.) But to give yourself flexibility down the line, you may want to keep the selection on its own layer. You can then reposition the selection, or even delete it, without affecting the underlying image.

PhotoDeluxe doesn't let you Undo the Paste command. If you don't like what you see after you choose the command, drag the new layer that contains the pasted selection to the Trash icon in the Layers palette.

Pasting a selection inside a selection

A variation on the Paste command, Paste Into, enables you to paste one selection inside another selection outline.

I can hear you now: "Oh. Uh, . . . huh?" and "Why would I want to do that?" Well, if you paste a selection from Image A into a selection that you draw in Image B, only the portion of the Image A selection that fits inside the Image B selection is visible. The rest is hidden behind Image B; the Image B selection serves as a frame for the Image A selection. You can use then move the pasted section around so that different areas show through the frame if you want.

Um, that didn't clear things up a whole lot, did it? Well, take a look at Figures 8-8 and 8-9. I wanted to put my grade-school face (love those pin curls) into the center of the one-dollar bill. Trying to select just the right amount of face to fill the hole in the dollar poses a real challenge, especially because the face image, as it stands, is a little too large to fit inside the opening. So I selected the entire face image, copied it to the Clipboard, selected the hole in the dollar bill using the Color Wand, and chose the Paste Into command. Finally, I used the Object Selection tool to reduce my face enough to fit inside the oval. In a few minutes, I created my very own currency. Sadly, Julie bucks have been devalued lately and don't buy spit anymore.

Figure 8-8:
The components of a new currency.

Like some of the other features described in this book, the Paste Into command is easier understood when you're working with actual images. So the following steps show you how to create your own custom bills. The dollar bill image is found on the PhotoDeluxe CD-ROM; plan on providing your own mug shot.

These steps assume that you have selected the Allow Multiple Document Windows option in the File⇨Preferences submenu (Version 2 only) and that your computer is sufficiently powered to enable you to have two images open at once. If neither is true, you can use the Hold Photo feature described in Chapter 2 to keep both images close at hand while you work, provided you're not using Version 3, which took away the Hold Photo feature.

Figure 8-9:
The Paste Into command made it easy to merge mug and money.

1. **Open the Layers and Selection palettes.**

   You need them both for this project. To open the palettes, head for the View menu.

2. **Open the dollar bill image.**

   The image is stored in the Pdart/Samples/Things folder on the PhotoDeluxe CD and is named Money1.ppd.

3. **Open your face image.**

4. **Size both images.**

   Use the Size⇨Photo Size command, discussed in Chapter 3. You can adjust the size of your face image slightly to fit the hole later, but get as close as you can to the approximate size now.

   Be sure to use the same Resolution value for both images. Otherwise, when you paste your face image into the dollar bill, the face is automatically converted to the resolution of the dollar bill. If the resolution of the dollar is higher than the face, the face gets smaller when you paste it. If the resolution of the dollar is lower, the face selection gets bigger.

5. **Select your face.**

   Select your face plus a generous margin of pixels around all sides. If your image is about the same height as the dollar bill image, like mine, you can just select the entire image (press Ctrl+A or ⌘+A).

6. **Press Ctrl+C (⌘+C on a Mac).**

   Your face is cloned and sent to the Clipboard.

7. **Select the hole in the dollar bill.**

   One click of the Color Wand in the center of the bill does the trick.

8. **Choose Edit⇨Paste Into.**

   Your face appears inside the hole selection. The face image is placed on a floating layer (a temporary layer), making it independent of the dollar bill. You see a dotted outline indicating the boundaries of the face image.

9. **Send your face to a permanent layer.**

   Because the face exists on a floating layer, you could size and position the face inside the hole at this point. But sending the face to its own layer gives you some added editing protection. Remember, a floating layer is only temporary, and if you click with any tool but the Move tool, PhotoDeluxe merges the floating layer with the underlying image. So just to be safe, go ahead and send the face to a permanent layer now. You can merge face image and money image later if you want.

   To put the face on a real layer, drag the Floating Layer item in the Layers palette to the New Layer icon. Or choose Make Layer from the Layers palette menu (click the right-pointing triangle to display the menu). Now you can resize, rotate, and otherwise manipulate your face so that it fits perfectly inside the frame, and you don't have to worry about merging the face and money by accident.

10. Grab the Object Selection tool from the Selections palette.

11. Click your face.

The resize and rotate handles appear, as discussed in "The Object Selection tool" earlier in this chapter. Use the techniques described in that section to adjust the face image as needed. Don't resize or rotate the image too much, because both can degrade the appearance of your lovely countenance.

When you drag inside the selection box to move the face layer, the entire image temporarily pops in front of the dollar bill, making it difficult to determine the right position for the face. So you may want to use this alternative method for moving the face around: Press Ctrl+G (⌘+G) to select the Move tool and then press the arrow keys on your keyboard to nudge the face into place. One press moves the face one pixel; Shift+arrow moves the face ten pixels.

12. Merge the layers, or not.

When you're happy with the face (well, satisfied with the positioning of images, anyway, if not the whole genetic package), you can permanently bond the face and dollar bill layer together by choosing Merge Layers. Or, if you prefer, you can keep the two layers separate so that you can easily replace your face picture when you pass through adolescence or get a decent haircut, whichever comes first. Just drag the face layer to the Trash icon in the Layers palette and use the Paste Into command to insert a more flattering picture.

Hopefully, you now understand the point of the Paste Into command. When you want to frame a selection with another image element, this command does the trick beautifully. You can use Paste Into to frame a selection with an element in the same image, by the way, instead of merging two images as you did in the preceding steps.

Deleting a Selection

If you want to get rid of the pixels inside a selection, just press Delete. Those pixels are forever banished from the image. Assuming that you're working on the background layer of the image, the empty image canvas appears where those selected pixels used to be, as shown earlier in the right-hand image in Figure 8-7.

When you delete pixels on any layer but the background image layer, however, you create a transparent hole in the layer. Pixels from the underlying image layer show through the hole. For more on this intriguing topic, see "Rubbing Out Pixels with the Eraser" in Chapter 10.

Selecting on Layers

If you're working on a multilayered image, keep in mind that selection outlines are layer-independent. Say that you select an element on Layer 1. If you then make Layer 2 active, the selection outline affects that layer, not Layer 1. You don't need to "move" the selection outline from one layer to another.

Remember that the selection tools themselves also affect the active layer only. Suppose that you have a blue sky on Layer 1 and a red airplane on Layer 2. If Layer 1 is active and you click on the red airplane with the Color Wand, for example, the Color Wand selects the blue sky pixels, not the red airplane pixels. If you want to select the airplane pixels, you need to make Layer 2 active. If all this makes no sense to you, turn to Chapter 10, where you can dig deeper into layers.

Deleting or Filling a Feathered Selection

Feathering a selection makes the edges of a selection outline fuzzy, so that instead of a harsh transition between the selected and deselected pixels, you get a soft, gradual transition.

In PhotoDeluxe, you can feather your selection outline and then fill the selection with a color or pattern. Or you can delete either the selection or the deselected pixels.

Perhaps the most common use of this feature is to give a photograph a soft, fade-into-nothingness frame, as I did for the lovely specimen in Figure 8-10. We love our farm animals here in Indiana and feel that they deserve all the dignity they can get, even when sneering at the camera.

To create a similar result, choose the Effects⇨Feather command after you create your selection outline. The Feather dialog box shown in Figure 8-11 appears. Enter a Feather value to tell PhotoDeluxe how fuzzy you want to make the edges of the selection. Higher numbers increase the fuzziness of the selection. I used a value of 13 to create the effect in Figure 8-10.

To delete everything but the selection, as I did in the figure, click the Delete Background icon. Alternatively, to delete the selection and keep the background, choose the Delete Selection icon.

Figure 8-10:
Such a
lovely smile
(left)
deserves a
special,
feathered
frame
(right).

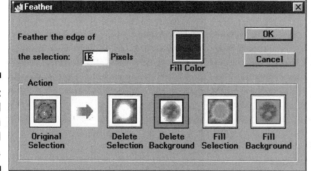

Figure 8-11:
You can fill
or delete a
feathered
selection.

If you instead want to pour a solid color into either the selection or the background, click the Fill Selection or Fill Background icon, respectively. Click the Color swatch icon to display the Color Picker, where you can choose the color that you want to apply. (See Chapter 9 for more information about the Color Picker.) Click OK to apply the effect to your image.

In the Business Edition, you can create similar effects by drawing your selection outline with the SmartSelect tool and raising the Feather value. You can read more about the SmartSelect tool earlier in this chapter.

And in Version 3, you can try out the automatic feathered-frame effect created by the Extensis PhotoFrame plug-in. Choose Effects⇨Extensis⇨ PhotoFrame to try out the plug-in. Choose the Soft Circle.frm option at the top of the resulting dialog box and deselect the CameraEdge.frm and WaterColor.frm options. (Click the Eyeball icon next to the options to turn the options on and off).

If you want to frame your entire image, cancel any existing selection outlines before you choose the command. The frame is centered on the image canvas. If you select a portion of the image before invoking the command, the frame is centered on the selection outline.

To find out more about the PhotoFrame plug-in and discover the other, cooler effects you can create with it, check out Chapter 13.

Part III

Amazing Feats of Digital Trickery

In this part . . .

One of the things I appreciate most about PhotoDeluxe is that it enables me to express creative notions that I simply can't put forth using traditional art tools. An art class washout, I can't paint a decent bowl of fruit to save my life. When I sketch people, they get sticks for arms and legs, circles for hands and feet. And if you're thinking of giving me a lump of potter's clay and asking me to sculpt a little something, you'd better be prepared to go home with a thumbprint ashtray. But with PhotoDeluxe, I can create acceptable and sometimes really terrific works of photographic art with a fair amount of ease.

Whether or not you share my artistic limitations, this part of the book aims to inspire your creative side by introducing you to some of the more advanced options available in PhotoDeluxe. You find out how to build photographic collages using image layers, how to use some of the program's more interesting special-effects filters, and how to create eye-catching text. I also share some ideas on how to use your image masterpieces, from turning them into on-screen jigsaw puzzles to incorporating them into a spreadsheet or other document.

If you are as inept as I am with traditional art tools, you'll be amazed at how PhotoDeluxe enables your artistic side to shine. And if you're the next Monet or Picasso, time spent in this digital art studio should advance your genius even further. And the best part is, you don't have to inhale any smelly paint-thinner fumes or get clay underneath your fingernails in the pursuit of your art.

Chapter 9
Open Up Your Paint Box

• •

In This Chapter

▶ Choosing your paint color

▶ Dabbing at pixels with the Brush tool

▶ Adjusting the size and opacity of your paint strokes

▶ Painting perfectly straight lines

▶ Smearing colors with the Smudge tool

▶ Filling a selection with a pattern or color

▶ Experimenting with blend modes

▶ Creating a gradient fill

• •

*I*f you've ever taken an oil painting class, you may be aware that many items in the typical paint box are, shall we say, user-unfriendly. Inhale too many paint-thinner fumes or absentmindedly chew on a brush handle that's coated with certain pigments, and you can do some serious damage to your health. Some people even speculate that one reason Van Gogh went bonkers and decided to divest himself of his ear was that he ingested too many toxic paints.

Thankfully, digital painting is less hazardous to your health. No toxins are involved, unless you count that major mug of caffeine I see curdling on your cup warmer. True, trying to paint just the right stroke with a mouse can sometimes lead to mental anguish, but I don't think you're at risk of severing any body parts. Hey, put those scissors down! You're going to want that ear later, really!

This chapter shows you how to work with the two major PhotoDeluxe painting tools, the Brush and Line tools. You also learn how to dump a whole bucketful of paint onto the canvas using the Selection Fill command, smear colors around your image using the Smudge tool, and perform a few other painting tricks as well.

Painting without Pain

As you ply the Brush, Line, or other painting tools, keep the following tips in mind.

✔ Unless your computer's memory is limited and you can't work with multilayered images, do your painting on a separate layer from the rest of your image. If you hate what you paint, you can simply delete the layer and start over. You haven't damaged your original image. To create a new layer, choose View➪Show Layers to display the Layers palette and click the New Layer icon (the double-square in the bottom-left corner of the palette). To find out more about editing on a layer, read Chapter 10.

✔ If you're trying to paint a specific area, select the area before you paint. As covered in Chapter 8, your paint strokes are then confined to the boundaries of the selection. You can't mistakenly paint over pixels that you didn't intend to color.

✔ The standard cursors for the paint tools can make seeing what you're doing difficult. For a better cursor option, press the Caps Lock key to switch to a crosshair cursor. For more about swapping cursors, read "Changing the Cursor Style" in Chapter 2.

✔ On the surface, the PhotoDeluxe assortment of paint tools seems rather limited. But by varying your brush size, shape, and opacity, you can create a real variety of shapes. Add to that different modes for blending painted pixels with original image pixels, and you actually have a wealth of creative possibilities. So be sure to explore the sections in this chapter that discuss the many ways to alter the performance of your paint tools.

Picking a Paint Color

You can carry two colors of paint in your PhotoDeluxe paint box at a time:

✔ The *foreground color* is the primary color. The Brush and Line tools always apply the foreground color. The foreground color is also used in some special effects.

✔ The *background color* is a minor role-player. It's used only when you apply some special effects, such as the Clouds and Bas Relief filters, both covered elsewhere in Chapter 12.

To set the foreground or background color, choose Effects➪Choose Colors. The Color Picker dialog box rushes onto the stage. Figure 9-1 shows the Version 2 dialog box, and Figure 9-2 shows the Business Edition and Version 3 dialog box.

Figure 9-1:
The Version
2 Color
Picker
dialog box.

Figure 9-2:
The
Business
Edition and
Version 3
Color Picker
dialog box.

The following color-picking rules apply to both versions of the dialog box:

✔ The Foreground and Background icons show the currently selected foreground and background colors.

✔ The icon surrounded by the double black border is the active color — the one you're about to change. The Foreground color is active in Figures 9-1 and 9-2. To set the other color, click its icon.

✔ At the bottom of the dialog box is a preview area that displays a spectrum of colors. When you move your cursor into the preview area, it becomes an eyedropper, as shown in Figure 9-1. Click the color that you want to use.

✔ If you want your paint color to match an existing image color exactly, move the eyedropper into the image window and use it to click the color in the image.

✔ You can display three different color spectrums in the preview: a full-color spectrum, a grayscale spectrum, and a spectrum that fades gradually from the current foreground color to the current background color. In Version 2, Shift+click the preview to cycle through the displays. In the Business Edition and Version 3, you can either do the Shift+click trick or click the icons to the right of the preview to select a color spectrum.

✔ If you're not able to choose just the right color using the eyedropper, double-click the icon for the color you're trying to set. PhotoDeluxe displays the Windows or Apple system color pickers, which give you some additional tools for specifying a color. The next sections explain how to use both system color pickers.

✔ After you set your Foreground and Background colors, click OK to close the Color Picker dialog box and get on with your painting chores.

The Business Edition and Version 3 Color Picker dialog box offers an additional feature not found in the Version 2 dialog box. In addition to clicking a color in the preview area at the bottom of the dialog box, you can click one of the squares in the Color Swatches area to select that color.

You can also add your own color swatches. After you choose a color — by clicking in the preview area at the bottom of the dialog box or clicking in the image window, or by using the Windows color picker (described next) — click the Add Swatch button to add that color to the Color Swatches display. To select that exact color again in the future, you can simply click the swatch.

The Color Swatches display has room for eight new swatches. After you fill up the eighth empty spot, you must replace an existing swatch if you want to add a new color to the display. Click a swatch that you no longer need and then click Remove Swatch. Now you can fill the empty swatch with another color.

The Windows color picker

To gain additional control over your color — and hey, who doesn't think colors should be more tightly controlled? — double-click the Foreground or Background icon in the PhotoDeluxe Color Picker, depending on which color you want to set. The Windows Color dialog box, shown in Figure 9-3, arises from the digital depths. (Actually, you initially see only the left side of the dialog box. More on that in a moment.)

The dialog box is a bit formidable, but not so difficult when you know how it works. Here's the inside skinny:

✔ If you want to use one of the colors in the Basic Colors area, click the color swatch, click OK, and then click OK again in the PhotoDeluxe Color Picker dialog box.

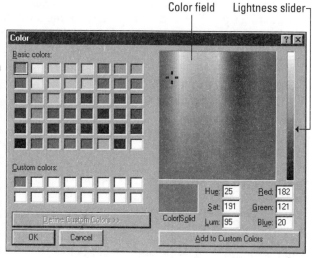

Color field · Lightness slider

Figure 9-3:
You can be more precise about your color choice in the Windows color picker.

✔ Don't care for any of the basic colors? Click Define Custom Colors to display the hidden half of the dialog box, which enables you to create your own color.

✔ To set the hue and saturation of your custom color, drag the cursor inside the color field (labeled in Figure 9-3). Drag the lightness slider to adjust the amount of black and white in the color.

✔ As you drag, the values in the Red, Green, and Blue option boxes indicate the amount of red, green, and blue in the color. As discussed in the sidebar "Why what you see isn't what you get" in Chapter 5, full-strength red, green, and blue make white. (A value of 255 indicates full-intensity color.)

The Hue, Sat, and Lum option boxes define the color according to another color model. The Hue value reflects the, er, hue; Sat indicates the Saturation; and Lum (luminosity) indicates the brightness.

You don't have to pay a gnat's breath worth of attention to these values, however, unless you want to be able to create the exact same color later. If so, jot down the values that appear in either set of option boxes. Then, when you come back to the Color dialog box, just enter those values again.

✔ If you expect to use a color on a regular basis, add it to the Custom Colors palette on the left side of the dialog box. You can put up to 16 custom colors in the palette. Click the Add to Custom Colors button to put the color in the palette. You can then simply click the swatch to select the color on your next trip to the Color dialog box.

- ✔ If you run out of empty spaces in the Custom Colors palette, you can replace an existing swatch with a new color. Click the swatch that you want to replace, define the new color, and click Add to Custom Colors.

- ✔ That Color/Solid swatch beneath the color field has to do with how a monitor creates color. A monitor can display only so many solid colors; it displays other colors by blending — or *dithering* — the available solid colors. Dithered colors don't look as good on screen as solid colors.

Today's monitors can typically be set to display 256, 32,000, or 16 million colors. Unless your monitor displays only 256 colors, you probably can't see much difference between the two sides of the Color/Solid swatch. I was running my monitor at 16 million colors when I captured the screen shown in Figure 9-3, and as you can see, the Color and Solid swatches are identical. Only concern yourself with the side-by-side comparison if you're creating images for viewers who use older systems limited to 256 colors. In that case, you may want to stick with the solid colors. Click the Solid half of the swatch to choose the closest solid — that is, undithered — version of your color.

Using the Apple color picker

On a Macintosh computer, double-clicking the Foreground or Background swatch in the PhotoDeluxe Color Picker dialog box displays the Apple color picker, shown in Figure 9-4.

You can choose a color using either of two color models, Apple RGB (Red, Green, and Blue) or Apple HSL (Hue, Saturation, and Lightness). Feel free to user whichever color mode is easier for you. Click the icon corresponding to your favored color model in the left side of the dialog box. (If you don't see the icons on the left side of the dialog box, click the More Choices button. Click Fewer Choices to hide the icons again and shrink the dialog box.)

As you work in the color picker, the New swatch shows you the color that you're creating. The Original swatch displays the current Foreground or Background color, depending on which color you're trying to set.

Figure 9-4 shows the Color Picker dialog box when the HSL color model is selected. Drag the crosshair cursor in the color wheel to set the basic hue and saturation of your color, and then drag the lightness slider bar to make the color lighter or darker. Or adjust the values in the Hue Angle, Saturation, and Lightness option boxes. A Lightness value of 50 percent gives you the most vivid version of the color.

Color wheel

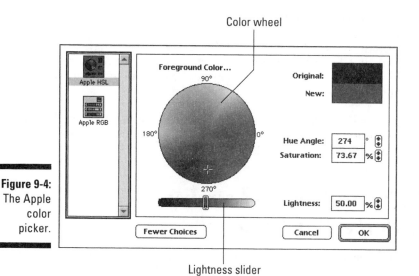

Figure 9-4:
The Apple
color
picker.

Lightness slider

If you opt for the RGB color model, create your color by dragging the R, G, and B color sliders. Or enter values into the R, G, and B option boxes.

Remember that you're mixing light to create color, so things may work differently than you expect. Full-strength red, green, and blue — a value of 255 for each color — results in pure white. Enter 0 in all three option boxes to create the blackest black.

After you create the perfect shade, you may want to jot down the values in the option boxes. If you ever want to paint with the color again, you can simply enter the same values into the option boxes.

Click OK to exit the Apple color picker and return to the PhotoDeluxe Color Picker dialog box. Click OK to close that dialog box and start painting.

Introducing the Painting Tools

Like most people, I use PhotoDeluxe to repair photographic images, not to paint masterpieces from scratch, which is why I rarely pick up the Brush or Line tools. These tools come in handy on occasion — for example, to repair a portion of a border that you accidentally deleted or dab a spot of color onto a scratch or other image defect. But as a general rule, the Brush and Line tools are more for creative expression than for fixing everyday images. If you're painting all over your pictures, after all, you're not exactly turning out 8-x-10 prints of reality.

Of course, I might feel differently about these tools if I possessed a smidgen of talent for painting. My skills at painting with a mouse are even less than my aptitude for painting with a real brush — which is to say, miserable to nonexistent. I do believe that most 5-year-olds produce better results. But if you're talented at traditional painting, you're likely to have a blast with the digital variety.

Whether you're making a small image correction or painting the masterpiece of the century, the following sections explain everything you need to know to ply the Brush and Line tools.

Painting freehand strokes with the Brush tool

To paint freehand brush strokes, choose Tools➪Brush or press Ctrl+J (⌘+J on a Mac). That's right, *J*, as in, um . . . hmmm. Not sure where they got that one from.

At any rate, just drag with the Brush tool to lay down a paint stroke. You can adjust the width, softness, and opacity of your stroke as outlined in the next two sections.

To paint a perfectly straight line, click at the spot where you want the line to start and Shift+click at the spot where you want the line to end. If you want to paint a perfectly horizontal or vertical line, press the mouse button to set the start of the line — press, don't click — and then Shift+drag to create the line.

Choosing a brush tip

You can alter the size and width of the stroke created by the Brush tool by choosing a different brush tip from the Brushes palette, shown in Figure 9-5. The palette appears automatically when you select the Brush tool. (A variation of this same palette appears when you work with the Clone, Eraser, and Smudge tools.)

Here's a quick guide to the palette:

   ✔ To choose a brush, just click its icon. In the top two rows of the palette, the icons reflect the actual size of the brush. The smallest brush is just one pixel big.

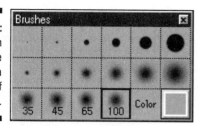

Figure 9-5:
You can choose from a variety of brush tips.

✔ Brushes in the last row of the palette are too large to show at their actual size. The number indicates the size of the brush in pixels.

✔ The brushes on the top row paint hard-edged strokes, as if you were drawing with a pen. The other brushes paint soft-edged strokes, more like you get with a traditional paintbrush.

✔ You can change your cursor so that it reflects the size of your brush tip. Press Ctrl+K (⌘+K on a Mac) to open the Cursors dialog box and choose Brush Size under the Painting Tools options. Or press the Caps Lock key to toggle back and forth between a brush-size cursor and a crosshair cursor. (Note that if you're zoomed out on your image and working with a small brush size, PhotoDeluxe surrounds the brush cursor with crosshairs so that you can see the cursor more easily.)

✔ To make a quick trip to the Color Picker dialog box and change your paint color, click the Color swatch.

✔ You can relocate the palette on-screen by dragging its title bar. Close the palette by clicking the Close button on the title bar.

Adjusting opacity

You can paint strokes that are fully opaque, or you can make your strokes partially transparent, so that some of the underlying pixels show through. Figure 9-6 and Color Plate 9-1 offer a look at the same stroke at different opacity levels.

Adjusting the opacity of the Brush tool — as well as the Clone, Line, Smudge, and Eraser tools — is as easy as pressing a number key. (If you're using your numeric keyboard, be sure that you turn on the Num Lock function.) Press 0 for fully opaque strokes. Press 9 for 90 percent opacity, 8 for 80 percent, and so on.

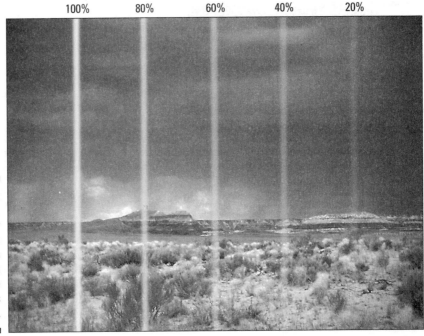

100%   80%   60%   40%   20%

Figure 9-6:
Lowering
the opacity
of the Brush
tool makes
underlying
image
pixels
visible.

PhotoDeluxe leaves it up to you to remember what opacity value you chose — the value isn't indicated in the Brushes palette or anywhere else. Furthermore, the value you set remains in force until you press another number key. So if a tool doesn't seem to alter your image in the way that you expected, check to make sure that you have the opacity value where you want it. Note that the opacity settings don't transfer from one tool to another; you set the value for each tool independently. If you set the Brush tool at 50 percent opacity, for example, the other tools aren't automatically set to 50 percent opacity as well.

Painting straight lines

Earlier, I mentioned that you can paint a perfectly straight line by Shift+dragging or Shift+clicking with the Brush tool. But when you paint lines using the Brush tool, you're limited to the brush sizes available in the Brushes palette. If you want to paint a line of some other size, choose Tools➪Line to use the Line tool instead. Keep in mind, however, that the Line tool can paint hard-edged strokes only; you can't paint a soft-edged line as you can with the Brush tool.

When you activate the Line tool, the Line Tool Options palette, shown in Figure 9-7, appears. Enter the line width you want in the option box. Then set the color of the line by clicking the Color swatch. PhotoDeluxe opens the Color Picker dialog box, where you can choose the line color, as discussed earlier in this chapter. Click OK to close the Color Picker and then drag to create your line.

Figure 9-7:
Set your
line color
and size
here.

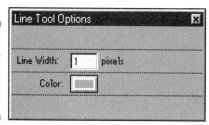

To constrain your line to an angle that's an increment of 45 degrees, Shift+drag with the Line tool. To envision this feature, imagine a 360-degree circle. If you put your tool cursor in the middle of the circle and try to Shift+drag to the outside edge of the circle, PhotoDeluxe allows you to drag only to the 0-degree point on the outside edge (the top), the 45-degree point, the 90-degree point, the 135-degree point, and so on. You're restricted to drawing lines at angles that are multiples of 45 degrees. Perhaps the most common reason to Shift+drag is to paint lines that are perfectly vertical or perfectly horizontal — to put a horizontal line under a piece of text, for example. (The PhotoDeluxe Text tool doesn't enable you to create under-lined text automatically.)

In addition, you can vary the opacity of the line by pressing the number keys, just as you do with the Brush tool. Press 0 for full opacity, 9 for 90 percent opacity, 8 for 80 percent opacity, and so on.

Dragging Your Finger through Wet Paint

The Smudge tool takes you back to the fun of yesteryear, when your kinder-garten teacher introduced you to the fine art of fingerpainting. When you drag with this tool, you smear your image pixels together, creating an effect that looks for all the world as if you dragged your paw through wet paint.

Choose Tools⇨Smudge to select the tool and then drag over the area that you want to smear. As you can see from Color Plate 9-2 and Figure 9-8, you can create some fairly entertaining effects with the Smudge tool. In the right image in the figure and color plate, I gave an unsuspecting feathered friend a makeover by dragging from the middle of the beak toward the edge of the picture. Just to make the poor bird look even sillier, I added a few long eyelashes by dragging outward from the dark rim around the eye. I do hope that all the Audubon Society members out there will forgive me.

You can adjust the performance of the Smudge tool as follows:

- ✔ Press a number key to adjust the pressure of your stroke. If you press 0, you get a full-pressure smudge, which means that the tool smears a color from the spot where you begin dragging to the spot where you release the mouse button. At lower pressure, the color is smeared for only a portion of your drag. Press 1 for 10 percent pressure, 2 for 20 percent, and so on.

- ✔ You can change the size and softness of the brush tip on the Smudge tool, just as you can for the Brush tool. When you select the Smudge tool, PhotoDeluxe displays the Smudges palette, which is the same as the Brushes palette except for the fact that it lacks a Color icon. For more information about available brush tips, read "Choosing a brush tip," earlier in this chapter.

Figure 9-8:
A few swipes of the Smudge tool was all it took to make this bird's beak and eyelashes grow.

✔ If you use the Smudge tool at full pressure and/or a large brush size, PhotoDeluxe may take a few moments to complete the effect of your drag. So if nothing happens right away when you let up on the mouse button, don't panic. Give the effect a second or two to materialize.

✔ The bird image in Figure 9-8 and Color Plate 9-2 is on the PhotoDeluxe CD-ROM. Look in the Pdart/Samples/Nature folder. The image is titled Bird.jpg.

Painting with a Power Roller

If you have a large area to color, you don't need to waste your time scrubbing at it with the Brush tool. PhotoDeluxe offers two tools that can paint as many pixels as you want at one time: the Selection Fill command and the Color Change tool. I describe both tools in the next page or so, but here's an up-front disclosure: I don't recommend the Color Change tool because it's not terribly precise. You usually wind up either painting more pixels than you intended or not coloring all those you did want to paint.

Using the Selection Fill command

The Selection Fill command, located on the Effects menu, can fill a selected area with either a solid color or a predefined pattern. You must create a selection before you can access the command, so if you need help selecting the pixels that you want to paint, check out Chapter 8.

After you create a selection outline, just press Ctrl+9 (⌘+9 on a Mac) to choose the Selection Fill command quickly.

However you choose the command, the dialog box shown in Figure 9-9 appears. The options work as follows:

Figure 9-9:
Use the
Selection
Fill
command
to paint a
selection
with solid
color or a
pattern.

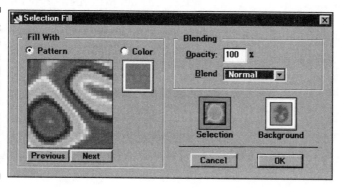

✔ To fill a selection with solid color, select the Color radio button. Then click the color swatch to open the Color Picker and choose your fill color. Click OK to close the Color Picker dialog box and return to the Selection Fill dialog box.

✔ Select the Pattern radio button if you want to fill the selection with one of the patterns provided by PhotoDeluxe. To see the available patterns, click the Previous and Next buttons. PhotoDeluxe displays a preview of the patterns in the dialog box.

✔ You can fill either all pixels inside the selection outline or all pixels outside the outline. Click the Selection icon to fill the selection; click the Background icon to color all the deselected pixels instead.

✔ Adjust the Opacity value to make the color or pattern more or less opaque. To fully cover the pixels you're painting, set the value to 100 percent. Any lower value makes the fill partially transparent, so some of the original pixels show through the fill.

✔ The options in the Blend drop-down list enable you to fool with the way that your fill pixels are blended with your original image pixels. The six available blend modes are illustrated in Color Plate 9-3 and explained in the next section.

✔ After you choose your fill options, click OK to dump paint or pattern into your image. Press Ctrl+Z (⌘+Z on a Mac) to undo things if you don't like the results. Unfortunately, you can't preview the effects of your settings inside the Selection Fill dialog box, so filling is sometimes a matter of trial and error.

✔ You can fill a selection with the foreground color in a snap by pressing Alt+Delete (Option+Delete on a Mac). Your color is applied at 100 percent opacity and with the Normal blend mode in force.

Filling a selection with a custom pattern

If none of the patterns available in the Selection Fill dialog box amuses you, you can fill a selection with your own custom patterns — provided that you're using the Business Edition or Version 3. In Figure 9-10, I filled a canvas with a custom pattern created from the bird image in Figure 9-8.

Here's how to fill a selection with your own custom pattern:

1. **Choose the Rectangle selection tool.**

   Press Ctrl+M (⌘+M on a Mac) to do it in a flash.

   You can create custom patterns from rectangular selections only.

2. **Select the area that you want to use as the basis for your pattern.**

Figure 9-10:
You can fill a canvas with your own custom patterns using the Define Pattern command.

3. **Choose Effects⇨Define Pattern.**

4. **Select the area that you want to fill with the pattern.**

5. **Choose Effects⇨Selection Fill.**

   Your custom pattern should appear in the pattern preview area.

6. **Click the Pattern button and then click OK.**

   PhotoDeluxe fills the selected area with the pattern, repeating the pattern as many times as necessary to fill the selection outline. You can use the Blend and Opacity options in the Selection Fill dialog box to vary the effect of your pattern fill if you like.

PhotoDeluxe can remember only one custom pattern at a time. If you create a second custom pattern, the first pattern is chucked from the Selection Fill dialog box. Also, PhotoDeluxe doesn't save any custom patterns when you shut down the program. So if you want to reuse a pattern in a future editing session, perform this saving routine immediately after you draw the initial selection outline to create your pattern:

1. **Press Ctrl+C (⌘+C on a Mac) to copy the selection to the Clipboard.**

2. **Choose File⇨New and click OK to create a new image.**

   PhotoDeluxe automatically sizes the new image to match the size and resolution of the image on the Clipboard.

3. **Press Ctrl+V (⌘+V) to paste the pattern into the new image.**

4. **Save the image as usual.**

   To reuse the pattern, simply open the saved pattern image, press Ctrl+A (⌘+A) to select the entire image, and choose Effects⇨Define Pattern.

Blending pixels in cruel and unusual ways

When you fill a selection using the Selection Fill command, you can choose from six different *blend modes.* Blend modes control how the fill pixels are mixed with the original pixels inside the selection. Color Plate 9-3 illustrates how you can vary the effects of the Selection Fill command by using different blend modes.

To create the different pumpkins, I started with the original pumpkin image in the center of the color plate. (This image is named Jackolan.jpg and is found on the PhotoDeluxe CD-ROM, in the Pdart/Samples/Things folder in Version 2 and Version 3 and the Pdart/Samples/Occasion folder in the Business Edition.) I selected the pumpkin "skin" — everything but the eyes, nose, mouth, and stem — using the SmartSelect tool. Then I filled the skin with one of the patterns available in the Selection Fill dialog box. The pattern is shown in the background of Color Plate 9-3.

The following list explains the different blend modes. But after you get past the Normal and Color modes, things grow a little complicated — and truthfully, predicting how the blend modes will affect your image isn't easy. So don't worry if you don't understand what's going on. Just experiment until you get results that you like.

To make these explanations a little simpler, I refer to the original image color as the *base color* and the color applied by the Selection Fill command as the *blend color.*

- ✔ **Normal:** The blend color completely obscures the base color. In Color Plate 9-3, the colors of the pattern completely cover the pumpkin skin. All highlights and shadows from the original pumpkin are lost. (For a look at the Normal mode when used with a solid color fill, see Color Plate 9-4.)

- ✔ **Color:** This mode applies the hue and saturation of the blend color or fill, but using the brightness levels of the base pixels. The result is a fill that retains the original shadows and highlights of the image. In the pumpkin image in Color Plate 9-3, for example, you can still see the ribbing in the pumpkin skin.

  If you want to change the color of an image element in a way that looks natural, the Color mode is one good option. Take a look at Color Plate 9-4 for further proof.

- ✔ **Lighten and Darken:** These two modes apply the blend color depending on the brightness of the blend pixels. With Lighten, the blend color is applied only if it is lighter than the base pixels. With Darken, the blend color is applied only if it is darker than the base pixels.

However, when PhotoDeluxe evaluates the brightness of the blend and base pixels, it considers the brightness of the red, green, and blue components of each pixel, not the overall brightness of the pixel. (Remember, images that you edit in PhotoDeluxe are based on the RGB color model, which mixes colors using red, green, and blue light.) So predicting the outcome of the Lighten and Darken modes isn't as easy as you might expect, as illustrated by the examples in Color Plate 9-3.

✔ **Difference:** Ready to have your mind totally boggled? With the Difference mode, PhotoDeluxe first evaluates the brightness value for the red, green, and blue components of the pixels in the blend and base colors. Then it subtracts the blend color from the base color or vice versa, depending on which one has the greater brightness value. Don't even try to figure it out — just keep in mind that the Difference mode gives you an inverted effect, similar to a photo negative.

✔ **Overlay:** Every bit as challenging as Difference, Overlay *multiplies* the base color information by the blend color information if the base color is darker than the blend color. If the base color is lighter, Overlay multiplies the inverse of the base color and blend color. And if you can understand *that,* please put your mind to use figuring out something more important than image editing.

In practical terms — albeit not crystal-clear terms — Overlay applies your blend color or pattern in a way that retains the highlights and shadows from both the blend pixels and the base pixels. When you want to replace the color of an image with another color, try the Overlay mode if you can't get the effect you want with the Color mode.

To expand your pixel-mixing range even further, the following list offers yet a few more ideas for using blend modes:

✔ The impact of all the blend modes is affected by the Opacity value you set in the Selection Fill dialog box. By playing with the Opacity and Blend options, you can create a seemingly endless variety of fill effects.

✔ These same blend modes are available in the Layer Options dialog box, where you can specify how you want PhotoDeluxe to mix the pixels in one layer with another layer. For information about working with layers, see Chapter 10.

✔ In fact, if you want to experiment with blend modes, the Layer Options dialog box is a better place to play around than the Selection Fill dialog box. You can preview the effects of the blend mode from inside the Layer Options dialog box; the Selection Fill dialog box has no preview option.

So, instead of setting your blend mode in the Selection Fill dialog box, draw your selection outline on a new layer, fill the selection using the Normal blend mode in the Selection Fill dialog box, and then open the Layer Options dialog box. As you choose different options from the Blend pop-up menu in the Layer Options dialog box, the image window shows the effect of the blend mode.

> ✔ You can blend colors you paint with the Brush or Line tools in the same way you blend colors applied with Selection Fill. Just do your painting on a layer separate from the underlying image and choose your blend mode in the Layer Options dialog box.

Trying the Color Change tool

Note the name of this section. I chose the headline because I think that after you try the Color Change tool once, you're likely to abandon it in favor of the more capable and precise Selection Fill command, explained in the preceding sections.

The Color Change command works like a combination of the Color Wand and the Selection Fill command. Color Change selects an area of the image and then fills the selection for you. The problem is that predicting which pixels will be selected and recolored is nearly impossible. Furthermore, the command is a bit awkward to use, as you can discover for yourself by giving the Color Change command a test drive, as follows:

1. **Choose Tools⇨Color Change.**

   A little Color Change palette, shown in Figure 9-11, appears.

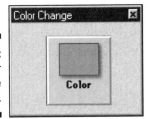

Figure 9-11: The Color Change palette.

2. **Click the Color icon to set the fill color.**

   The Color Picker dialog box, explained in "Picking a Paint Color" earlier in this chapter, appears. Choose the fill color that you want to apply and then click OK.

3. **Set the tool opacity.**

   Press a number key to set the opacity of the color you apply, just as with the Brush tool. Press 0 to make your fill completely opaque, 9 for a fill that's 90 percent opaque, 8 for 80 percent opacity, and so on.

4. **Click the color that you want to replace with the fill color.**

   PhotoDeluxe selects all adjacent pixels that are similar in color to the pixel you clicked, just as if you had clicked with the Color Wand. Then, before you can say "Stop, that's not the area I wanted to select!" the fill is applied to the selection.

You do have the power to vary the sensitivity of the Color Change tool — just as you can with the Color Wand. Press Ctrl+K (⌘+K on a Mac) to open the Cursors dialog box. Then adjust the Tolerance value. Lower the value if you want the Color Change tool to be more selective so that pixels must be closer in color to the pixel you click in order to get the fill. Raise the value to include a greater spectrum of colors in the selection.

When you work with the Color Wand, you rarely get the selection outline just right the first time, and the same is true with the Color Change tool. But with the Color Change tool, you don't have the opportunity to refine the selection before the fill is applied. In Figure 9-12, I set the Color Change tool opacity to 100 percent, chose light gray as my fill color, and clicked at the spot on the collar marked by the Paint Can cursor (the standard cursor for the Color Change tool). By clicking a few pixels away, I could fill an entirely different area of the collar.

If the Color Change tool alters too few pixels, you can keep clicking to fill more areas. But if too many pixels were changed, you have to click Undo and start the whole procedure over. Because it's difficult (at best) to gauge which pixels the Color Change tool will select, I suggest that you avoid this option. Instead, create an exact selection using the Selection tools discussed in Chapter 8 and then apply your fill using the Selection Fill command explained earlier in this chapter. You get more control over the selection and you also get the advantage of the blend and opacity options available in the Selection Fill dialog box.

Replacing One Color with Another

When you want to redecorate your image, changing the colors of some elements, you have several options available to you. Some work better than others, as illustrated in Color Plate 9-4. I decided to create a new type of grape, so I selected the grapes in the original image (top left) and then filled the selection in three different ways:

- ✔ In the top-right image, I applied the Selection Fill command with the Blend mode set to Normal, the Opacity value set at 100 percent, and orange as my fill color. The result is a solid expanse of flat color — hardly a natural-looking effect. Forget this option.

   You get the same unhappy results if you paint over the grapes with the Brush or Line tools with the opacity value set to 100 percent, by the way. Again, not a good choice.

- ✔ To create the glowing green grapes in the bottom-left image, I once again used the Selection Fill command. This time I choose green as the

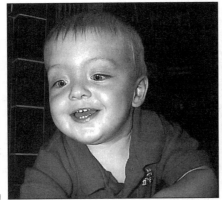
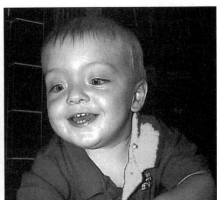

Figure 9-12: The Color Change tool selects and fills an area with one click, but it's often imprecise.

fill color, set the Blend mode to Color, and the Opacity value to 100 percent. Because the Color mode retains the brightness values of the original grapes, you don't lose any image details and you achieve more lifelike results. Another possibility is to choose the Overlay mode, which retains the brightness values of both the grapes and the fill color.

You can get the same results by painting with the Brush tool on a new layer. Select the grapes, create a new layer immediately above the grape layer, set the layer blend mode to Color or Overlay in the Layer Options dialog box, and then paint inside your selection. See Chapter 10 for more information about layers.

✔ In the bottom-right example in Color Plate 9-4, I selected the grapes and then chose the Quality⇨Hue/Saturation command and adjusted the Hue slider in the Hue/Saturation dialog box.

To understand how the Hue value works, think of a circular graph of all the available image colors — also known as a *color wheel*. Red is situated at the 0-degree position on the circle, green at 120 degrees, and blue at 240 degrees. When you drag the Hue slider, you move so many degrees around the color wheel. Suppose that you select a blue pixel before choosing the Hue/Saturation command. If you drag the Hue slider to 120, your pixel becomes red. Blue occupies the 240-degree mark on the color wheel, and 240 degrees plus 120 degrees equals 360 degrees — or 0 degrees, whichever way you want to look at things (a circle is 360 degrees total, for all those who skipped math class).

Note how the shadows and highlights in the grapes were affected differently when I applied the Hue/Saturation command than when I used the Color blend mode. In the Color example (bottom left in Color Plate 9-4), all pixels are some shade of green. But in the Hue/Saturation example (bottom right), the areas that were dark in the original grapes become almost black.

✔ Also give the Quality⇨Color Balance command a whirl. Using this command, explained in depth in Chapter 6, you can adjust the amount of red, green, and blue in your color. You don't get quite the range of color-shifting possibilities as when you use the other methods I just described, however.

✔ Don't forget that you can adjust the color shift achieved through any of these modes by playing with opacity. If you apply your new color on a layer, raise or lower the Opacity value in the Layer Options dialog box to make the new color more or less transparent. If you apply the new color by using the Selection Fill dialog box, adjust the opacity value in the Selection Fill dialog box.

All the techniques in this section replace an existing color in a way that gives you some semblance of reality. If you want to create color shifts that are obviously unrealistic, check out the special-effects color filters discussed in Chapter 12.

Creating a Gradient Fill

A gradient fill? Sounds like something you pour on a driveway to repair cracks and the like, doesn't it? Well, in the ever-odd world of digital nomenclature, a *gradient* refers to a gradual transition from one color to another. If you fill a selection with a black to white gradient — apply a gradient fill, in techie terms — you get something like the image in Figure 9-13.

Figure 9-13:
A black-to-white circular gradient.

Gradient fills are great for spicing up a boring background. If your image features an object set against a plain white background, for example, you can apply the gradient to the background to add some depth and interest to the background.

The following steps explain how to create a simple gradient fill:

1. **Select the area that you want to fill.**

   Alternatively, select the background. The Gradient Fill command enables you to fill either the selected or the deselected area with a gradient.

2. **Choose Effects⇨Gradient Fill.**

   Or press Ctrl+8 (⌘+8 on a Mac). The Gradient Fill dialog box, shown in Figure 9-14, appears.

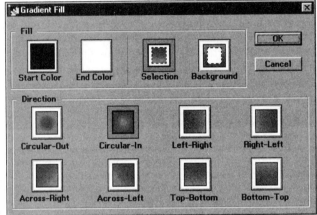

Figure 9-14: Set the style and colors of your gradient fill here.

3. **Set the start and end colors of the gradient.**

   Click the Start color icon to display the Color Picker dialog box, and choose the initial gradient color. Then click the End Color icon and select the other gradient color. (If you need help, the Color Picker is described in detail earlier in this chapter, in the section "Picking a Paint Color.")

4. **Specify whether you want to fill the selected pixels or deselected pixels.**

   If you want to apply the fill to the pixels inside the selection outline, click the Selection icon. To fill the pixels outside the outline, click the Background icon.

5. **Choose a gradient direction.**

   Click one of the eight icons at the bottom of the dialog box to choose the style and direction of the gradient.

6. **Click OK.**

For some fun special effects, try creating your gradient fill on a separate layer from the rest of the image. Then reduce the layer opacity to something less than 100 percent, so the underlying image remains visible, and blend the gradient with the underlying image using one of the layer blend modes, as discussed in Chapter 10.

Chapter 10

Better Living through Layers

. . . .

In This Chapter

▶ Using layers for editing safety and flexibility

▶ Understanding how layers work

▶ Navigating with the Layers palette

▶ Shuffling the order of your layers

▶ Creating a transparent window in a layer

▶ Changing layer opacity and blend mode

▶ Adding, deleting, and merging layers

. . . .

*I*f you want to become proficient at image editing, this chapter is a must-read. Here you find out about the professional's secret weapon: layers. By taking advantage of layers, you can save yourself an enormous amount of time and heartache. Just as important, you can explore a whole spectrum of creative effects that are impossible to achieve without layers.

In other words, don't miss this chapter!

Peering through Layers

After such a glowing introduction, you're no doubt drooling over the concept of layers. Except — well, maybe you're not quite sure what a layer *is*.

Perhaps an analogy can help. Imagine that instead of creating a digital image, you're creating transparencies to use with an overhead projector. You know — those old-fashioned sheets of clear acetate that people relied on before whiz-bang multimedia presentations came into vogue.

Anyway, you put an image of a house on one transparency. The house image is completely opaque (solidly colored) and covers the middle of the transparency; the rest of the sheet is clear. On another transparency, you put an image of a peaceful mountainside. That image covers the whole sheet and, like the house, is fully opaque.

If you put the house transparency on top of the mountain transparency and project the two images, the result is a scene of a house set against a mountain backdrop. Where the house transparency is clear, the mountain image is visible. If you reverse the order of the two transparencies, however, the mountain image totally obscures the house image.

Now suppose that you want to add a third transparency with some notations about urban sprawl and the decay of our natural resources or something like that. So you pick up a marker and start scribbling away on a new sheet of acetate. But instead of writing *environment,* you mistakenly write *eviroment.* No problem — you just trash that sheet of acetate and grab a new one. You haven't damaged your house image or your mountain image in any way.

Fine, you think, but what does all this have to do with digital images? Well, image layers are like digital sheets of acetate. Every image starts out with one layer, but you can create as many additional layers as you like. You can put different image elements on different layers, just as you put that house, mountain, and text on different transparencies. And just as with overhead transparencies, portions of layers that do not contain image elements are completely transparent, allowing elements from underlying layers to show through.

The benefits of using layers include the following:

- ✔ You can edit an element on one layer without affecting the rest of the image. If you want to change the color of your house image, for example, you can paint on the house layer without fear that you'll spill some paint on the text or mountain image.

- ✔ You can experiment freely. If you want to try out a special effect, for example, you can apply the effect on a separate layer from the rest of the image. If you don't like the results, you just delete the layer. Your original image isn't affected in the least.

- ✔ You can shuffle the stacking order of your layers to combine image elements in different ways. You can put your house layer on top of your mountain layer, so that you create the house-on-a-mountainside image. Or you can swap the layers, so that the mountain obscures the house.

- ✔ You can move the elements on one layer around to reposition them with respect to elements on other layers. If all the elements are on a single layer, you can't move any of them without leaving background-colored holes in the image.

- ✔ You can adjust the opacity of any layer — something you can't do with real-life transparencies — to give yourself even more creative possibilities. For example, if you had your mountain layer stacked on top of your house layer but made the mountain layer 50 percent opaque, you could see a faint house image peeking through your mountain image.

✔ You can create some interesting special effects by blending the pixels in one layer with those in the underlying layer, using the same blend modes available in the Selection Fill dialog box, discussed in Chapter 9.

These and other techniques are explained fully throughout the rest of this chapter. Although working with layers may seem like the long way to do things at first, after you compare editing with layers to editing without them, you'll never again want to be caught layerless.

Working with the Layers Palette

The key to creating, arranging, and editing layers is the Layers palette, shown in Figure 10-1. To display the palette, choose View⇨Show Layers.

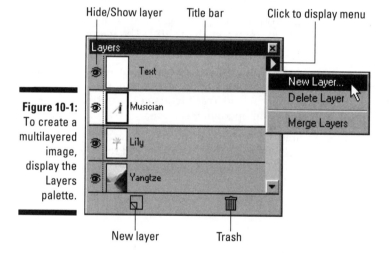

Figure 10-1: To create a multilayered image, display the Layers palette.

For such a small creature, the palette is loaded with options for creating and managing layers. Later sections offer more details about various aspects of the palette, but here's a brief introductory guide:

✔ The palette lists each layer in your image and includes a little thumbnail view of the layer contents next to the layer name. By default, every image contains a background layer, called Layer 0, and a text layer, called, oddly enough, the Text layer.

✔ Only one layer is active at a time. The active layer is the layer that's affected by any edits that you make. In the Layers palette, the active layer name is set against a highlighted background (in Figure 10-1, the Musician layer is active). To make a different layer the active layer, click its name in the palette.

✔ Use the Eyeball icon to the left of the layer name to hide or display individual layers on-screen. If the Eyeball icon is visible, the layer is visible. Click the eyeball to hide the layer; click again in the same space to bring back the eyeball and redisplay the layer.

✔ To hide all layers but one, Alt+click the eyeball next to the layer that you want to see (Option+click on a Mac). Alt+ or Option+click the eyeball again to redisplay all layers.

✔ You can resize the palette, if needed. In Windows, place your cursor at a corner of the palette. When the cursor turns into a double-headed arrow, drag to make the palette larger or smaller.

On a Mac, drag the size box in the lower-right corner of the window. Click the box in the top-right corner of the window (on the title bar) to expand and collapse the palette.

✔ To move the palette to a different on-screen location, drag the title bar. To close the palette, click the close button in the title bar.

✔ Click the right-pointing arrow in the upper-right corner of the palette to display the palette menu, as shown in Figure 10-1. The menu contains three important commands for managing layers.

✔ You really need to visit the menu only for choosing the Merge Layers command, however. You can access the other two commands more quickly by using the New Layer and Trash icons at the bottom of the Layers palette, as explained in upcoming sections.

✔ Double-click a layer name to display the Layer Options dialog box, where you can rename the layer, adjust the opacity of the layer, and choose a layer blend mode. See "Making Layer Elements Transparent" and "Fooling Around with Blend Modes," later in this chapter, for more information.

Creating New Layers

When you open an image for the first time, PhotoDeluxe automatically generates two layers. The bottom layer, called Layer 0, holds your image pixels. The top layer, the Text layer, is reserved for holding text that you create with the Text tool (explained in Chapter 11).

If you want to create more layers, you have several options:

✔ Click the New Layer icon, labeled in Figure 10-1, or choose the New Layer command from the palette menu. The New Layer dialog box, shown in Figure 10-2, appears. Here you can give your layer a name, set the opacity of the layer, and choose a layer blend mode. You can revisit this dialog box at any time by double-clicking the layer name in the Layers palette, so don't worry if you're not sure just yet what opacity or blend mode you want to use. See the next section for more information on these two options.

After you click OK, PhotoDeluxe adds your new layer directly above the layer that was active when you clicked the New Layer icon or chose the New Layer command.

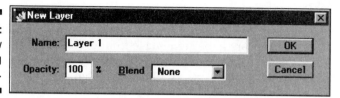

Figure 10-2:
The New
Layer dialog
box.

✔ To copy the contents of an entire layer to a new layer, drag the layer name to the New Layer icon. The duplicate layer is placed directly above the original layer.

✔ You can create a new layer without bothering with the New Layer dialog box by Alt+clicking the New Layer icon (Option+click on a Mac). PhotoDeluxe creates a new layer using 100 percent as the Opacity value and Normal as the Blend mode. The new layer is assigned a name — Layer 1, Layer 2, and so on, depending on how many layers already exist in your image.

✔ When you paste a selection from the Clipboard, the selection is automatically placed on a new layer, as explained in Chapter 8. If you drag and drop a selection or paste a selection with the Paste Into command, the selection goes on a temporary layer, called a *floating layer*. To turn the floating layer into a permanent layer, drag the Floating Layer item in the Layers palette to the New Layer icon.

✔ Every new layer you add increases the size of your image file and the amount of RAM and scratch disk space PhotoDeluxe needs to process your edits. (The concept of the scratch disk is explained in Chapter 2, in the section "Telling PhotoDeluxe Where to Scratch.") If your computer starts complaining about overload, either delete some of your layers or merge several layers together into one, as described in "Flattening Your Image," later in this chapter.

Shuffling Layer Order

The individual layers in your image are listed in the Layers palette according to their positions in the image. The bottom-most layer is at the bottom of the palette and serves as the background for your image. The Text layer is always the top layer of any image, even if you don't create any text.

You can rearrange the order of your layers to combine image elements in different ways. For example, both images in Figure 10-3 contain three image layers: one for the Yangtze River image, one for the lily image, and one for the musician image. The river image is the background — bottom — layer in both images.

In the left example, I placed the musician layer on top of the lily layer, so that the musician appears to be standing in front of the lily, with his feet resting on the lily petals. In the right example, I switched the two layers so that the lily layer is the top layer and the musician layer is the middle layer. Now the musician appears to be standing amid the lily petals at the back of the image. I didn't move the musician or the lily in the image frame to come up with these images — I merely rearranged the order of the two layers.

You shuffle the order of your layers by dragging the layer names in the Layers palette. Click on the layer name that you want to move, and then drag it up or down to the new position. As you drag, your cursor changes into a clenched fist to show that you grasped the layer correctly. A heavy black line indicates where the layer will be dropped if you release the mouse button (see Figure 10-4).

With PhotoDeluxe, the Text layer always stays put — you can't move it. This special layer resides as the top layer of the image, as discussed in Chapter 11. However, using the techniques I discuss in Chapter 11, you can work around this limitation if you want.

Figure 10-3:
Swapping the stacking order of the lily and musician layers creates two different scenes.

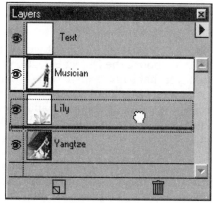

Figure 10-4:
Drag a layer up or down the list to change its placement in the layer stacking order.

Another alternative for changing the layer order is to grab the Object Selection tool and then click in the image window on any element on the layer that you want to move. (You must click on an area of the layer that contains image elements; if you click on a transparent area of the layer, you don't select the layer.) Then click the Stacking Order icon in the image window, labeled in Figure 10-5, to display a menu containing four options.

Choose Send to Front to send the selected layer to the top of the layer stack. Send to Back sends your layer to the bottom of the stack, and Send Back One and Send Forward One move the layer up or down one level.

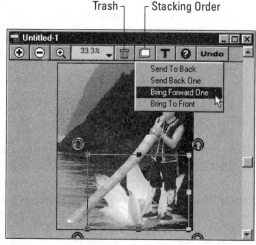

Figure 10-5:
The Stacking Order and Trash icons give you alternative ways to rearrange and delete layers.

Manipulating Layer Contents

You can move, rotate, and resize the contents of a layer at will without affecting the rest of the image. First, choose the Object Selection tool, and then click on any portion of the layer that's not transparent — that is, any area that isn't empty. The layer contents become surrounded by the standard rotate and resize handles, as discussed in Chapter 8 and shown in Figure 10-5. You can then use any of the techniques covered in Chapter 8 to reposition and resize the layer.

Note that if you want to manipulate only some of the layer elements, you must select them individually, using the other selection tools discussed in Chapter 8. All the rules for moving, copying, and transforming standard selections apply, as discussed in Chapter 8.

Editing on a Layer

For the most part, the selection and editing tools work the same as they do when you work on a single-layer image. But multilayered images present a few differences, so keep the following tips in mind:

✔ Any edits that you make, with the exception of resizing the image via the Photo Size command, affect the active layer only. Ditto for the selection tools — the Color Wand and SmartSelect tool "see" pixels on the active layer only, for example. (The active layer is the highlighted layer in the Layers palette; click a layer name to make it active.)

✔ Selection outlines, however, are independent of layers. If you select an element on Layer 1, for example, and then make Layer 2 active, the selection outline remains, and affects pixels on Layer 2. In other words, the selection outline "floats" over the image and affects the current active layer, regardless of what layer was active when you drew the outline.

✔ When saving your image, you must save in the PDD or PSD formats — the native formats for PhotoDeluxe and Photoshop, respectively, if you want to retain your image layers. Other formats flatten all your layers into one layer.

✔ If you paste an element from Image 1 into Image 2, the pasted element retains its original pixel count. But PhotoDeluxe automatically changes the image resolution to that of Image 2. Unless you set the image resolution of both images to the same value before you paste, the element from Image 1 either grows or shrinks as a result of the change in resolution. For more on this mind-bending issue, see Chapter 3.

Trashing Layers

To delete a layer, you have several options:

- ✔ Drag the layer name to the Trash icon in the Layers palette.

- ✔ Click a nontransparent area of the layer with the Object Selection tool and then press Delete or click the Trash icon.

- ✔ Click the layer that you want to delete in the Layers palette. Then click the Trash icon.

Remember that you're not just deleting the layer, but every image element that resides on the layer. If you want to reduce the number of layers in the image without destroying any image elements, use the Merge Layers command, discussed next.

Flattening Your Image

Because every layer you add to an image increases the image file size, merge layers together whenever possible. When you merge layers, they become permanently fused together, so that all elements from the individual layers reside on the same layer.

In image-editing parlance, merging layers is also known as *flattening the image*.

To merge all your image layers into one, choose the Merge Layers command from the Layers palette menu. Your multilayered image now has just two layers — one with all your regular image pixels, plus the Text layer that PhotoDeluxe automatically creates for every image. In case you're wondering, you can't delete that Text layer or merge it with the image layer — Adobe wants you to have that layer at all times, whether or not you need it. The only way to get rid of the independent Text layer is to save the image in some format other than the PhotoDeluxe native format. See Chapter 11 for more on this intriguing topic.

After you flatten your image, you lose the ability to move, resize, and otherwise manipulate the individual image elements without affecting the rest of the image. So you may want to make a copy of the layered image in case you're ever interested in working with the separate layers again. Be sure to save your image in the native PhotoDeluxe format, PDD, using the File⇨Save command, or in the Photoshop format, PSD, using the File⇨ Send To⇨File Format command. Any other format automatically flattens your image during the saving process.

Making Layer Elements Transparent

All layers are initially transparent. After you place an element on a layer, you can make the pixels in that element transparent again by using these methods:

- ✔ Select the pixels that you want to erase, using the selection tools discussed in Chapter 8. Then press Delete. All pixels inside the selection become completely transparent, and any pixels on the underlying layer become visible inside the selection outline.

- ✔ Rub out the offending pixels with the Eraser tool, discussed in the next section. By varying the opacity of the Eraser, you can make the pixels you rub more or less transparent. You can make the pixels either completely transparent, as if you had deleted them, or partially transparent, so that both the layer pixels and the underlying pixels are partially visible.

- ✔ Adjust the opacity of the layer inside the Layer Options dialog box, as discussed in the upcoming section, "Adjusting layer opacity." If you set the layer opacity to 0, all pixels on the layer are completely transparent. If you set the opacity to 100, all pixels are completely opaque, obscuring any pixels in the underlying layer. Anything in between creates a partially opaque layer.

Rubbing out pixels with the Eraser

The Eraser tool is one of the coolest weapons in the PhotoDeluxe arsenal. This tool erases pixels — or, to put it another way, paints on transparency. Figure 10-6 offers an example. In this image, the musician image is on the top layer, with the lily image on the layer immediately below. The right image catches me in the act of erasing the musician's leg. Wherever the Eraser tip touches the leg, the pixels are made transparent, allowing the underlying lily image to show through.

Here's how to use the Eraser:

1. **Choose Tools⇨Eraser.**

   Or just press Ctrl+E (⌘+E on a Mac). Either way, PhotoDeluxe activates the tool and displays the Eraser palette, which is just like the Brushes palette discussed in Chapter 9.

2. **Choose a brush tip from the Eraser palette.**

   Review "Choosing a brush tip" in Chapter 8 to understand your options here.

Figure 10-6:
Rub the
Eraser tool
over image
pixels to
make them
transparent.

Don't forget that you can set your cursor to reflect the actual size of the brush tip you choose. Press Ctrl+K (⌘+K) to open the Cursors dialog box, choose the Brush Size option in the Painting Tools section of the dialog box, and then click OK. For more about cursor options, read "Changing the Cursor Style" in Chapter 2.

3. Set the Eraser opacity.

If you want to make pixels completely transparent, press 0 (zero). Press any other number from 1 to 9 to make the pixels you touch with the eraser partially opaque. Press 1 for 10 percent opacity, 2 for 20 percent opacity, and so on.

4. Drag over the pixels you want to erase.

Or click the pixels one by one.

If you set your background display to be white inside the Background Options dialog box (as discussed in Chapter 2) and then stroke pixels on the bottom layer of the image, the pixels you touch appear to turn white. But if you change the background display to one of the checkerboard options, you can see that you are indeed making the pixels transparent, not white.

Adjusting layer opacity

If you want to make an entire layer more or less opaque, double-click the layer name in the Layers palette. PhotoDeluxe displays the Layer Options dialog box, which looks just like the New Layer dialog box shown in Figure 10-2, except for the name on the title bar.

To set the layer opacity, enter a value in the Opacity option box. A value of 100 percent makes your layer perfectly opaque, so that any pixels on the layer completely obscure any pixels on underlying layers. Any value less than 100 percent makes the layer pixels partially transparent, so that the underlying pixels become partially visible.

In Figure 10-7, I set the layer opacity for both the lily image and the musician image to 50 percent, giving the two elements a ghostly appearance. Note that you can't adjust the opacity of the Text layer; if you want semitransparent text, you have to use the special workaround technique covered in Chapter 11.

Figure 10-7: I turned the lily and musician into ghosts of their former selves by reducing the layer opacity to 50 percent.

Fooling Around with Blend Modes

Blend modes enable you to mix the pixels in one layer with the pixels in another layer in a variety of ways to create special effects. When you work with multilayered images, you have access to the same blend modes available in the Selection Fill dialog box, discussed in Chapter 9 and illustrated in Color Plate 9-3.

You can set the layer blend mode when creating a new layer by selecting an option from the Blend drop-down list inside the New Layer dialog box. Or double-click the layer name in the Layers palette and choose the blend mode in the Layer Options dialog box.

The various blend modes work just the same as described in Chapter 9. In fact, you could create the images in Color Plate 9-3 by using either the Selection Fill command or by relying on layer blend modes. In the Color Plate, I selected the pumpkin, filled it with a pattern available inside the Selection Fill dialog box, and chose a different blend mode for each example. But I could just have easily put the pattern fill on a separate layer from the pumpkin, set the blend mode to Normal inside the Selection Fill dialog box, and then selected a blend mode in the Layer Options or New Layer dialog box.

Working with blend modes via the New Layer dialog box has one advantage over using the Selection Fill dialog box, though. When you choose different blend modes inside the New Layer dialog box, you can preview the effect on your image without leaving the dialog box. The Selection Fill dialog box doesn't offer an image preview. So you have to try one option, close the dialog box, and then Undo the edit and return to the dialog box if you don't like the result.

With the exception of the Color and Overlay modes, the blend modes are primarily useful for creating special effects. Review "Blending pixels in cruel and unusual ways" in Chapter 9 for a thorough discussion of how each blend mode works. Or better yet, experiment for yourself to see what kinds of wacky image combinations you can create.

Creating a Multilayered Collage

To get a better understanding of how to put all the advantages of layers to use, set your sights on Figures 10-8 and 10-9, as well as their color counterparts, Color Plates 10-1 and 10-2. In Figure 10-8 and Color Plate 10-1, you see a collection of images that I shot on a recent trip to China. Figure 10-9 and Color Plate 10-2 show the collage that I created by layering all those individual elements.

The following list explains how I combined the elements into the collage. Reviewing these tactics can give you some ideas about how to build your own multilayered masterpiece.

✔ First, I opened each individual image and did any necessary color correction, sharpening, and so on.

✔ I wanted to keep all my original images intact in case I needed them again in the future. So I saved each corrected image under a new name, as explained in Chapter 4.

✔ Working on the duplicate images, I selected the portion of the image that I wanted to use in the collage. In most cases, I relied on the SmartSelect tool as the primary selection tool (see Chapter 8 for a review of selection tools).

Figure 10-8:
These six images form the basis of a collage commemorating a recent trip to China.

Figure 10-9:
By using layers, I was able to move each image element around freely until I arrived at a good layout for the collage.

✔ One by one, I copied and pasted the elements onto the Yangtze River image. Figure 10-10 shows you the order of the layers in the image.

✔ After pasting in each element, I moved it into position by using either the Move tool or the Object Selection tool. I resized a few image elements — but only slightly, because too much resizing can damage image quality, as explained in Chapter 3. I slightly rotated the lily image, and I flipped the lion image horizontally. I kept all the other images at their original orientation.

✔ Using the Eraser tool with a soft, fuzzy brush and an opacity value of 50 percent, I nipped at the edges of the stone lion's feet to create a softer transition between the lion's paws and the background water. I did the same thing along the bottom and right corner of the golden statue image so that the statue appears to be tucked behind the mountain and sunk into the water. I set the Eraser opacity at 50 percent when erasing along the water edge and 100 percent when rubbing along the mountain edge.

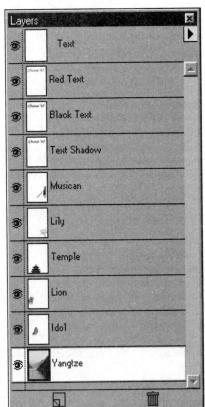

Figure 10-10:
The stacking order of the layers in the China collage.

✔ Next, I dragged with the Eraser over the inside leg of the musician. Originally, the leg obscured the lily petals rather than the other way around (check out the left image in Figure 10-3 to see the original placement). By erasing the leg pixels, I brought the lily pixels back into view so that the musician appears to be perched inside the flower.

✔ I created the shadowed text by using the special text techniques outlined in Chapter 11. This text actually comprises three separate components: a block of red text, a block of black text, and a drop shadow.

✔ For all layers, I set the layer opacity to 100 percent and the blend mode to Normal.

The image in Figure 10-9 would have been impossible to create without using layers. Sure, I could have pasted all the image elements directly onto the river image. But without layers, I wouldn't have been able to position, size, and erase the elements as I did in the multilayered version. For maximum creative potential, layers are without a doubt the image editor's best friend.

Chapter 11

Text Expressions

*T*hey say that a picture is worth 1,000 words. But on occasion, you may need 1,001, 1,002, or even 1,003 words. That's the time to pick up the Text tool. Using the Text tool, you can add captions, callouts, or other words of wisdom to your images.

In this chapter, you find out how to create simple text using the Text tool and the special Text layer that PhotoDeluxe reserves for your pithy phrases. But you also discover how to work around some inherent limitations in the Text tool and create some pretty snazzy text effects, such as the ones in Color Plate 11-1.

Laying Down Language

The PhotoDeluxe Text tool is a special animal. If you're using Version 2 or the Business Edition, you can create solid, colored text — and that's it. Version 3 users can also create semitransparent text. But to create special text effects such as the ones in Color Plate 11-1, you have to use a top-secret text formula that's outlined in the next part of this chapter.

For basic text, however, the Text tool is more than adequate. Here's how to imprint some words on your image:

1. **Select the Text tool.**

   You can pick up your digital typewriter by pressing Ctrl+T (⌘+T on a Mac), choosing Tools⇨Text, or by clicking the T button at the top of the image window.

   After you activate the tool, the Text Tool dialog box, shown in Figure 11-1, appears. The top dialog box in the figure is from Version 2; the bottom dialog box is the Version 3 edition. The Business Edition dialog box is similar to the Version 3 dialog box except that it lacks the Transparency option.

2. **Type your text.**

   Click inside the text box on the left side of the dialog box. If you want to create a line break, press Enter if you're using a PC. Press Return if you're using a Mac.

3. **Select the font.**

   When you choose a font from the Font drop-down list, your text appears in that font inside the text box.

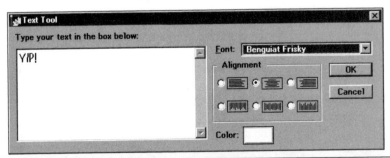

Figure 11-1: The Version 2 Text Tool dialog box (top) and the more advanced Version 3 dialog box (bottom).

In the Business Edition and Version 3, you can also enter a type size. You can always resize your type later, but if you have a specific size in mind, enter it into the Size dialog box. The type size is measured in _points,_ the traditional unit of measurement for type.

4. Choose an Alignment option.

These options determine whether your text runs horizontally across the image, like normal book text, or vertically. In addition, if you enter multiple lines of text, the options determine how the rows of text align with respect to each other. For example, if you click the first alignment option in the top row, text lines are aligned by the left edge.

The top three alignment options are for left alignment, centered alignment, and right alignment, respectively. The bottom three options orient your text into columns, so that it runs vertically on the page rather than horizontally. Here, you can opt for top, centered, or bottom alignment.

5. Set the text color.

The Color swatch shows the current text color. If you want to change the color, click the swatch and choose a color from the Color Picker dialog box. Then click OK to close the dialog box and return to the Text Tool dialog box.

6. Set the text opacity.

Version 3 gives you the option of varying the opacity of your text. To create solid, fully opaque text, set the Transparency value to 0. Raise the value to create characters that are semitransparent.

If you haven't upgraded to Version 3, you can create semitransparent text by using the technique outlined in "Basic recipe for cooler text," later in this chapter.

7. Click OK.

PhotoDeluxe creates your text and places it on the special Text layer. The Object Selection tool and the text are both selected automatically for you so that you can resize, rotate, or reposition your text if needed, as explained in the next section.

Inside the Business Edition and Version 3 Text Tool dialog box, you can click the Reset button at any time before you click OK to return to the original values that were in place when you opened the dialog box. If you're using Version 2, you can click the Cancel button and then reopen the dialog box to accomplish the same thing.

You can create as many blocks of text as you like. Just repeat the steps to add more text. All your text blocks are kept on the Text layer, independent of the rest of the image. (For more on layers, read Chapter 10.)

However, your text remains separate from the rest of the image only if you save the image in the PDD file format, as explained in Chapter 4. If you save to some other file format, the text and image are fused together, and you can no longer reposition or edit the text without affecting the rest of the image. The exception is the Photoshop format, PSD. When you save to this format, PhotoDeluxe adds a new layer to your image and moves the text to that layer — a fact that can come in handy for creating some special text effects, as explained later in this chapter.

Positioning and Sizing Text

After you create text, PhotoDeluxe selects the text and the Object Selection tool so that you can adjust the size, angle, and placement of the text. You see the standard rotate and resize handles around the text, as shown in Figure 11-2. These are the same handles that appear when you select a layer or entire image with the Object Selection tool. You can enlarge, reduce, rotate, distort, and flip your text as described in Chapter 8, in the section related to the Object Selection tool.

Because of the way PhotoDeluxe treats text, the standard warnings about enlarging image elements don't apply here. You can scale text as large or as small as you like without damaging the quality of the letters. Also, because your text always remains on the Text layer — independent of the rest of the image — you can move it around at will without affecting the underlying image one whit.

However, any text created in a painting program is, by nature, a little jaggedy — remember, you're "writing" with square blocks of color (pixels). And the larger you make your text, the more noticeable the jagged edges become. If you need really large text, try creating the text according to the instructions in "Basic recipe for cooler text," later in this chapter, and then apply one of the Blur commands to soften the edges of the letters. Mind you, this approach doesn't totally solve the problem, but it can help in many cases.

Editing Existing Text

Editing text in PhotoDeluxe is surprisingly easy. Just pick up the Object Selection tool, explained in Chapter 8, and double-click the text. Then revise the text in the Text Tool dialog box as needed. You can also choose another font, alignment, or color if you want. When you click OK, PhotoDeluxe replaces the selected text with the new text.

Text tool button

Stacking Order   Rotate handle   Resize handle

Figure 11-2:
Drag the
rotate and
resize
handles to
spin, shrink,
or enlarge
your text.

If you simply want to move, resize, or rotate your text, click the text with
the Object Selection tool instead of double-clicking. The rotate and resize
handles reappear, and you can then use the techniques outlined in Chapter 8
to manipulate your text.

Remember that you can edit text in this fashion only if you save your image
in the PDD file format. Saving to any other format merges the text with the
underlying image, and you lose the ability to manipulate or edit the text
without affecting the rest of the image. If you save to the Photoshop format,
PSD, you can move, resize, and rotate your text (as well as perform many
other text tricks), but you can't double-click the text to edit it inside the
Text Tool dialog box.

Creating Special Text Effects

Because PhotoDeluxe treats text differently from other image elements,
you're somewhat limited in your creative possibilities if you stick with the
"official" method of adding text. You can't vary the opacity of the text layer,
you can't apply any of the special effects or correction filters to your text,
and you can't slip text behind an image element. You can create solid,
straightforward text that rests at the top of the image, and that's it.

Unless, of course, you follow the highly guarded secret workaround for creating text. Using this method, you can do just about anything you want with your text, from painting on it to filling it with an image. Color Plate 11-1 shows some examples of some typographical treatments for inspiration; the following sections give you some specific how-to's to get you started on your text adventure.

Basic recipe for cooler text

The key to making your text more flexible is to free it from the restrictive bounds of the Text layer. Here's how to add a better breed of text to your image:

1. **Create your text.**

   Use the methods described in the first part of this chapter. Double-check your text to make sure that the words are spelled correctly; after you complete this process, you can't use the controls in the Text Tool dialog box to edit individual words. Nor can you change the font or text alignment (how multiple lines of text align with each other). If you're using Version 3, set the text opacity to 100 percent — you can always change the opacity later. You also can alter the text size and color later, so don't concern yourself with those text characteristics too much.

2. **Save the image in the Photoshop native format, PSD.**

   See Chapter 4 for information on how to save to a format other than the PhotoDeluxe native format. Be sure that the Flatten Image option is not selected when you save.

3. **Close the on-screen image.**

   You don't need to bother saving this version if you don't want to.

4. **Open the PSD version of the image.**

   After you open the image, take a look at the Layers palette. Magic! In the process of saving the image, PhotoDeluxe sent everything from the Text layer onto a new, regular layer. The official Text layer is empty, but all the text you created is intact on the new layer.

Note that if you used white as your text color and the canvas color is also set to white, your text may seem to disappear when you save to the PSD format. The text is still intact; you just can't see it. To make the text visible, change the canvas to the checkerboard pattern instead of solid white. Choose File⇨Preferences⇨Background and follow the instructions given in Chapter 2.

Now your text behaves like any other part of the image, which opens up a zillion creative possibilities. You can do all the following, and more:

✔ Select your text and then paint it, stroke it, or do anything else you would do to regular selections.

Because the text pixels are all by their lonesomes on the layer, you can easily select the characters. To select just one or two characters, click each character with the Color Wand (click the Add icon in the Selections palette before you start). Or to select many characters, use the Color Wand to select the background instead. Be sure to click inside the "loops" of any letters — such as the interior of the letter *O*. After you have selected all the background, invert the selection by clicking the Invert icon in the Selections palette or pressing Ctrl+I (⌘+I on a Mac). Now the text characters, and not the background, are selected.

If you want to select just some of the text characters, use the Polygon tool to drag around them. After you enclose a character in a selection outline, you can use the Color Wand to deselect any background areas inside a closed loop. For example, to select the letter O, drag around the letter with the Polygon tool, select the Color Wand, click the Reduce icon in the Selections palette, and click inside the O. The pixels inside the O become deselected.

✔ Apply the Outline command to selected text to create effects like the one in the top example in Color Plate 11-1. In that image, I applied the Outline command twice, once to create the white outline and once to create the dark purple outline.

✔ Fill selected text with a pattern using the Selection Fill dialog box. You can even fill the text with an image, as explained a little later in this chapter and illustrated in the middle image in Color Plate 11-1. (If you want to change the color of the text, you can do that via the Selection Fill dialog box, too.)

✔ Paint stripes across characters with the Brush tool. Or polka dots, or squiggles, or whatever your heart desires. To keep the Brush tool within the outlines of your text, select the text before you paint.

✔ Make your text more or less transparent. Just change the Opacity value in the Layer Options box for the layer that holds the text, as described in Chapter 10. In the bottom image in Color Plate 11-1, for example, I reduced the opacity of the text to 90 percent so that the underlying money image was visible through the letters.

As explained earlier, Version 3 does enable you to set text opacity by using a Transparency control in the Text Tool dialog box, but adjusting the text opacity via the Layer Options dialog box is easier. You can preview the effects of different Opacity values from within the Layer Options dialog box, but not the Text Tool dialog box.

✔ Blend the text pixels with the image pixels, using the Blend modes in the Layer Options dialog box.

✔ Apply any special effect, from a distortion filter to a color-effects filter. The bottom image in Color Plate 11-1 shows the results of applying the Effects⇔Distort⇔Sphere command to my text.

✔ Get rid of the jagged edges of your text by selecting the entire text layer and then applying a slight blur with the Effects⇨Soften command. I used this trick to smooth out the edges of all the text examples in Color Plate 11-1. Inside the Soften dialog box, use the lowest Radius value that smooths the text edges. Too high a Radius value creates fuzzy text.

✔ On the other hand, maybe you *want* a fuzzy-text effect. If so, use the Soften filter with a high Radius value. Your text appears as if you sprayed it on your image with an airbrush.

✔ Create a feathered drop-shadow, as described shortly and illustrated in the middle example of the color plate.

✔ Place the text in any position in the image stacking order. You can use your text as the background layer of the image, sandwich it between two other image layers, or put it at the very top of the image.

✔ You can even spread the individual characters in your text farther apart or move them closer together — both of which are known as *kerning* in the typesetting world. Just use the Color Wand or Polygon tool to select the character that you want to move, press Ctrl+G (⌘+G on a Mac) to select the Move tool, and nudge the character with the arrow keys.

In other words, you are king of the text hill. So go bonkers — let your imagination rule. And never again be limited to the boring effects you can create with the standard PhotoDeluxe Text layer.

Shadowed text

You can place a drop shadow behind your text, as in Figure 11-3, by following these easy steps:

Figure 11-3:
A drop shadow gives text the illusion of depth.

1. **Create your text, as explained in the preceding basic recipe steps.**

2. **In the Layers palette, click the name of the layer that holds your text.**

Note: The layer that you need here is not the official Text layer — you want the layer created when you saved to the Photoshop (PSD) file format.

3. **Select the text.**

The Color Wand is usually your best selection tool here.

4. **Choose Effects⇨Drop Shadow.**

The Drop Shadow dialog box, introduced in Chapter 6, appears. Select the size, direction, and color of your shadow. For now, leave the Opacity value set to 100 percent. Click OK to apply the shadow.

PhotoDeluxe creates two new layers: One layer holds the shadow, and the other holds a duplicate of the text.

5. **Adjust the drop shadow if needed.**

If you're not happy with the position of the shadow, click the Shadow layer in the Layers palette. Then press Ctrl+G (⌘+G on a Mac) to activate the Move tool. You can now press the arrow keys to nudge the shadow into place.

To alter the opacity of the text, double-click the Shadow layer name and change the Opacity value in the Layer Options dialog box. And if you want a fuzzy shadow instead of a hard-edged shadow, click the Shadow layer in the Layers palette and then use the Effects⇨Soften command to blur the edges of the shadow. I used this technique to create the text in Figure 11-3.

To give your text a glowing background, as in Figure 11-4, create a huge, fuzzy shadow using white as the fill color.

For more information about the Drop Shadow command, head to Chapter 6.

Figure 11-4:
A fuzzy white drop shadow lends a spooky touch to this text.

Outlined text

Outlining your text can help the characters stand out from the background image. For an example of outlined text, turn your gaze to Figure 11-5 and the top example of Color Plate 11-1.

Figure 11-5:
Use the
Outline
command
to create
this double-
border
effect.

To create outlined text, walk this way:

1. **Create your text as explained earlier in "Basic recipe for cooler text."**

2. **Select the text.**

   Your old pal the Color Wand can usually do the trick in no time. For fastest results, click on a non-text area to select the background of the text layer — don't forget about the holes in the letters — and then invert the selection to select the text itself.

3. **Create a new layer to hold the outline.**

   Click the New Layer icon in the Layers palette. When the New Layer dialog box appears, name the layer *Outline* and click OK. This time, you want the new layer to be one step above the original text layer in the Layers palette, which is just where PhotoDeluxe puts it.

4. **Choose Effects⇨Outline.**

   Specify the size, position, and color of the outline and then click OK. (You can read more about options found in the Outline dialog box in Chapter 6, in the section "Adding a Border.")

To create the double-border look shown in Figure 11-5 and Color Plate 11-1, click through these invigorating mouse exercises:

1. **Follow the preceding steps.**

   But in Step 4, choose a larger size for the outline. This first outline that you create is the outside outline — the purple outline in Color Plate 11-1, for example. Make the outline larger than you want it to actually appear, because it will be partially covered by the second outline (the white outline in Color Plate 11-1). In the Color Plate, I created a 10-pixel purple outline using the Outside placement option in the Outline dialog box.

2. **Click the New Layer icon.**

   This layer is for your second outline.

3. **Choose Effects⇨Outline and apply your second border.**

   In Figure 11-5 and Color Plate 11-1, I applied a 5-pixel white outline, again using the Outside placement option. The white outline rests atop the purple outline.

Keep in mind that the text in the figure and color plate is really big. For smaller text, the 5- and 10-pixel outline values mentioned in the steps are probably too large.

Image-filled text

Want to unleash some really eye-catching text? Fill your text with an image, as I did in Figure 11-6 and the middle example in Color Plate 11-1. Here, I filled the text characters with an image of all kinds of currency. The currency image, which I also used as the background for the bottom example in the color plate, is from the PhotoDeluxe CD-ROM. The image is named Money.jpg and is found in the Pdart/Samples/Background folder in Version 2 and in the Pdart/Samples/Webart folder in the Business Edition. Sadly, the image is gone from Version 3; evidently somebody took the money and ran.

Figure 11-6:
Filling text
with an
image gives
new power
to the
printed
word.

To create image-filled text, take these steps:

1. **Create your text in the image that you want to use as the fill.**

   Follow the steps presented earlier in this chapter in "Basic recipe for cooler text." In my example, I created my text in the currency image. Save your image in the Photoshop format (PSD) when you're done creating the text. Then close the version of the image on-screen and open the PSD version.

2. **Click the layer that holds your text.**

   Remember, the layer you want is not the official PhotoDeluxe Text layer, but the new layer that the program created when you saved to the PSD format.

3. **Select the text background.**

   You want to select everything on the text layer except the text itself. As you may have gathered if you read the rest of this chapter, I think the Color Wand is the cat's meow for this particular task.

4. **Click the image layer name in the Layers palette.**

   Now the image layer is active.

5. **Press Delete.**

   Deleting the selection on the background layer leaves you with text-shaped image areas. However, because your text layer is still intact on the layer above, you may not be able to see the results of your handiwork.

6. **Click the Eyeball icon next to the text layer name to hide the layer.**

   Now your image-filled characters come into view. If you like what you see, proceed to the next step. If you don't, press Ctrl+Z (⌘+Z) to undelete the background and start all over.

7. **Drag the text layer to the Trash icon.**

   You don't need those original text characters anymore. If you want to add further text effects, such as a drop shadow like the one in Color Plate 11-1, select the image-filled text and use that selection outline to create your drop shadow, as explained earlier in this chapter.

A few final text tips

The effects you see in this chapter represent just the tip of the iceberg when it comes to creating fun text in PhotoDeluxe. Spend some time experimenting, and you'll no doubt come up with all sorts of other interesting treatments for text.

As you play with text, keep these tips in mind:

✔ When possible, create your effects on a separate layer from your original text. You can copy your original text layer to a new layer and experiment on the copy. You may want to hide the original text layer (by clicking its Eyeball icon in the Layers palette) while you experiment. See Chapter 10 if you need help working with layers. That way, you can dump the layer and start over if you don't like the results.

✔ In addition to playing with the special filters on the Effects menu, try fooling around with the Size⇨Perspective and Size⇨Distort commands, which are discussed in Chapter 12. You can create some interesting perspective effects as well as twist your text into unusual shapes by using these commands.

✔ Performing all the text tricks in this chapter requires some familiarity with the Layers palette and the selection tools, explored in Chapters 10 and 8.

✔ Most text effects look best on big, blocky typefaces like the one you see in Color Plate 11-1, especially if you want to fill the characters with an image.

✔ Remember that if your text looks jaggedy, applying the Effects⇨Soften command can smooth out the edges a little.

✔ Finally, PhotoDeluxe (and any painting program) is best used to create small bits of decorative text. If you need to create a text-based logo, large banner headlines, and the like, you're better off doing so in a word processing or drawing program.

Chapter 12

Wild and Wooly Pixel Adventures

· ·

In This Chapter

▶ Sending reality out the window

▶ Giving pixels a dye job with the color filters

▶ Sucking the color out of a picture

▶ Putting color into the cheeks of grayscale images

▶ Creating faux clouds

▶ Applying petroleum jelly to the camera lens (blurring an image)

▶ Creating psychedelic backgrounds by using multiple filters

· ·

*O*ne of the things I appreciate most about PhotoDeluxe is that it offers many of the same great special-effects filters found in Adobe's higher-end (and much higher-priced) image editor, Photoshop. It's like sipping expensive French champagne for the price of a wine cooler — you get to sample some of the really good stuff without forking out major bucks.

Of course, with PhotoDeluxe, the servings of special effects aren't as generous as in Photoshop. But as this chapter proves, you still get more than enough to make you a little tipsy with power. You can apply all sorts of wacky color effects, bend and twist your image, and even turn a dull, overcast sky into a brilliant blue sky dotted with fluffy white clouds. In short, with a few choice selections from the Effects menu, you can give your pixels a night they'll never forget.

Throwing Colors to the Wind

PhotoDeluxe offers several filters that shift the colors in your image. Chapter 9 introduces you to the Hue/Saturation command, which sends all your pixels on a trip around the color wheel, and Chapter 6 explains the Color Balance and Variations command, both of which adjust the balance of different color components in your image. You can see examples of the results of the Hue/Saturation filter in Color Plate 9-4 and the Color Balance command in Color Plate 6-3.

For more bizarre color effects, though, head for the Effects menu, where you can find several filters that alter the colors in your image in ways you probably never imagined.

Here's a quick guide to some of the more intriguing color filters:

✔ **Negative:** This filter inverts your image to create an effect similar to a photographic negative. The top-right image in Color Plate 12-1 shows what happened to my colorful but rather sedate paddleboat image (top-left) after a pass through the Negative filter.

✔ **Stylize⇨Solarize:** This filter gives you an effect similar to what happens if you expose a real photographic print to light during the development process, if that means anything to you. If not, take a look at the bottom-left image of Color Plate 12-1.

The Solarize filter can make your image look a little dark, so you may want to tweak the brightness and contrast after applying the filter, as I did to the image in the Color Plate.

✔ **Artistic⇨Posterize:** The Posterize filter reduces your image to a certain number of brightness levels, which you specify in the Posterize dialog box that appears when you choose the command. You can use this command to achieve a comic-book-like effect. The lower the value you enter in the Levels option box, the more dramatic the effect. Try applying this filter to a grayscale image for the most entertaining results.

Before applying one of these filters, copy your entire image to a new layer. Apply the filter to the new layer and try different layer blend modes to mix the filtered layer with the underlying image. Using this technique, you can create many variations on the basic filter effect. In the lower-right image in Color Plate 12-1, for example, I applied the Negative filter to the new layer and then blended the filtered layer with the underlying image, using the Difference blend mode. (For more about layers and blend modes, check out Chapter 10.) The result is a bolder, more colorful version of the Negative filter.

Playing with Gray

Although bright, eye-popping colors seem to be in vogue these days, especially in print and television advertising, don't overlook the power of black-and-white images. As anyone who has ever seen an Ansel Adams photograph can attest, a black-and-white image can be every bit as arresting — if not more so — than a color photograph.

In the image-editing world, what most folks commonly call a black-and-white photograph is known as a *grayscale* image. That's because the image is made up of many different shades of gray — typically 256 — rather than just pure black and pure white.

The following sections give you the background information you need to understand how PhotoDeluxe handles grayscale images and give you the step-by-step for creating the two grayscale effects shown in Color Plate 12-2.

Real gray versus faux gray

PhotoDeluxe treats grayscale images a little differently than most graphics programs. When you open any image in PhotoDeluxe, the program determines whether or not the image file was saved in the native PhotoDeluxe format, PDD. If not, the program creates a copy of the image, converts the copy to the PDD format, and opens the copy for you to work on. In other words, any image you see on-screen is a PDD image, regardless of the format of the original image. For more on this PDD stuff, see "Pulling Out of the Driveway: Opening Images" in Chapter 1.

PDD images are *always* full-color RGB images, regardless of whether the original image was full-color, grayscale, indexed color, or whatever. That *doesn't* mean that PhotoDeluxe adds colors to your image that weren't there before. What it does mean is that *you* can add colors to your image if you want. If you open a 256-color grayscale image, for example, you can stroke on red paint, if you want, or blue, or green, or any other color. You're no longer bound by the original 256 grayscale color limitation.

In addition, the Effects⇨Color to Black/White command, which you use to suck the color out of an image, doesn't create a true grayscale image. It merely desaturates your colors so that they all appear gray, the same as if you had dragged the Saturation control all the way to the left in the Hue/Saturation dialog box. Your image is still an RGB image. And if you want to bring the image into a program that only supports real grayscale images, you may have trouble.

If you need to convert your image to a true, 256-colors-or-fewer grayscale image, save the image by using the Grayscale File command. (See the next section for details.) This approach may seem a little bizarre if you're used to working with other image editors, where grayscale is grayscale is grayscale. But the PhotoDeluxe take on gray can actually come in handy for creating certain effects.

Turning gray

To turn your image into a gray version of its former self, you have two options:

✔ To convert the on-screen, working image to gray, choose Effects⇨Color to Black/White. As discussed in the preceding section, this command shifts all your colors to a shade of gray.

After you choose the Color to Black/White command, you can't retrieve your original image colors. So you may want to make a backup copy of the image before you apply the command.

✔ To save your image as a true, 256-color grayscale image, choose File➪Send To➪Grayscale File command in Version 2; File➪Export➪Grayscale File in Version 3; and File➪Save As➪Grayscale File in the Business Edition. PhotoDeluxe makes a copy of your image, converts all colors to gray according to a 256-color grayscale spectrum, and saves the copy to disk. Your on-screen image is unaffected.

If you choose the Color to Black/White command, you can elect to make just a portion of your image gray, as I did in Color Plate 12-2. The top image in the color plate is the original image. I selected the car and then inverted the selection so that the background was selected. Then I applied the Color to Black/White command to the background only, creating the middle image in the color plate. Desaturating the background in this way adds extra emphasis to the subject.

Colorizing a grayscale image

One of the benefits of the PhotoDeluxe approach to black-and-white images is that you can add color back into the image at any time. This feature enables you to colorize your grayscale images to create a variety of effects, including the antique photograph effect shown in the bottom image in Color Plate 12-2.

To create a similar image, march along this simple trail:

1. **Choose Effects➪Color to Black/White.**

2. **Click the New Layer icon in the Layers palette.**

    PhotoDeluxe creates a new layer. (See Chapter 10 if you need help.)

3. **Press Ctrl+A (⌘+A on the Mac).**

    This shortcut selects the entire new layer.

4. **Choose Effects➪Selection Fill.**

    The Selection Fill dialog box opens.

5. **Click the color square to open the Color Picker dialog box.**

6. **Choose a shade of rusty yellow that looks like what you see in antique photographs.**

    Close the Color Picker dialog box to return to the Selection Fill dialog box.

7. **Click the Fill Selection option, set the Opacity value to 50 percent, and the Blend mode to Color.**

8. **Click OK.**

   Your image now appears as though it's peering through a semitransparent, rusty yellow window. If you're not 100 percent satisfied with the effect, double-click the layer name of the yellow layer in the Layers palette to open the Layer Options dialog box. (Find out more about layers in Chapter 10.) In the color plate, I used an opacity value of 65 percent.

   Play with the Opacity value until you get the amount of coloring you want. Also experiment with using the Overlay blend mode instead of the Color mode.

Turning Cloudy Skies to Blue

Many a picture has been spoiled by nature's refusal to provide an idyllic blue sky. The left image in Color Plate 12-3 is a case in point. This image was shot on a day so cloudy that the sky actually looks white in the image.

With the help of the Effects⇨Render⇨Clouds command, however, you can turn any cloudy sky into a clear blue sky dotted with fluffy clouds, as in the right image in the color plate. To create a similar effect for your sky, click this way:

1. **Select the sky area.**

   Chapter 8 describes different selection techniques.

2. **Choose Effects⇨Choose Colors.**

   In the next step, the Clouds command creates your new sky using the foreground and background colors selected in the Color Picker dialog box. I find that using a light and dark shade of blue, rather than blue and pure white, creates more-natural results.

3. **Choose Effects⇨Render⇨Clouds.**

   PhotoDeluxe fills the selection with a random pattern based on your foreground and background colors.

   If your clouds appear too harsh or unnatural, try applying one of the blur filters to soften the transition between the sky and cloud areas. You can find out more about the blur filters in "Blurring the Focus," later in this chapter.

For an otherworldly variation on the clouds effect, choose the other command on the Render submenu, called Merge Clouds in Version 2 and Cloud Texture in the Business Edition and Version 3. This filter blends the cloud image with the underlying image using the Difference blend mode. You can get the exact same effect by applying the Clouds command on a separate layer from the original image and then setting the layer blend mode to Difference.

Tracing Edges with Color

Several of the filters on the Effects menu apply special color treatments based on the *edges* in your image — areas where light pixels meet dark. Color Plate 12-3 shows the results of applying three of these filters: Stylize⇨Find Edges, Stylize⇨Glowing Edges, and Artistic⇨Neon Glow. The following list explains a bit more about each effect.

- ✔ **Stylize⇨Find Edges:** This command searches out areas of contrast. Then it colors low-contrast areas with white and emphasizes edges with dark outlines. The upper-right image in Color Plate 12-3 shows the result of applying the Find Edges command to my original image (upper-left).

- ✔ **Stylize⇨Glowing Edges:** A variation of Find Edges, this filter turns low-contrast areas dark and highlights edges with white — so that the edges in your image "glow." When you choose this command, PhotoDeluxe displays a dialog box in which you can adjust the width and brightness of the glowing edges. You can also adjust the sensitivity of the filter by playing with the Smoothness control. If you use a high Smoothness value, the filter applies the glowing effect only to major edges (areas of highest contrast). A lower value finds more edges and thus gives you more glowing lines. In the bottom-left image of Color Plate 12-3, I applied the filter using an Edge Width value of 5, Edge Brightness value of 6, and Smoothness value of 5.

Refer to "Communicating with a Dialog Box," in Chapter 1, for some tips on working inside the Glowing Edges dialog box as well as other filter dialog boxes.

- ✔ **Artistic⇨Neon Glow:** This animal is a bit difficult to explain, but in essence, it repaints your image using the foreground and background colors you set in the Color Picker dialog box (choose Effects⇨Choose Colors). Then it adds glowing highlights around the edges of your image, giving the picture a neonlike appearance.

  Choosing the Neon Glow command brings up a dialog box with several options. Drag the Glow Size slider to adjust the, er, size of the glow. Negative values give you an inverted photograph effect. The Glow Brightness value determines the opacity of the glow. Higher values make more of your original image detail visible. Click the Glow Color swatch to choose a color for the edge glow.

Predicting the outcome of this filter is difficult at best, so just play around until you arrive at an effect that makes you happy. And don't forget to experiment with blending a filtered version of your image with the original, using the layer blend modes discussed in Chapter 10. Copy your entire image to a new layer, apply the filter to the new layer, and then select your blend mode and layer opacity in the Layer Options dialog box. In the bottom-right image of Color Plate 12-3, I blended the filtered image with the original using the Difference blend mode at 100 percent opacity. I used dark blue and pale yellow as my foreground and background colors, set the Glow Brightness to 28, the Glow Size to 14, and the Glow Color to red.

 ✔ **Brush StrokesíAccented Edges:** The Business Edition offers one additional interesting edge effect, Accented Edges. This filter traces edges — areas where light pixels meet dark pixels — with either black or white halos. The Edge Width value determines the width of the halos; raise the value for a more visible effect. The Edge Brightness value determines whether you get dark or light halos. Low Edge Brightness values give you dark halos; high values give you light halos. The Smoothness value adjusts the sensitivity of the filter — if you use a low value, the filter traces more edges than if you use a high value.

Blurring the Focus

The filters on the Effects⇨Blur menu do just what the name implies: blur the image so that the focus appears overly soft. In other words, they do the opposite of the sharpening filters covered in Chapter 7.

For the most part, the blur filters are reserved for creating special effects. But on occasion, they can come in handy for corrective editing as well. For example, applying a slight blur can lessen the jaggedy appearance that sometimes results from overcompressing an image. Blurring the background of an image, as I did in the car images in Color Plate 12-2, can lend more emphasis to the foreground subject and can even make the focus of the subject seem sharper in comparison to the blurry background.

PhotoDeluxe offers you five options for blurring your image. For corrective blurring, choose one of these blur filters:

✔ **Blur:** Apply this command for a gentle softening effect.

✔ **Blur More:** If Blur doesn't do the trick, Blur More just might.

 ✔ **Soften:** Actually, this is the filter I'd go with all the time if I were you. Whereas Blur and Blur More give you no control over the extent of the softening effect, Soften enables you to specify just how fuzzy you want that image to look. When you choose the Blur⇨Soften command,

PhotoDeluxe displays a dialog box that includes a Radius control. Raise the Radius value to increase the blur. Be sure to check the Preview check box so that you can preview the results of your changes in the image window.

The remaining blur filters send your pixels on a bit of a wild ride, adding a feeling of motion to the blur. The next two sections fill you in on the details.

Blur⇨Circular

This command spins your pixels in a circular direction. As an example, see Figures 12-1 and 12-2. Figure 12-1 shows my original image of a china elephant. In Figure 12-2, I selected the background and applied the Circular command, creating the "world-spinning-out-of-control" effect. You have no doubt seen this effect a zillion times in old movies and cartoons.

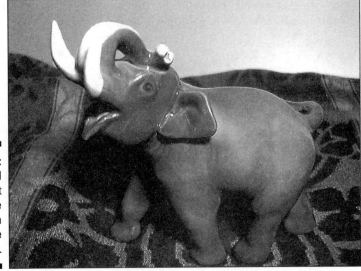

Figure 12-1:
My original elephant image seems a little ordinary.

Choosing the Blur⇨Circular command displays the dialog box shown in Figure 12-3. The Circular filter is really quite sophisticated, and the options aren't very self-explanatory — which is a good thing, or you wouldn't need me.

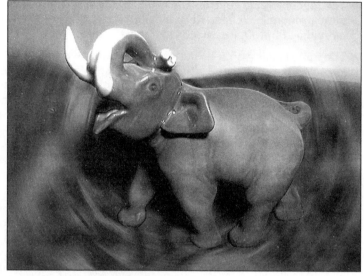

Figure 12-2:
Applying a circular blur to the background sends this pachyderm's world spinning.

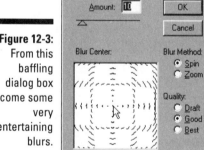

Figure 12-3:
From this baffling dialog box come some very entertaining blurs.

Here's what the various controls do:

- ✔ The Blur Method options determine the direction of the blur. With Spin, the blur appears to rotate around a central point, as in Figure 12-2. With Zoom, the direction of the blur is from the edge of the image inward, making the image appear to be rushing outward. Imagine looking through a camera viewfinder as you zoom in on a subject, and you have the idea behind the Zoom option.

- ✔ By default, the blur occurs from the exact center of your image or selection (if you select a portion of your image, the filter affects the selection only). But you can relocate the origin of the blur by dragging the center point inside the Blur Center box. (The cursor is pointing to the center spot in Figure 12-3.) Or click at any spot inside the Blur Center box to move the center point to that position.

✔ The Amount value controls the extent of the blur. Raise the value for a more pronounced effect. Keep in mind that the higher the value, the more time PhotoDeluxe needs to apply the filter.

✔ The three Quality options determine how well and how quickly PhotoDeluxe applies the filter. If you choose Best, PhotoDeluxe applies the highest quality blur, giving you a smoother result than the Draft or Good option. But the Best option also takes more time to complete than Draft, which gives you the least-smooth blur, or Good, which gives you middle-of-the-road blur quality.

Blur⇨Motion

Whereas the Circular blur filter sends pixels spinning, the Motion blur filter moves them along a straight line. This filter can add a sense of movement to your image, as in Figure 12-4. Again, I blurred just the background in the image. The elephant now appears to be racing across a textile savanna. Or maybe holding on for dear life as someone attempts to pull the rug out from under him.

In any case, you can create a similar effect by selecting the area you want to blur and choosing Effects⇨Blur⇨Motion. In response, PhotoDeluxe whips out the Motion Blur dialog box, shown in Figure 12-5. Set the direction of the blur by clicking on the circle next to the Angle option box, as shown in the figure. Or just enter a value in the option box (0 or 180 gives you a perfectly horizontal blur). The Distance value determines the extent of the blur; higher values create a more dramatic effect.

Figure 12-4:
Applying the Motion blur filter to the background creates a sense of movement.

Figure 12-5: Adjust the direction and extent of the motion blur here.

Filtering with a Purpose

Although special-effects filters are mostly for fun — distorting your least-favorite coworker's face, for example — you can also use them for a more serious intent: producing interesting backgrounds for photo collages or simple photographic subjects. In Color Plate 12-5, you can see three such backgrounds that I created from an ordinary field-of-flowers image (top-left). Here's how I created each background:

✔ To produce the top-right image, I applied the Effects⇔Distort⇔Funnel filter to the original image with the Rectangular to Polar option selected. You can find out more about the Funnel filter and other Distort filters in the next chapter.

✔ To create the bottom-left image, I applied the Effects⇔Sketch⇔Bas Relief filter to the top-right image. I set the Detail value to 13, the Smoothness value to 3, and the Light Direction value to Bottom. Because the Bas Relief filter colors your image with the current Foreground and Background colors, I selected sky blue as my Foreground color and pale yellow as the Background color before applying the filter.

✔ Taking things a few steps farther, I distorted the bottom-left image by using the Effects⇔Distort⇔Shear filter. (Chapter 14 describes this filter in detail.) Then I chose the Effects⇔Negative command to invert all colors in the image.

By applying filter on top of filter, you can create an unlimited variety of effects. So spend some time playing around to see what develops. To add even more possibilities to your repertoire, apply your special-effects filters on a separate layer from the rest of the image and then blend the effects layer with the image layer, using the blend modes discussed in Chapter 9.

Putting Your Picture in a Frame

After you finish editing your image, you may want to give it a snazzy frame to help set the right tone for the picture. All versions of PhotoDeluxe include frame templates that you can apply to your image. To use the frames in Version 2 and 3, click the Cards & More button on the Guided Activities panel and then click the Frames & More option. Choose the Frames option and follow the on-screen prompts to select and apply a frame. In the Business Edition, click the Projects button, the Presentations tab, and then the Frames option. Regardless of what version you use, you must have the PhotoDeluxe CD-ROM in your CD drive to access the frames.

In addition to the PhotoDeluxe frame templates, Version 3 includes a nifty plug-in called PhotoFrame, from Extensis. This program-within-a-program enables you to apply several cool framing effects to your image. For two examples, see Figure 12-6. The old-time effects are perfect for this old-time photograph, which captured my older sister and me performing some odd Christmas ritual that evidently required us to wear boys' t-shirts and bad pants. I'm a bit blurry because I'm doing a little holiday dance to entertain the relatives. But you just can't let a little blur stop you from taking the opportunity to embarrass your siblings when you get the chance, you know?

If you get a similar urge to decorate your family history — or any other photographs — choose Effects⇨Extensis⇨PhotoFrame to display the PhotoFrame dialog box, shown in Figure 12-7.

The PhotoFrame options work as follows:

✔ You can apply three separate framing filters — CameraEdge, WaterColor, and SoftCircle. The left image in Figure 12-6 illustrates the kind of frame possible with the CameraEdge filter, and the right image shows the WaterColor filter. The SoftCircle filter places your image in a feathered, circular frame much like the one shown in Figure 8-10, which was created with the PhotoDeluxe Feather command.

✔ You can apply all three frames at once or just select one or two. To apply a filter, click the Eyeball icon next to the effect name at the top of the dialog box. If the eyeball is visible, the frame is applied. Click the eyeball to turn off the frame.

✔ The WaterColor and SoftCircle frames can't be altered in design or placement. But if you choose the CameraEdge filter, you can vary the look of the frame by using the options on the Background and Border tabs. If you want to lift a color from your image to use as the frame color, click the Eyedropper button at the bottom of the dialog box and then click inside your image.

Figure 12-6:
Two framing effects created by the Extensis PhotoFrame plug-in in Version 3.

✔ You can also change the angle and layout of the CameraEdge frame by using the Orientation options found just above the tabs. To change the angle of the frame, drag the little ball around the Orientation circle (labeled in Figure 12-7). Or enter an angle of rotation in the Orientation option box.

✔ Additionally, you can adjust the placement of the CameraEdge frame with respect to your image by using the Move tool. Click the Move tool icon and move your cursor inside the preview area. A selection outline with four square handles appears around the frame. Drag inside the outline to move the frame. Drag the square handles to change the size and shape of the frame.

✔ After you make an adjustment, click the Undo button if you don't like the results. Click the Reset button to change all the dialog box settings back to the way they were when you first opened the dialog box.

✔ Use the controls beneath the preview area to zoom in on your image. The Zoom buttons, the Zoom tool, and the Hand tool all work just as they do in the standard PhotoDeluxe window. Click with the Zoom tool to zoom in; Alt+click to zoom out. Drag with the Hand tool to pull a hidden portion of the image into view.

✔ If you create an effect that you really like, click the Save button and save your settings. You're asked to give your settings a name; type in the name and click OK. To use those same settings again later, just select the name from the Settings pop-up menu.

Drag to adjust frame angle

✔ When you're ready to place the frame on the image for good, click the Apply button.

✔ The SoftCircle effect applies the feathered frame around the center of the image (or the selected area, if you draw a selection outline before you choose the PhotoFrame command). Unfortunately, you can't move the frame from this position, which means that sometimes the frame may hide a portion of your image that you prefer to show.

But if you apply the frame to a separate layer in your image, you can get around this problem. Before choosing the PhotoFrame command, create a new layer as explained in Chapter 10. Press Ctrl+A to select the entire layer and then choose the PhotoFrame command. After you apply the frame, drag the layer with the Object Selection tool to reposition it.

✔ As a matter of fact, applying your frame to a separate layer is always a good idea, no matter which framing effect you choose. Then if you decide later that you want to remove the frame, you can simply trash the layer.

Chapter 13

Projects for a Rainy Day

· ·

In This Chapter

▶ Creating a custom screen saver

▶ Pasting up some new digital wallpaper

▶ Adding your picture to stationery

▶ Inserting images into a spreadsheet, multimedia presentation, or word processor document

▶ Sending an image via e-mail

▶ Stitching images together to create a panoramic image

▶ Slapping your mug on everything but the kitchen sink

▶ Morphing Version 3 clip art

· ·

*A*fter hours of sweat-inducing labor, you sit back to survey the absolutely magnificent image you created. Now what? Well, you could do the obvious: Print out three dozen copies and pass them out to every unsuspecting friend and family member you can find. But frankly, in this age of digital media, plain-paper printouts are just a tad dull. For some really fun and a few practical ways to use that image, browse through the project ideas in this chapter.

Staring at Your Face in the Monitor

Back in the good old days of computing, when only the wealthy few had personal computers, leaving the same data displayed on the computer monitor for a long time resulted in a condition known as "burn-in." Burn-in left a faint representation of the data display on the monitor, serving as a ghostly reminder of your computing past.

This phenomenon led to the creation of the screen saver, a program that displays random images or text during times when the computer is inactive — or rather, when the computer operator is inactive. By continually changing the on-screen image, the screen saver prevents burn-in from ruining the monitor.

With today's monitors, you really don't have to worry about burn-in. But over the years, so many fun and entertaining screen savers have been designed that people like to use them anyway. After all, when you're daydreaming instead of working, wouldn't you rather watch a really cool screen saver than stare at the half-completed project on-screen?

With PhotoDeluxe, you can do the computer geeks in your office one better by designing a custom screen saver using your own images. The following steps show you how.

Sadly, this function is provided in the Windows versions of PhotoDeluxe only.

1. **Open the first image that you want to include in the screen saver.**

2. **Choose File➪Send To➪Screen Saver.**

   In Version 3, choose File➪Export➪Screen Saver instead.

   PhotoDeluxe hems and haws a little and then creates a copy of the image. The copy is saved in a file format appropriate for use as a screen saver.

   After the copy is made, the EasyPhoto image browser opens, and a thumbnail of your screen saver image appears on a new browser tab, appropriately named Screen Saver.

3. **Add the rest of your images.**

   Just keep repeating Steps 1 and 2 until you have all the images you want. To remove an image from the screen saver, just click its thumbnail on the Screen Saver tab in the EasyPhoto browser and press Delete.

After you create your screen saver, you need to tell your operating system that you want to use the thing. Here's the drill:

1. **Choose Start➪Settings➪Control Panel and double-click the Display icon.**

   Or right-click an empty area in the Windows 95 desktop and choose Properties from the menu that appears. Either way, the Display Properties dialog box opens.

2. **Click the Screen Saver tab.**

3. **Choose EasyPhoto Slide Show from the Screen Saver list of screen saver options.**

4. **Click the Settings button.**

   A tiny dialog box opens, containing one option. If you want the screen saver to display the image caption along with the image, check the Show Captions check box. (You can find out how to add captions to

EasyPhoto thumbnails in Chapter 4, in the section "Adding captions and viewing information.") Click OK after you make your choice.

5. **Click the Preview button.**

   Windows shows you how the screen saver will look.

6. **Set the delay time.**

   Tell Windows how many minutes you want the computer to be idle before the screen saver appears by entering a value in the Wait option box.

7. **Add a password (if you dare).**

   If you work in an office full of snoops, you can attach a password to your screen saver. That way, nobody but you can turn off the screen saver and poke about in your computer files. To add the password, check the Password Protected box and then click the Change button. Enter the password that you want to use in the top option box and then confirm the password by typing it again in the bottom option box.

   Don't forget that password, or *you* won't be able to get back into your computer files, either!

8. **Click OK.**

Hanging New Computer Wallpaper

Tired of looking at the same old background on your computer desktop? You can create a custom background featuring your favorite digital image, as shown in Figure 13-1.

In computereze, the background is known as *wallpaper,* if you must know.

The process for changing wallpaper is different for Windows and Mac systems. But on either system, you may want to do a little preparatory work on your image before turning it into wallpaper. If you want the image to fill the entire screen, use the Size⇨Photo Size command to make the image size match that of your monitor. For example, if your monitor is set to display 640 x 480 pixels, size your image to 640 x 480 pixels. Use the Pixels option as your unit of measurement inside the Photo Size dialog box to resize your image. (Make a backup copy of the original image before you create the wallpaper version, because you'll probably dump pixels in the process of sizing the image. See Chapter 3 for more information on the Photo Size command and sizing images for the screen.)

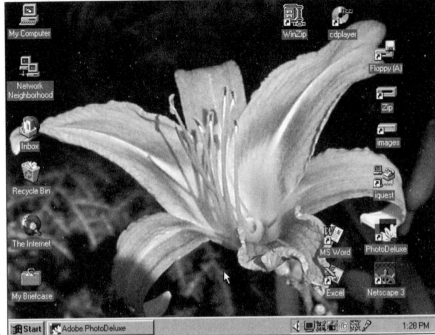

Figure 13-1:
Replace
your boring
desktop
wallpaper
with a
favorite
image.

Putting up Windows wallpaper

After you prepare your image, follow these redecorating steps in Windows:

1. **Open your image.**

2. **Choose File⇨Send To⇨Wallpaper.**

   Or, if you're a Version 3 user, choose File⇨Export⇨Windows Wallpaper.

   PhotoDeluxe makes a copy of your image and saves the copy in the BMP file format, which is the right format to use for on-screen resources in Windows. The file is called PhotoDeluxe and is stored in the main Windows folder with the regular Windows wallpaper files. PhotoDeluxe automatically selects the new file as your system wallpaper.

You can control whether your wallpaper displays just one image or repeats the same image several times across the screen. Here's how:

1. **Right-click an empty area on the Windows desktop.**

2. **Choose Properties from the menu that appeared when you right-clicked.**

   The Display Properties dialog box appears.

3. **Click the Background tab.**

4. Choose Tile or Center.

The Tile option repeats your image as many times as necessary in order to fill the screen. The Center option displays the image once, in the center of the screen.

5. Click OK.

PhotoDeluxe can store only one image as wallpaper at a time. If you want to change the wallpaper image, open the new image and choose the Wallpaper command again from the File↪Send to or File↪Export menu. PhotoDeluxe asks whether you want to replace the existing wallpaper image. Click OK to go ahead.

However, you can keep several images on hand to use as wallpaper by saving your image "manually" as a BMP file (see Chapter 4 for information on how to save in the BMP format). Then, to select an image for use as your wallpaper, head for the Background tab of the Display Properties dialog box, as covered in the preceding steps. Click the Browse button, track down the BMP image file you want to use, and click Open.

To switch back to the PhotoDeluxe-sponsored wallpaper — wallpaper created by using the File↪Send To↪Wallpaper command — choose the PhotoDeluxe option from the list of wallpaper options in the Display Properties dialog box.

Redecorating on a Mac

PhotoDeluxe doesn't offer an automatic command for converting an image into wallpaper on a Macintosh. But you can do the job yourself in a few simple steps.

If you're using System 7.5, you must start with a 128-x-128-pixel image, and you can only create wallpaper that repeats that tiny square image across the screen. If those limitations don't offend your design sensibilities too much, save the image in the PICT format (see Chapter 4 for details). Then take a dance across this floor:

1. Open the image.

2. Select the entire image by pressing ⌘+A.

3. Press ⌘+C to copy the image to the Clipboard.

4. Open the Desktop Patterns program.

I can't tell you exactly where to locate this program because I can't see how your Macintosh is set up from here. But you can probably find the program in the Control Panels folder. After you open the program, the Desktop Patterns dialog box appears.

5. Press ⌘+V to paste your picture into the dialog box.

6. Click the Set Desktop Pattern button.

System 8 users take a little different approach to wallpaper creation. You can use a JPEG or PICT image as wallpaper, and you can fill the entire screen with one image, if you want. To try out a new wallpaper, waltz through these easy-to-follow steps:

1. Open the Desktop Patterns program.

Normally, you access the program via the Control Panels item on the Apple menu, but your system may be set up differently. After you launch the program, you see the dialog box shown in Figure 13-2.

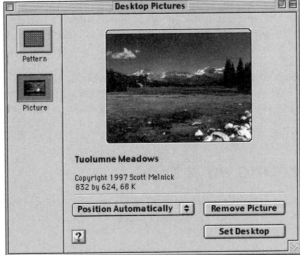

Figure 13-2:
The OS 8 Desktop Patterns dialog box enables you to create a custom wallpaper.

2. Click the Picture icon and then click Remove Picture.

After you click, the Remove Picture button magically changes into the Select Picture button.

3. Click the Select Picture button and choose your image.

When you click the Select Picture button, a dialog box appears. Select the image that you want to use as wallpaper and then click Open.

4. Set the display option.

The pop-up menu at the bottom of the dialog box offers several options for the wallpaper display. Fill Screen covers the entire screen with your image. Scale to Screen enlarges or reduces the image so that it fits in its entirety on the screen, just in case you didn't bother to make that size adjustment before you started. Center on Screen positions your image in the center of the screen. Tile on Screen repeats the image as many times as needed to cover the entire screen. And if you choose Position Automatically, the Desktop Patterns program either scales the image or fills the image with the picture, depending on the image size.

5. **Click the Set Desktop button to paste the wallpaper onto the screen.**

Putting Your Face on a Letter

One of the many projects you can do using the PhotoDeluxe Guided Activities is to create personalized stationery that includes an image. You may want to add your face or a picture of your company's product to your stationery, for example.

The Guided Activities are fairly easy to follow, but many may leave you with a few questions along the way. So I'm including this example to clear up a few issues that arise when you're using the Guided Activities. The following steps give you a general idea behind most of the Guided Activities.

Before you begin, do any cropping, color correcting, or other necessary editing to your image. Save the image and then step this way (you can either have your image open or not):

1. **Click the Cards & More button on the Guided Activities panel.**

   In the Business Edition, click the Projects button instead.

2. **Track down the Stationery activity.**

   In Version 2, click the Pages tab and click the Stationery icon. In Version 3, click the Pages & Certificates icon and choose Stationery from the drop-down menu. And in the Business Edition, click the Forms tab and then the Letterhead icon. (In the stuffy business world, *stationery* is called *letterhead,* you know.)

3. **Click the Choose Stationery tab.**

   In the Business Edition, click the Choose Letterhead tab instead.

   At this point, PhotoDeluxe may prompt you to edit your image, if you so desire, before you start using the Guided Activities. If you're using the Business Edition or Version 2, the prompts come in the form of Clue Cards; in Version 3, the Assistant Drawer slides out with the hint.

   Clue Cards and the Assistant Drawer tips pop up throughout the Guided Activities process, but this is the only one I'll mention. To find out more about the Clue Cards and the Assistant Drawer — including how to prevent them from interrupting your progress — meander back to Chapter 2.

   If your image is open and you're using either Version 2 or the Business Edition, PhotoDeluxe displays the Hold Photo window and asks you to store your image in the Hold Photo area. Give the image a name and click OK. (For more about Hold Photo, see Chapter 1.) A thumbnail of the image is placed in the Hold Photo area on the left side of the PhotoDeluxe window, and the image window itself is put away.

In Version 3, your image window closes and a thumbnail of the image appears in the Open Photos area on the left side of the program window.

4. **Click the Choose Stationery icon on the Choose Stationery tab.**

An EasyPhoto browser window appears showing thumbnails of all the stationery designs you can use.

5. **After you find a design you like, drag it into the image-editing window.**

At this point, PhotoDeluxe may ask you to insert the PhotoDeluxe CD-ROM into your CD-ROM drive. Do as you're told and then click OK. (If you have your CD-ROM player's autoplay feature enabled, the PhotoDeluxe installation program may take over your screen after you put the CD in the drive. Click the Close button in the installation program to get rid of the intrusion.)

After much buzzing and spinning, PhotoDeluxe opens the stationery image in a standard image window, as shown in Figure 13-3. This image is actually a template that you can customize by adding your own text and photo.

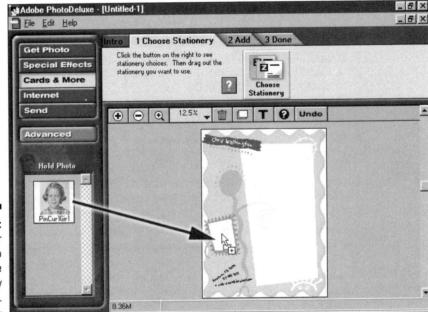

Figure 13-3:
Drag your image onto the Stationery template.

6. Click the Add tab in the Guided Activities area.

PhotoDeluxe displays the same tab that you see if you use the Guided Activities to open an image. You can use the icons to open your image or use the standard image-opening procedures offered up in Chapter 1 (File⇨Open and so forth).

If the image that you want to use is in the Hold Photo or Open Photo area, simply drag the thumbnail onto the card, as illustrated in Figure 13-3.

PhotoDeluxe automatically formats and sizes your image to match the layout of the stationery. The image is then pasted into the card on a separate layer, just like any other selection you paste (see Chapter 8 for more information).

7. Size and position the image as needed.

Use the Object Selection tool and the techniques discussed in Chapter 8 to size and position the image.

8. Click Done.

You're not really done — you still have to edit the text, as covered in the next several steps.

In Version 3, an Edit Photo tab appears between the Add tab and the Done tab. But if you click it, you see that this tab simply tells you to click the Done tab if you want to edit your image. So go ahead and feel free to ignore the Edit Photo tab altogether.

9. Choose View⇨Show Layers.

Your image likely contains several layers, which you can inspect in the Layers palette as discussed in Chapter 10. The top Text layer contains the prefab text provided on the template; another layer holds the artwork, and one or more additional layers are provided for photos.

10. Edit the text.

To edit a block of text, double-click it with the Object Selection tool, which opens the Text Tool dialog box. You can then replace the text, change the font, or otherwise modify the text, as discussed in Chapter 11. To add new text, click the Text tool icon in the image window or press Ctrl+T (⌘+T on the Mac) and create your text just as you normally do.

To resize, rotate, or move text, click it with the Object Selection tool and then drag the selection handles, as described in Chapter 8 in the section "The Object Selection tool."

11. Delete any extra Photo layers.

Some templates include several different layers for photos. You see the word *Photo* anywhere the design calls for you to add a photo to the card. After you add your image, the *Photo* usually disappears. But check the Layers palette to make sure that you don't have any stray Photo layers that contain the word *Photo* rather than an image.

To do this, Alt+click the Eyeball icon next to any Photo layer in the Layers palette. (Alt+clicking hides every layer but the layer you click.) If the layer is empty except for the *Photo* placeholder text, drag the layer name to the Trash icon in the Layers palette to delete the layer. No sense having extra layers in your image — they just increase the file size. Keep Alt+clicking on the Photo layers until you inspect each one. To bring all layers back into view, Alt+click again on the last Eyeball icon you clicked.

If you change your mind and want to add an additional photo, just do so as you normally add photos to an image. See "Moving and Copying Selected Pixels" in Chapter 8 for details.

12. Click the Done tab.

Your click closes the Guided Activity.

13. Save the image.

If you want to preserve the separate layers of the stationery, save the card in the PDD or PSD (Photoshop) file format. You can read more about saving images and the PDD and PSD formats in Chapter 4. Be sure to click the Done tab — that is, take Step 12 — before you save, or your layers are merged together during the save process.

Note that the special text technique described in Chapter 11 works for images created with the Guided Activities. If you save the project to the PSD format, all the text on the Text layer is sent to a new, fully editable layer, enabling you to later create special text effects. But you must be sure to click the Done tab to close the Guided Activities before you save to the PSD format. Otherwise, your text, artwork, and photo are merged into a single layer when you open the PSD file.

You can't delete the Artwork layer or edit the components on the layer. But if you just want to use the layout of the template and not the artwork, here's a workaround. In the Layers palette, click the Eyeball icon next to the Artwork layer to hide the layer. Then save the image in any format other than the PDD or PSD format. Other formats merge all layers together, and only visible layers are saved with the image file. Close the on-screen version of the stationery and then open the image you just saved. No more artwork!

Importing Images into Other Documents

Adding an image to a spreadsheet, word processor document, multimedia presentation, or any other document is a fairly easy process. Figure 13-4 shows an Excel spreadsheet that I created to track inventory for a little antiques business that I run when I'm not chained to my computer. If the spreadsheet contained only the text descriptions, remembering what each item looks like would be a test of my own mental RAM. The images make it easy to find a particular item when I'm checking inventory. So whenever I purchase an item, I snap a quick picture with a digital camera and then add the photo to the spreadsheet along with the pertinent purchase information.

The following steps give you a generic instruction for adding images to an Excel spreadsheet. The process should be nearly identical for almost any other spreadsheet, word processor, multimedia, or Web page-creation program:

1. **Prepare your image.**

   Do all your retouching and resizing in PhotoDeluxe.

2. **Save the image in a file format that can be recognized by the other program.**

   In Excel, you can use TIFF, GIF, or JPEG formats, among others. Most programs can work with these same file formats, but to find out specifically what format your program recommends, check the program's help system. Look for information regarding importing files or adding graphics. See Chapter 4 for additional background on file formats.

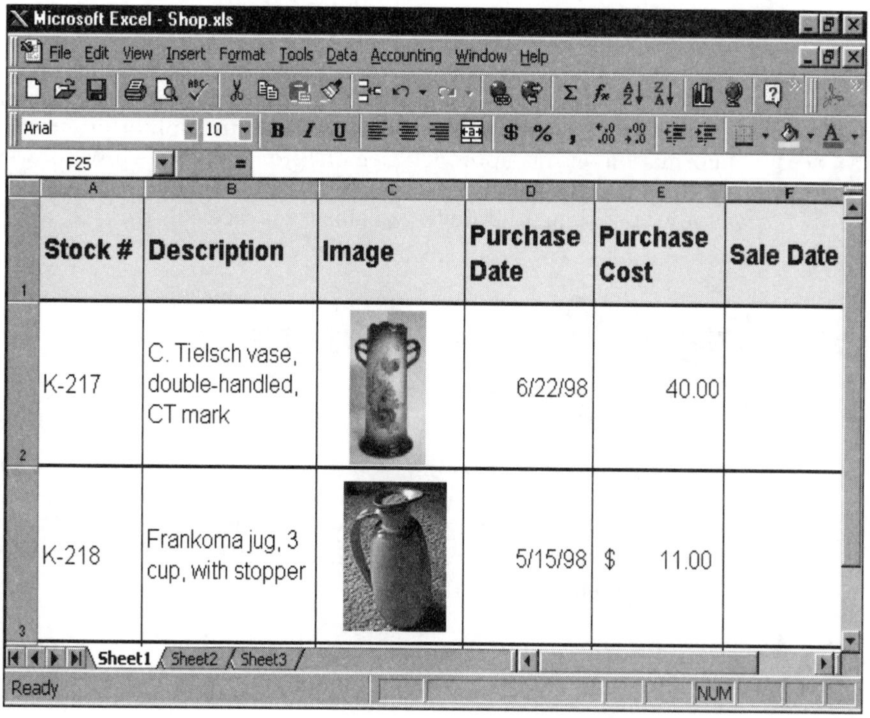
Microsoft Excel - Shop.xls
File Edit View Insert Format Tools Data Accounting Window Help
Arial
10
F25
Stock #
Description
Image
Purchase Date
Purchase Cost
Sale Date
K-217
C. Tielsch vase, double-handled, CT mark
6/22/98
40.00
K-218
Frankoma jug, 3 cup, with stopper
5/15/98
$ 11.00
Sheet1
Sheet2
Sheet3
Ready
NUM

Figure 13-4: Images are a helpful addition to an inventory spreadsheet.

Some programs have trouble reading TIFF files that have been saved using LZW compression, as well as JPEG files that have been saved using the Progressive option. If you experience difficulty opening the file inside the other program, try resaving the image with these options turned off.

3. **Open the document to which you want to add the image.**

4. **Choose the program's import command.**

This command varies from program to program, so check the Help system for information about importing files or adding graphics. In Excel as well as Microsoft Word, the command is Insert⇨Picture⇨From File.

After you choose the command, an Import dialog box opens (or, in programs other than Excel, a dialog box with a similar name). Locate the image file that you want to add and click the Insert button, which may be named Open or Import or something like that in other programs.

5. **Position your image.**

The image is pasted into the document and surrounded by black resize handles that work much like those in PhotoDeluxe. You can move the image and also resize it. Again, check the Help system for specifics related to your program. But be careful about resizing too much, because doing so can degrade the image quality.

You can also usually use the standard Cut, Copy, and Paste commands to copy or move an image from PhotoDeluxe into another program. For more information on this approach, see Chapter 8. If you're a Windows 95 user, you may be able to use the drag-and-drop method of copying images to another program. Chapter 8 explains the process.

Sending a Picture with an E-Mail Message

If you have an e-mail account, you can attach your image to an e-mail message and send your photo to folks all over the world in seconds. The process varies depending on what e-mail software you're using, so check the online help system to find out the exact commands that you need to use to attach an image.

Version 2 and the Business Edition include a wizard for adding an image to an e-mail message, but it's designed to work with Windows Messaging and also requires a bit of system configuring to set up. More importantly, the wizard sends the image file in the PhotoDeluxe native file format, which means that your recipient needs PhotoDeluxe to open the image.

For these reasons, I recommend that you prepare and send your image without using the wizard, as follows:

1. **Size your image for screen display.**

   See the instructions in Chapter 3 if you need help. Remember, the size at which the image displays is determined by the resolution of the viewer's monitor. You need to either size your image using Pixels as the unit of measurement or, if you prefer to use a traditional unit of measurement, set the image resolution in the 72-to-96-ppi range with the File Size check box turned *off*.

   Remember to make a backup copy of your original image before you resample it for on-screen use! Again, see Chapter 3 for the complete story.

   If you need to send someone an image file for a use that requires high-resolution images, don't take this step. Keep in mind that large images take a long time to download; you may want to consider putting that file on a disk and sending it in the mail or via overnight courier instead.

2. **Save the image in JPEG format.**

   JPEG is the most widely recognized format for e-mail image transfer. But if the person who receives your e-mail has trouble with the image, try resending it in the GIF format instead. (You can find out more about saving images in Chapter 4.)

   Again, however, if the person receiving the image has requested another format, don't take this step. The person's browser can still download the file, although it may not be able to display the image on-screen in the browser window.

3. **Compose your e-mail message.**

   Fire up your e-mail software and write a witty aside to go along with that image.

4. **Attach the image file.**

   Again, the specific procedure varies depending on whether you're using Internet Explorer, Netscape Communicator, or some other e-mail program. Check the Help system for your specific program to locate the exact commands that you need.

5. **Send the message.**

   Your image file is appended to the e-mail message and shoots down the wire with your text when you send the message.

Several software companies offer a jazzier approach to e-mailing images: You can create and send digital "postcards" that have your image on one side and a text message on the other. Check out the postcard option at the Kodak Web site, www.kodak.com, for an example. Another fun choice is NetCard, a postcard program from PictureWorks (www.pictureworks.com). Using this program, you can even add an audio message to your postcard.

Stitching Together a Panorama

You know how some cameras enable you to shoot a panoramic picture — an image that's much wider than a standard snapshot? Well, using an *image stitching program*, you can combine two or more photos to create a panoramic digital image. And — bonus time — with a digital panorama, you can make your panorama as wide as you want; you're not limited to a set size as you are with a film camera.

On the CD accompanying this book, you can find a full working version of a terrific stitching program, Spin Panorama from PictureWorks. Yep, you read me right — PictureWorks is providing this software to you on the CD at no charge. In return for this generous gift, be sure to visit the PictureWorks Web site at www.pictureworks.com to find out about some other cool imaging tools the company offers.

Spin Panorama enables you to create both panoramic pictures and 360-degree QuickTime VR movies that you can view on a computer. Figure 13-5 shows three images of a city landscape that I stitched together to create the simple panorama in Figure 13-6. (These images are found in the sample image folder that comes with the Spin Panorama program.)

Figure 13-5:
These three images were the starting point for the panorama in Figure 13-6.

Figure 13-6:
Using Spin Panorama, from PictureWorks, I stitched the three images into this panoramic view.

You can include your panorama or movie in a presentation, use it on a Web site, include it in a printed document, or just impress the heck out of your friends. When people display the image on a computer monitor, they can scroll around the image to see different portions of the scene.

Spin Panorama is remarkably easy to use, but not so simple that I can give you all the details here. After installing the program, read the online help instructions for using the software, and you can expect to be up and running in no time. Make sure that you read the information about shooting your original panoramic images, because the program's ability to create good panoramas depends on your ability to give it the right pictures to work with.

Version 3 and the Business Edition offer a built-in stitching utility that you may want to investigate as well. The Panorama Guided Activity, which is actually a limited version of SmoothMove PhotoStitcher program from Infinite Pictures, enables you to stitch as many as three pictures together. To check out the process in Version 3, click the Get & Fix Photo button on the Activities panel, click the Special Effects icon, click the Collage option on the drop-down menu, and choose the Panorama option. In the Business Edition, click the Special Effects button, click the Collage tab, and click the Panorama icon. Work your way through the tabs in the Guided Activity panel to complete the panorama.

The complete version of SmoothMove is included on the PhotoDeluxe CD, but you can't access all the features unless you pay for the full version ($24.95), at which point you're given a code to unlock the program. After you unlock SmoothMove, you can stitch an unlimited number of photos together and create 360-degree panoramas. For more information, go to the following Web site: www.smoothmove.com/adobe.html.

Pasting Clip Art into Your Image

All three versions of PhotoDeluxe include clip art — little drawings that you can add to your photos. Here's how to add a piece of clip art to your image:

1. **Open the image that you want to decorate.**

2. **Put the PhotoDeluxe CD-ROM in your CD drive.**

   (If you have autoplay enabled and the installation window takes over your screen, just click the window Close button to get rid of it.)

3. **Choose File⇨Open Special⇨Clip Art.**

   The EasyPhoto browser appears, displaying thumbnails of the available clip art.

4. **Drag the thumbnail for the art that you want to use into the image window.**

   The clip art is added on its own layer. You can resize, move, and rotate the clip art using the Object Selection tool, just as you do with any layer or a text block. See Chapter 8 for details on using the Object Selection tool.

   Because the clip art resides on a layer, you can also adjust the opacity of the art and blend it with the underlying image using the various layer blend modes. For more about using layers, book a flight to Chapter 10.

Version 3 includes a special, morphable brand of clip art called Changeables. You can adjust the shape, design, and color of the clip art objects before you add them to your photos. To access this special clip art — it's very cool, by the way — choose File⇨Open Special⇨Changeables. An EasyPhoto browser window displays thumbnails of the changeable art.

To add a changeable object to your image, drag the thumbnail into the image window. Either way, the Changeable window appears. The dialog box includes several controls for varying the look of the object; the exact options differ depending upon the specific piece of art. Play around with the controls to see what's possible. When you're happy with the object, click OK. Like regular clip art, the changeable clip art is added to its own layer, so you can resize, reshape, and otherwise manipulate the art just as you do any layer object.

If you want to open a piece of clip art — changeable or not — in its own image window, double-click the thumbnail in the EasyPhoto browser. Or drag the thumbnail to an empty part of the image-editing area (not into an open image window). PhotoDeluxe then places the clip art in a new image window.

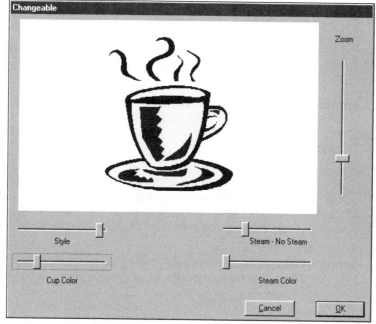

Figure 13-7:
Version 3
includes
morphable
clip art to
add to your
images.

Creating T-Shirts, Mugs, and More

With more and more consumers getting into digital imaging, more and more companies are offering products you can use to display your digital artwork. Here are just some of the ways you can show off your creative genius:

✔ Kodak, Epson, Hewlett-Packard, and others offer special paper stock for creating greeting cards, business cards, postcards, and other print media. You can buy kits of paper specially designed for use in today's color inkjet printers at local office supply and electronics stores.

✔ Put your favorite image on a coffee mug using special accessory kits available for certain inkjet and dye-sub printers. The Fargo Foto-FUN! dye-sub printer is one model that offers mug kits. You print your image, clamp it onto the mug included in the kit, and bake the mug in the oven to transfer the image.

✔ You can also transfer an image to a T-shirt or other piece of clothing. After creating your image, you print it on special transfer paper and then iron the image onto the shirt.

✔ Several software programs enable you to turn your image into an on-screen jigsaw puzzle. You open your image, specify how many pieces you want in your puzzle, and the program "cuts" the image into that many pieces. You can then use your mouse to "work" the puzzle on-screen. *Warning:* These programs are every bit as addictive as working traditional jigsaw puzzles!

Windows users can try out one jigsaw program, BrainsBreaker, by installing the demo included on the CD at the back of this book. Mac users can also get in on the puzzle fun by installing the Jigsaw Deluxe demo on the CD.

✔ You can print your image on small peel-and-paste stickers. The stickers are great for creating instant name badges, for example, or for marking kids' books and other belongings. A few printer models are designed expressly to create these stickers, but you can also print them on standard inkjets using sticker paper available from Kodak, Alps, and other manufacturers.

✔ If you're using Version 3, be sure to check out the PhotoParade Guided Activity. This Guided Activity walks you through the steps of creating a multimedia show featuring your images. To send your images to the parade, click the Cards & More button on the Guided Activities panel and then click the PhotoParade icon. Follow the on-screen instructions that appear when you click each tab in the Guided Activities area.

✔ Finally, you can create calendars, sports cards, and all sorts of other fun printed pieces using the Guided Activities in PhotoDeluxe. Be sure to investigate the Guided Activities to see what fun stuff you can create.

If you don't want to invest in special printer media, don't have a good printer, or need to create a large quantity of customized pieces, you can have your creations printed at a commercial printer or at a quick-printshop such as Kinko's. You can even find companies offering these printing services by mail or the Internet, so you may be able to get the job done without ever leaving home. (See Chapter 17 for a few leads.) Is this a great world or what?

Part IV
The Part of Tens

The 5th Wave — By Rich Tennant

"Look, I've already launched a search for 'reanimated babe cadavers' three times and nothing came up!"

In this part . . .

This part of the book is like a strong blast of information espresso. Containing scads of hints, tips, and suggestions that you can digest in mere moments, the chapters in this part give you a quick jolt that leaves you refreshed, awakened, and heady with newfound knowledge.

You not only find the answers to the most frequently asked questions about PhotoDeluxe, but you also get a run-down of PhotoDeluxe keyboard shortcuts, a look at ten great distortion filters, and a list of online sites that offer still more tidbits of digital imaging information. I've condensed everything so that even the quickest swig of text can have a big impact on your image-editing prowess.

In fact, this part is the perfect pick-me-up if you find yourself nodding off during your next office meeting. While your boss drones on about some meaningless subject, you can sneak glances at these pages (being careful to look up periodically and nod in thoughtful agreement, of course). Before that meeting is done, you can soak up a bunch of great information without anyone being the wiser — but you.

Chapter 14

Ten Ways to Wreak Havoc on an Image

*M*any chapters in this book show you how to make subtle improvements to your images — to enhance, rather than alter, the original scene. But in this chapter, you're invited to toss reality to the wind and explore some of the more entertaining special effects in the PhotoDeluxe bag of tricks.

This chapter introduces you to the seven filters on the Effects⇨Distort submenu and their counterparts on the Size menu, all of which enable you to bend, stretch, warp, and otherwise distort your image. Applied with a light touch, these filters are the perfect partner in crime when you want to make a despised coworker or neighbor look silly — not that I'm advocating such treachery, of course. Taken to their extreme, the filters remove any semblance of the original photograph and lead to some interesting pixel productions.

Throughout this chapter, I use the highly decorated specimen shown in Figure 14-1 as a subject. This same fellow gets an application of the Smudge tool back in Chapter 9, and I suppose I should pick on some other poor creature for this chapter. But given that face and those feathers, this bird surely takes some ridicule from the rest of the animal kingdom already, so what harm could a little more digital foolishness do?

Figure 14-1:
A well-decorated bird agrees to be distorted in the name of art throughout this chapter.

Effects⇨Distort⇨Funnel

For complete obliteration of your image, you can't top the Funnel filter. According to the PhotoDeluxe online help information, you can use this filter to make your image appear as if it were either reflected in a curved mirror or wrapped around the inside of a funnel. Personally, I think this description is a little off, but I can't come up with anything better.

When you choose the Funnel filter, PhotoDeluxe displays a dialog box containing two options: Rectangular to Polar or Polar to Rectangular. Um . . . huh? What does that have to do with a funnel? Or a mirror, for that matter? Actually, nothing. You see, the folks at Adobe took the Funnel filter from their other image-editing product, Photoshop. In Photoshop, the filter is called the Polar Coordinates filter. The filter name was changed for PhotoDeluxe, but not the option names in the dialog box.

At any rate, if you select the Rectangular to Polar option, you get the image-going-down-a-funnel look that's shown in the image on the left in Figure 14-2. If you select Polar to Rectangular, you get the gooey mess shown in the right-hand image.

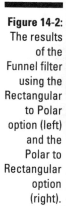

Figure 14-2:
The results
of the
Funnel filter
using the
Rectangular
to Polar
option (left)
and the
Polar to
Rectangular
option
(right).

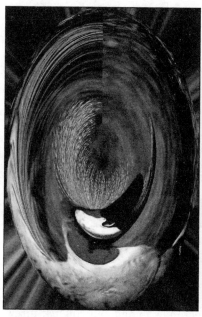 

Efffects⇨Distort⇨Pinch

If you want to make someone look really goofy, give the Pinch filter a go. Using this filter, you can pinch your image inward, as I did in the left-hand image of Figure 14-3, or outward, as in the right-hand image.

When you select the filter, PhotoDeluxe displays a dialog box containing a single option, Amount. If you use a positive Amount value, you pinch inward, creating that shrunken-head look in the image on the left in Figure 14-3. Enter a negative Amount value to pinch outward, which gives you the simulated fish-eye lens effect in the right-hand image.

For a variation on the theme, select just a portion of your image before you apply the filter. The selection gets pinched while the rest of the image looks normal.

Figure 14-3:
I applied the Pinch filter with a positive Amount value (left) and a negative Amount value (right).

Effects⇨Distort⇨Pond⇨Ripple

The Pond Ripple filter does pretty much what the name implies: creates the illusion that your image is reflected in a pond and you just threw a stone into the water. Figure 14-4 shows two examples of different applications of this filter; Figure 14-5 shows the Pond Ripples dialog box that appears when you choose the filter.

Using the three options in the dialog box, you can vary the effects of the filter, as follows:

- ✔ Enter a positive Amount value to create pond ripples that protrude above the surface of the image. Negative values invert the ripples.

- ✔ Adjust the Ridges value to control how many ripples are created. High values give you lots of sharp, tightly spaced ripples; low values produce softer, more watery-looking ripples.

- ✔ The Style options determine how your pixels are shifted around the image. Choose Pond Ripples to both move pixels outward from the center and rotate them around the center of the image — which, technical blather aside, creates your classic, stone-in-a-pond effect. I used this option with an Amount value of 100 and a Ridge value of 5 to create the left image in Figure 14-4.

Figure 14-4: I applied the Pond Ripples filter using the Pond Ripples option (left) and the Around Center option (right).

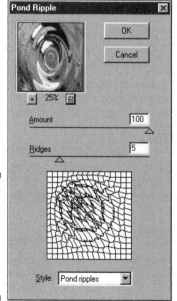

Figure 14-5: The settings used to create the effect in the left image in Figure 14-4.

Out From Center moves pixels outward but doesn't spin them around. I'm not sure what real-world analogy to apply to this effect, so just take a gander at the right image in Figure 14-4 to get the general idea. I used the same Amount and Ridge values as in the left image (100 and 5, respectively) but changed the Style option to Out From Center to create this effect.

Around Center rotates pixels in alternating directions around the center of the image but doesn't move them outward. The result is a ripple that has a zigzag look to it.

Effects⇨Distort⇨Ripple

For another watery effect, dive into the Ripple filter (yuk, yuk). This filter also gives your image an underwater appearance, but this time the water washes over the picture in parallel rather than in circular ripples.

The Ripple filter dialog box, which appears when you choose the Ripple command, contains two options. Raise the Amount value to change the magnitude or width of the waves. The Size value affects the length of the ripples. Choose the Small option to create more, shorter waves; choose Large for fewer, longer waves; choose Medium for something in-between.

Figure 14-6 shows the results of two different Ripple filter settings. To create the left image, I used an Amount value of 400 and selected Medium for the Size option. For the right image, I set the Size option to Small and cranked the Amount value all the way up to the maximum, 999. With this second set of values, the Ripple filter creates an effect more like textured glass than watery ripples.

Effects⇨Distort⇨Shear

If you want a little more control over how your image is distorted, choose Effects⇨Distort⇨Shear to access the Shear filter. Using this filter, you can distort your image according to a freeform curve of your own making, creating effects like the ones shown in Figure 14-7.

When you choose the Shear command, the dialog box shown in Figure 14-8 appears. You use the grid in the bottom-left corner of the dialog box to bend and twist your image. Initially, the grid contains a vertical line containing two control points. The top control point represents the top of your image, and the bottom point represents the bottom of your image.

Figure 14-6:
An underwater effect (left) and a textured-glass effect (right), both courtesy of the Ripple filter.

Figure 14-7:
An example of the Shear filter using the Wrap Around option (left) and the Repeat Edge Pixels option (right).

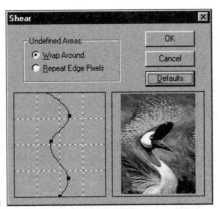

Figure 14-8:
Create a
custom
curve in the
Shear
dialog box
to distort
your image
at will.

To manipulate your image, do the following:

✔ Drag a control point to move the corresponding area of your image.

✔ Click anywhere on the line or in the grid to add new control points. PhotoDeluxe automatically redraws the line to accommodate the new control point. You can add as many control points as you want.

✔ To delete a control point, drag it out of the grid area.

✔ To get rid of all your custom control points, click the Defaults button. The original, two-point vertical line is restored, and your image appears as it did before you opened the Shear dialog box.

When you distort an image this way, gaps may appear along the edges of the image. The two options at the top of the dialog box determine how PhotoDeluxe fills in those gaps. If you choose the Wrap Around option, PhotoDeluxe fills the gaps on one side of the image with pixels that were shoved off the opposite side by the distortion, as in the left image in Figure 14-7. If you choose Repeat Edge Pixels, PhotoDeluxe simply repeats pixels from the edge of the selection as many times as necessary to fill the gap. The result is typically a striped effect, as shown in the right image of Figure 14-7.

Effects⇨Distort⇨Sphere

Figure 14-9 shows two examples of effects you can produce with the Sphere filter, which is a close cousin of the Pinch filter discussed earlier in this chapter.

Figure 14-9:
The result of applying the Sphere filter using the Normal mode (left) and the Vertical Only mode (right).

When you choose the Sphere command, PhotoDeluxe presents a dialog box containing a Mode option and an Amount option. The options work as follows:

✔ Select Sphere from the Mode pop-up menu to wrap your image around the inside or outside of a perfect sphere. Enter a positive Amount value to wrap the image around the outside of the sphere, as I did in the left-hand example in Figure 14-9; enter a negative value to wrap around the inside of the sphere. As you can see from the example in the figure, applying Sphere with a positive Amount value produces similar results to applying the Pinch filter with a negative value (see the right-hand image in Figure 14-3). Likewise, applying Sphere with a negative Amount value generates almost the same effect as applying Pinch with a positive Amount value (see the left-hand image in Figure 14-3). The difference is that the Sphere filter maps your pixels around a true sphere, whereas Pinch maps them on a sort of rounded cone.

✔ Note that the Sphere filter can distort only elliptical areas of an image. When you choose the command, PhotoDeluxe applies the distortion to the largest elliptical region within the bounds of your image or selection. The rest of the image is unaffected, which usually creates a distinct boundary between distorted and undistorted pixels. If you don't like that effect, use the Pinch filter instead of Sphere.

✔ Choose Vertical Only or Horizontal Only from the Mode menu to wrap your image on the inside or outside of a vertical or horizontal cylinder, respectively. Again, a positive Amount value puts your image on the outside of the cylinder, and a negative value puts the image on the inside of the cylinder. The right-side example in Figure 14-9 shows the results of selecting the Vertical Only option with an Amount value of –100.

Effects⇨Distort⇨Twirl

Not for those prone to motion sickness, the Twirl filter spins the center of the image around in circles while leaving the sides in place. Figure 14-10 offers two illustrations of the filter.

Figure 14-10: The Twirl filter applied at the maximum value of +999 (left) and a more modest –40 (right).

When you apply this filter, you can control the extent and direction of the twirling by adjusting the Angle value inside the Twirl dialog box. Enter a positive value to rotate pixels in a clockwise direction; enter a negative value to spin them counterclockwise.

You can enter values as high or low as +999 or –999. At these extreme values, you create a geometric spiral pattern that has little to do with your original image, as verified by the left example in Figure 14-10, where I used a value of +999. Use lower Angle values to create a more subtle twisting of your subject, as I did in the opposite example. An Angle value of −40 created just a slight counterclockwise rotation of the head and neck pixels.

If you want to create a spiral effect, experiment with applying the filter several times while using a moderate Angle value — in the 100 or 200 range, for example. You get a smoother spiral by applying the filter repeatedly at smaller values than by applying it once with a high value.

Size⇨Distort

If none of the filters on the Effects⇨Distort menu suits your fancy, check out the distortion options available on the Size menu: Distort, Perspective, and Free Resize.

Using the Distort command, you can skew your image as I did in Figure 14-11. After you choose the command, the image is surrounded by black resizing handles, just like the ones you use to resize a selection or image when using the Object Selection tool (see Chapter 8). But this time, you can drag the corner handles independently of each other, enabling you to skew the proportions of the image.

Figure 14-11:
Size⇨Distort
enables you
to skew your
image.

Here are a few rules to keep in mind as you're distorting:

- ✔ If you don't see the handles, zoom out on your image. When you're zoomed in tight on the image, the handles may be hidden from view.

- ✔ After you tug at a handle, PhotoDeluxe previews the effect for you in the image window. The preview can take several seconds to appear, so be patient. If you don't like the results, press Ctrl+Z (⌘+Z on a Mac) or click the Undo button. The handles reorient themselves to the positions that they held before your drag. You can drag as many times as you want, on as many corners as you want, until you get an effect that you like.

- ✔ To apply the transformation for good, click inside the selection outline or press Enter on a PC or Return on a Mac. To cancel out of the distortion anytime before applying it, press Esc.

- ✔ If you drag a handle off the canvas, a portion of your image disappears from view — you've stretched that area so that it no longer fits on the canvas. However, the pixels are still intact. To display them, use Size⇨Canvas Size to enlarge the canvas. Alternatively, you can move the image around on the canvas by using the Object Selection or Move tool after you apply the transformation. Just drag the image to reorient it on the canvas. Of course, when you move hidden portions of the image into view, other areas are shoved out of view.

- ✔ As long as you save the image in the native PhotoDeluxe format (PDD), any hidden pixels are retained. But if you save to another format, any pixels not on the canvas are clipped away.

- ✔ Keep in mind that resizing your image in this way can degrade your image quality. For best results, apply all your distortions in one pass.

- ✔ As with all special effects and most other commands in PhotoDeluxe, the command affects the entire image unless you select an area with one of the selection tools before choosing the command. In that case, only the pixels inside the selection outline are distorted. Review Chapter 8 if you need help creating selection outlines.

Size⇨Perspective

The Perspective command works similarly to Distort. After you choose the command, PhotoDeluxe displays the familiar black resize handles around the perimeter of the image. When you drag a corner handle, the opposite handle moves in tandem, creating a pseudo-perspective effect, as shown in Figure 14-12. I dragged a bottom handle inward and a top handle outward to achieve the effect in the figure.

For more tips on using the Perspective command, read the bulleted list in the preceding section. All the hints for using the Distort command apply to the Perspective command as well.

Figure 14-12:
You can simulate perspective effects by using the Size⇨ Perspective command.

Size⇨Free Resize

Using this command, you can resize your image without regard to the original image proportions. You can make an image tall and skinny, as I did in the left example in Figure 14-13, or short and fat, as in the right example.

When you choose the command, your image is surrounded by ordinary-looking resize handles. Drag a top or bottom handle to alter the vertical dimensions of the image; drag a side handle to stretch or shrink the image horizontally. To reshape the image in both directions at the same time, drag a corner handle.

Another way to perform the same trick is to simply click an image with the Object Selection tool or choose Size⇨Resize. The resize handles appear, and you can drag a top, bottom, or side handle as just described to mess up the image proportions. In this case, however, dragging a corner handle resizes the image without changing the image proportions.

Figure 14-13:
I used the
Free Resize
command
to stretch
the image
vertically
only
(left) and
horizontally
only (right).

For more information about distorting using Free Resize, read the bulleted list in the Size⇨Distort section. Those same tips apply to Free Resize as well as Distort.

Chapter 15

Top Ten PhotoDeluxe Brain Teasers

*E*ver hear the expression, "Ask a simple question, get a simple answer?" Well, this chapter gives you simple answers to *tough* questions. These stumpers can keep you sitting in front of your monitor, scratching your head and saying "huh?" for hours — or however long it takes you to find some precocious neighborhood teen who can offer some assistance.

The questions posed (and answered) in this chapter trip up almost every newcomer to image editing and PhotoDeluxe. But you, lucky reader, have the answers right here at your fingertips, unlike all those other poor slobs who weren't clever enough to buy this book. So while those folks are transfixed by confusion, you can be turning out one terrific image after another. Heck, you may even find yourself with enough spare time to enjoy a long walk and conversation with that local teenager. Mind you, that experience may also leave you scratching your head and saying "huh?" but at least you'll get to enjoy some fresh air and exercise in the process.

What does it mean when my scratch disk is full?

While processing images, PhotoDeluxe uses a portion of your hard disk to temporarily store data. This hard disk storage area is called a *scratch disk* in PhotoDeluxe parlance.

If your disk has limited free space, PhotoDeluxe may display a whiny little message about the scratch disk being full and refuse to carry out your commands. You need to delete some files on your hard disk to correct the problem. Another option is to flatten the layers in your image, if said image has many of them; each layer eats up more scratch disk space. (See Chapter 10 for information on layers and flattening.)

For more on the issue of scratch disk space, including some tips on how to assign a drive as your scratch disk, check out Chapter 2.

My computer has plenty of RAM, so why does PhotoDeluxe say "not enough memory?"

PhotoDeluxe, like other image-editing programs, requires an enormous amount of RAM to carry out your digital imaging whims. The amount of RAM the image consumes is indicated in the File Information box in the lower-left corner of the program window (the image window on a Mac), as discussed in Chapter 1. On average, the amount of memory an image consumes is about three times the image file size. So if you're working with very large images, even a well-equipped computer can hiccup.

Many times when PhotoDeluxe complains about memory, though, the problem isn't the amount of RAM but the amount of free scratch drive space (see the preceding section on scratch disks). You must have at least as much scratch drive space as you have memory — for example, if you have 64MB of RAM, you need 64MB of free scratch drive space. That's because PhotoDeluxe sometimes has to dump everything in RAM into the scratch disk space in order to carry out a command. If you have 64MB of RAM but only 40MB of scratch disk space, the program limits itself to using 40MB of RAM so that it doesn't get into trouble if it needs to dump data to the scratch disk.

To sum up, if you get an "out of memory" error, check both your available RAM and scratch disk space. You may also want to allocate more of your system memory to PhotoDeluxe. For more on memory issues, check out Chapter 2.

Why isn't the paint/line/smudge/ eraser/clone tool working?

One of the great things about the PhotoDeluxe editing tools is that you can vary their impact. You can adjust the opacity of the strokes that you apply with the paint, line, clone, and eraser tools, and you can set the smudge tool to smudge pixels over a shorter or greater distance. To adjust the tools, just press a number key. Press 0 for full opacity or full-intensity smudging, press 9 for 90 percent opacity/smudging, 8 for 80 percent, and so on. (If you use the number keys on your keyboard's numeric keyboard, be sure that the Num Lock key is turned on.)

On the downside, PhotoDeluxe gives you no on-screen indication of what tool setting is in force. And because the tool settings stay active until you change them again — even if you move on to another image — you can easily forget that you altered the tool's performance. So if one of these tools isn't having the effect that you anticipated, press a number key to reset the opacity or smudging setting you want to use.

Also remember that if you draw a selection with one of the selection tools, your editing tools do not affect any pixels outside the selection outline. You can swipe over those deselected pixels all you want, but PhotoDeluxe isn't going to alter them one iota, no matter what tool setting you're using.

In addition, both the painting and selection tools affect pixels on the active layer only, so check the Layers palette to make sure that the name of the layer you're trying to edit is highlighted. If not, click the layer name to activate the layer, as discussed in Chapter 10.

Why do my pictures look great on-screen, but terrible when I print them?

The problem is most likely that your image resolution is acceptable for display on a monitor, but not high enough for good print reproduction.

You see, different output devices have different resolution demands. Computer monitors and television screens are designed to display images at a resolution of only 72 to 96 pixels per inch (ppi). Printers, on the other hand, need far more pixels to produce a quality image. Most consumer inkjets are engineered to do their best work with images that have a resolution in the 250- to 300-ppi range. Ditto for commercial printing devices. That's why a low-resolution image can look perfectly fine on-screen but downright disastrous when printed. For the complete story on screen and printer resolution needs, check out Chapter 3.

Why does my image get so big when I display it on-screen?

When you display an image on a computer monitor, the resolution is controlled by the monitor, not by the image resolution you set in the Photo Size dialog box. On-screen images automatically default to the monitor's resolution, which typically ranges from 72 to 96 ppi.

Therefore, if you size an image in PhotoDeluxe and assign it a resolution of, say, 150 ppi, the image gets bigger when you display it on-screen, because you're spreading only 72 pixels across each inch rather than 150.

To avoid this confusion, use Pixels as your unit of measurement in the Photo Size dialog box when you're sizing images for on-screen display. And to see the approximate size at which the image will appear, choose the 100 percent zoom size in the PhotoDeluxe image window.

For more mind-numbing insights on sizing images for the screen, flip backward through this book to Chapter 3.

Why do my images look worse after I enlarge them?

At their core, digital pictures are nothing more than square blocks of color, known hither and yon — well, maybe not yon but definitely hither — as *pixels*. Each image starts life with a specific number of pixels.

When you enlarge an image, one of two things has to happen:

1. The number of pixels stays the same, and the existing pixels grow to cover the expanded image area. The resolution — number of pixels per inch — goes down. If the pixels get too big, your image looks jaggedy because the individual pixels become more noticeable to the naked eye.

2. The software adds pixels to fill in the gaps, and the resolution of the image is unchanged. But adding too many pixels usually results in a blurry image. The software has to guess at the color and brightness of the pixels that it adds, and even the smartest editing program doesn't get it right all the time — or most of the time, for that matter.

The moral of the story: To preserve the best image quality, don't enlarge your images. If enlarging is a must, try not to resize by more than 25 percent.

For more about these resizing issues and how to avoid turning your images to muck, refer to Chapter 3, which tells you more about pixels and image sizes than you probably ever cared to consider (but really should know).

I scanned an image into PhotoDeluxe. Where'd it go?

In Version 2 of PhotoDeluxe, scanned images are automatically saved to disk in the JPEG format and stored in the PhotoDeluxe/EZPhoto/Photo folder. A thumbnail of the scanned image appears on the Acquire tab in the EasyPhoto browser. You can open the scanned image by double-clicking its thumbnail.

If you don't want your scanned image saved in JPEG or stored in this fashion, do your scanning outside PhotoDeluxe, using your scanner's software.

Those using the Business Edition or Version 3 don't have to deal with this scanning issue. Images are scanned and placed directly into an image window. If you want to save the image to disk, you have to do so yourself.

For more on scanning into PhotoDeluxe, head for Chapter 1.

How do I put a PhotoDeluxe image into a brochure or other document?

You can easily export PhotoDeluxe images to text documents, multimedia presentations, Web pages, spreadsheets, or just about any other type of document. First, edit and size your image in PhotoDeluxe, and then save the image in a format that can be read by the program you're using to create the text document, Web page, or whatever. In that other program, check the Help system to find out what specific command you use to import the image.

Alternatively, just use the Cut, Copy, and Paste commands as described in Chapter 8. Select the entire image in PhotoDeluxe and choose Edit⇨Copy or Edit⇨Cut. Then switch to the other program and choose Edit⇨Paste. In Windows 95, you can drag and drop images to the Windows 95 taskbar to copy images into some programs. You can find more information about these options in Chapters 8 and 13.

Why don't my printed colors match my on-screen colors?

One of the headaches of dealing with digital images is that colors frequently look different on-screen than they do on the printed page. The problem occurs because printers and monitors create colors in two different ways. Printers combine cyan, magenta, yellow, and black ink to create color, whereas monitors combine red, blue, and green light to create color. For this reason, printers are said to use the CMYK color model; monitors, televisions, and other screen displays follow the RGB color model. Any image than you open or edit in PhotoDeluxe is also an RGB image.

RGB devices can create a broader spectrum — or *gamut* — of colors than CMYK printers. That's why very vivid, neon colors that you see on-screen emerge from the printer as duller versions of their former selves. If a color in your image is beyond the printer's capabilities — or *out of gamut* — the printer substitutes the closest available color.

Some printer software enables you to adjust the print settings so that printer and monitor colors are more in sync with each other. Version 3 includes an additional color matching tool in its File⇨Adjust Color Printing command, which is described in Chapter 5.

If print colors are more important than accurate on-screen colors, you can always play with the image colors using the color balance controls covered in Chapter 6. Experiment with the settings until your printed colors suit your taste.

The paper you use can also have an effect on your printed colors; try different weights and grades of paper to see which ones deliver the best results. For more on getting good printouts, dip your big toe into Chapter 5.

How do I save in a format other than the PhotoDeluxe native format?

As explained in gruesome detail in Chapters 1 and 4, PhotoDeluxe only works on images saved in the PhotoDeluxe native format (PDD). If you open an image that was saved in another format, the program makes a copy of the image, converts the copy to the PDD format, and opens the copy for you to edit.

PhotoDeluxe wants you to work in the PDD format because that format is optimized to work with the program. The software can work more efficiently when you use PDD, and you can take advantage of some features, such as layers, that other formats don't support.

Because of this setup, always save images in the PDD format until you're completely through editing them. If you then want to save the image in another format, you have to look beyond the ordinary File⇨Save menu. In Version 2, choose File⇨Send To⇨File Format to access other formats; in Version 3, choose File⇨Export⇨File Format. In the Business Edition, choose File⇨Save As and select a format from the resulting submenu. If you don't see the format that you want on the submenu, choose the Other option to access additional choices.

Chapter 16

Ten PhotoDeluxe Shortcuts

So much time, so little to do — that's the story of my life.

No, wait a minute, that's somebody else's life. My life is "So much to *do*, and not a prayer of getting it all done before this week's episode of *Buffy, the Vampire Slayer.*"

If you, too, feel the pressure of a ticking clock, you'll appreciate the keyboard shortcuts listed in this chapter. Instead of clicking your way through menus, you can access commands and tools by pressing a few handy keys. You not only save time, but you also save arm strength because you don't have to reach for the mouse so much.

Yep, if you commit these shortcuts to memory, you can finish in plenty of time to catch the Buffster and her vampire-slaying pals *and* have enough energy left to lift some potato chips out of the bag and into your mouth.

No need to thank me — helping people lead more artful, fulfilled lives is just part of my job.

Opening, closing, printing, and saving

Here's a batch of shortcuts that you can use every day. To open an existing image, press Ctrl+O (⌘+O on a Mac) and then choose your file from the Open dialog box, as explained in Chapter 1.

After you finish destroying . . . er, I mean, editing . . . your image, save your work to disk in a flash by pressing Ctrl+S (⌘+S on a Mac). The first time you save a document, PhotoDeluxe asks you to give the image a name, specify a location on disk (your hard drive, a floppy disk, Zip disk, and so on), and provide a few other saving instructions, as explained in Chapter 4. Thereafter, pressing the shortcut saves the image without making you bother with all those pesky details.

You can't use this shortcut to save in a format other than PDD, the native file format. Instead, you must use the File➪Send To➪File Format in Version 2, File➪Export➪File Format in Version 3, and File➪Save As in the Business Edition.

Ready to print your image? If your print settings are already established, press Ctrl+P (⌘+P on a Mac) to open the Print dialog box. Before you print, you may want to press Ctrl+/ (forward slash) on a PC (⌘+/ on a Mac) to see how the image fits on the selected page size.

To close an open image, press Ctrl+W (⌘+W on a Mac). Or just click the close button at the top of the image window.

You can find a bundle of other opening, closing, and saving tips in Chapters 1 and 4, if you're so inclined. More printing info is yours for the taking in Chapter 5.

Undoing bonehead moves

Ah, now here's a shortcut you should never be without. In fact, if you remember only one shortcut in this chapter, pick this one.

If you screw up and do something you didn't mean to do — or you just don't like the results of something you *did* mean to do — whack the Ctrl key and the Z key. On a Mac, press ⌘+Z instead. Alternatively, click the Undo button at the top of the image window.

You have to choose Undo immediately after you make a mistake. If you choose another command or take some other editing action, you lose your opportunity to Undo. The exception is choosing the Print command: You can print your image and then undo the move you made just before you printed the image.

You can also choose File➪Revert to Last Saved to restore your image to the way it appeared immediately after you last saved it using the File➪Save command. Chapter 6 offers more details.

Selecting and deselecting stuff

To limit the effects of your edits to a certain portion of your image, you have to select that area first. Use these shortcuts to breeze through your selection chores, and turn to Chapter 8 for the complete scoop on selecting:

- ✔ Select the entire image: Ctrl+A (⌘+A on a Mac)
- ✔ Cancel a selection outline: Ctrl+D (⌘+D)
- ✔ Invert the selection outline: Ctrl+I (⌘+I)
- ✔ Activate the Rectangle tool: Ctrl+M (⌘+M)
- ✔ Activate the Color Wand: Ctrl+F (⌘+F)
- ✔ Activate the Trace tool: Ctrl+L (⌘+L)
- ✔ Activate the Move tool: Ctrl+G (⌘+G)
- ✔ Relocate a selection outline: Ctrl+Alt+drag (⌘+Option+drag) to move large distances; select the Move tool and press the arrow keys to nudge short distances.

Zooming in and out on your image

Want to zoom in for a closer look at your pixels? Press Ctrl along with the plus key. Press ⌘ and the plus key on a Mac. (No need to press the Shift key to activate the plus key, by the way.) To zoom out, press Ctrl and the minus key. Press ⌘ and minus on a Mac. And turn to Chapter 1 for more details about viewing your images on-screen.

Opening the Cursors dialog box

The Cursors dialog box is Grand Central Station for choosing how your cursors appear on-screen and also for setting the Tolerance value for the Color Wand and the Color Change tool. To get to the dialog box quickly, press Ctrl+K (⌘+K on a Mac).

Activating the painting and editing tools

Some of the more popular painting and editing tools are also available at the press of a key. Jot these shortcuts down on your palm so that they'll always be close at hand (sorry, too much caffeine makes me punny):

- ✔ Brush tool: Ctrl+J (⌘+J on a Mac)
- ✔ Text tool: Ctrl+T (⌘+T) or click the T button on the image window
- ✔ Eraser tool: Ctrl+E (⌘+E)

✔ Selection Fill: Ctrl+9 (⌘+9)

✔ Gradient Fill: Ctrl+8 (⌘+8)

Adjusting tool opacity

You can control the opacity of the Brush, Eraser, Line, and Clone tools by pressing the number keys. Press 0 to create strokes that are completely opaque, press 9 to switch to 90 percent opacity, 8 to choose 80 percent opacity, and so on.

If you're using the Smudge tool, pressing the number keys changes how far the tool smudges the pixels that you drag across. Press 0 to smudge for the entire length of your drag. Lower settings smudge pixels for only a portion of the drag. See Chapter 9 for additional information about all these tools.

Applying image correction filters

Use these shortcuts to access commands that you can use to correct common image problems. Chapter 6 can fill in any gaps in your understanding of these issues.

✔ Color Balance: Ctrl+Y (⌘+Y on the Mac)

✔ Brightness/Contrast: Ctrl+B (⌘+B)

✔ Hue/Saturation: Ctrl+U (⌘+U)

Copying, moving, and pasting selections

To choose the always popular Cut, Copy, and Paste commands, covered thoroughly in Chapter 8, use these shortcuts:

✔ Cut: Ctrl+X (⌘+X)

✔ Copy: Ctrl+C (⌘+C)

✔ Paste: Ctrl+V (⌘+V)

Nudging a selection into place

When the Move tool is selected, you can nudge a selection into place by pressing the arrow keys. Press an arrow key once to nudge the selection one pixel in the direction of the arrow. Press Shift and an arrow key to nudge the selection ten pixels. More information about moving selections around your image awaits you in Chapter 8.

Chapter 17

Ten Online Resources

*A*t the moment, the community of folks working with digital images is fairly small and scattered. Unless you live in Silicon Valley or some other computing mecca, you're probably not going to be in the right neighborhood for an over-the-garden-fence chat about digital imaging. Not that your neighbors aren't perfectly nice people, of course — why, if they'd get rid of that tacky lawn art and take down those infernal wind chimes, you might even become fast friends. Even so, they're not likely to have a digital darkroom in their house yet.

But if you have a modem and Internet access, you can easily mingle with all sorts of people who share your enthusiasm for digital imaging. Via special chat rooms, message boards, and newsgroups, you can dish with fellow digital photography buffs all over the worlds. And by exploring various Web sites devoted to digital imaging, you can discover a wealth of technical information, buying advice, and creative ideas.

This chapter points you toward some of my favorite online resources for digital imaging information. Keep in mind that the URLs listed here were current as of press-time, but things change quickly on the Internet, so some sites may have changed since I wrote this.

For quick access to these Web sites, be sure to check out the CD at the back of this book. The CD includes a Web page listing all the links mentioned in this chapter. Save the page to your hard drive and then open it in your browser the next time you go online. You can then just click the links on the Web page to check out sites that interest you.

www.adobe.com

First and foremost on the hit parade is the Adobe Web site. Here, you can access and download additional Guided Activities projects (assuming that you're a Windows user — sorry, Mac users). You can also exchange questions, answers, and comments with other PhotoDeluxe users via a special Adobe online forum area. Finally, you can find out about any updates or fixes to your current edition of PhotoDeluxe.

www.hylas.com

A treasure trove of information waits at this site, which is a search engine dedicated to digital imaging topics. If you're looking for information on a specific topic, you can use this site's search tool to track down leads more quickly than by using a general purpose search engine such as Alta Vista or Yahoo! Or you can just explore a huge list of links that take you to Web sites of companies selling digital imaging hardware and software as well as to sites that offer reviews of new products, background information for beginning image editors, and artistic inspiration.

www.photo-on-PC.com

Offered by the same outfit behind the www.hylas.com site, this site offers counsel on what to look for when choosing a digital camera, plus tips on editing images, choosing software, and other topics related to digital imaging.

A great feature of the site is a page where you can download freeware and shareware image-editing and cataloging software. You can also read about the latest products to hit the market and request e-mail notification of product announcements from digital imaging vendors. If you find yourself baffled by a term you run across in an article on this site or elsewhere, you can check the site's glossary page for enlightenment. And for those wanting to buy or sell equipment, the site offers a classified ad section.

www.dcforum.com

This Web site is loaded with information about digital cameras, image editing, printing, removable storage, and memory. In addition to offering product reviews, the site provides forums where users can exchange information on a variety of topics and a price-search engine that tracks down the best online prices for products you may want to buy.

Before you buy a camera, printer, scanner, or other piece of equipment, definitely take a look-see. And after you buy that new toy, visit regularly to find out how to use the thing to its best advantage.

www.dcresource.com

This URL jets you to the Digital Camera Resource Page, which, as the name suggests, is devoted to issues related to buying and using digital cameras. But you can also find information on other digital imaging products, including printers, removable memory, and scanners. The site has a reviews section where you can find out about equipment before you buy, a message board where digital imaging enthusiasts can exchange ideas and tips, and links to other related Web sites.

www.kodak.com

A major player in the digital imaging industry, Kodak recognized that in order for people to really latch onto this new technology, they have to gain a better understanding of the science behind the art. To that end, Kodak offers the Digital Learning Center at its Web site. You can get good, entry-level information on subjects such as resolution, preparing Web images, and sending an image via e-mail, or you can really go gearhead and make your way through higher-end pages that explain some of the technology used in digital imaging equipment.

To access the learning center, click on the Digital Cameras and Technology link on the Kodak home page and then click the Digital Learning Center link. (If you buy a newer Kodak digital camera, the Learning Center is provided on CD-ROM, so you can get the same information offline if you like.)

www.digitalphoto.com.nf/

Tap into this URL, and you hit the front pages of two great online magazines, *dpi* and *photOZine*. The first magazine features articles on digital photography and imaging as well as reviews of new equipment and links to other good photography sites on the Web. The *photOZine* articles focus more on traditional film photography, but you can apply the artistic tips to digital photographs as well.

Stock photography sites

When you can't find just the right image for a project in your own photo album, you can search for and buy the image from several stock photo companies. Sure, you pay for the privilege — stock images don't come cheap, especially for commercial use such as advertising a product or service. But the image quality is good, and with online ordering and downloading of images, you can't ask for a more convenient way to get the perfect picture.

For royalty-free images, check out the following big names in the business. (Royalty-free doesn't mean free. You pay a one-time licensing fee for the right to use the image; you just don't pay royalties each time the image is published. Some licensing agreements do limit the kind of publication in which you can print the image, however.)

In many cases, you can either buy an entire collection of images or purchase a single image. The price varies depending on whether you need high- or low-resolution images. Before you buy, read the licensing agreements at the company's Web site to make sure the purchase agreement suits your needs.

- **PhotoDisc,** www.photodisc.com: One of the premiere royalty-free stock agencies, PhotoDisc offers 60,000-plus high- and low-res images. A 100-image CD collection runs $249; single images range from $19.95 to $129.95, depending on the resolution you need.

- **Corbis,** www.corbis.com: Corbis is owner of Digital Stock, another leader in the royalty-free game, as well as about 20 million non-royalty-free images. You can access all the Digital Stock goodies via the Corbis site or go directly to Digital Stock at www.digitalstock.com. CD collections cost $249; single images cost $29.95, $69.95, or $139.95, depending on whether you need low, high, or ultrahigh resolution.

- **Adobe Studios,** www.adobestudios.com: At this extension of the main Adobe Web site, you can buy collections of clip art, type, and Web art in addition to stock photography. The photography collections range in price from $80 to $299.99 per CD.

- **Corel,** www.corel.com: Corel, maker of CorelDRAW and Corel Photo-Paint, also offers a huge supply of royalty-free images. You can buy single images ranging in price from $8.99 to $39.99, depending on the image resolution. Corel also offers CD collections for $39.95.

Online printing and scanning services

Want to get some high-quality prints made of your digital artwork? Have some favorite photographs scanned to disk? Transfer a batch of images to Photo CD? You could go out and buy all the necessary equipment to do those jobs yourself — if you have a ton of cash, time, and spare space in your office for all that equipment. Or you can contact the following companies, which are some of the many vendors offering scanning, printing, and archiving services for digital imaging enthusiasts.

- ✔ `Fujifilm.net`: This site offers a wealth of services. First, you can drop off your undeveloped rolls of 35mm or APS film at a participating retail photo lab and have it sent to Fujifilm.net for scanning. You then download the digital images from the online site. The negatives are returned to you with or without prints, depending on your preference.

  If your computer's storage space is limited, you can store the digital images at the site rather than on your own computer. You can upload images to the Web site for storage as well as store images that you had digitized from film. Printing services are also available.

  The best part about this type of service is that friends and family members can log into the site and, using a special ID and password that you provide, view your images and order prints of the pictures they like. The site also offers an e-mail postcard option that enables you to force your favorite pictures on other people rather than relying on them to log into the site to view the images.

  All this photographic stuff isn't free, however. You pay $4.95 a month for the right to store up to 125 images at the site, and a penny a piece for each additional image. Film processing and scanning is extra, of course.

- ✔ **Kodak PhotoNet,** `www.kodak.com`: A joint offering from Kodak and PhotoNet, this online service offers similar goodies as the Fujifilm.net site. The pricing structure is different, however. After your film is developed and scanned, the digital images are stored online at no charge for 30 days. After 30 days, you can extend the storage time for about $3 a month for 36 images.

- ✔ **Firehouse Image Center,** `www.fire-house.net`: This company has been doing business in my neck of the woods (Indianapolis) for 25 years and has a high reputation among the graphics professionals in the area for photographic printing and pre-press services. But ordinary mortals can also take advantage of the company's offerings, which include scanning, printing, and Photo CD duplication.

  Here's a sampling of the kind of projects Firehouse can provide: Scanning slides or film negatives to Photo CD costs $1 per slide plus $10 for the CD; transferring existing digital images to writeable CD, $37.50 for the first 1-150MB of data, $25 per 150MB thereafter; 8-x-10-inch custom color print, $17.40 for the first print, $9.75 each for two to five additional copies. Shipping is extra, of course.

  If you want to try out Firehouse services, check out the coupon at the back of this book.

You can no doubt find scads of other companies offering similar services both online and in your own city. I mention these three because they're known entities to me and I've found them to be professional and reliable. For recommendations on other providers, talk to graphics professionals who use these services on a regular basis.

Internet newsgroups

If you have yet to discover the world of Internet newsgroups, also called discussion groups, now is the time to take the plunge. In these online forums, people from around the world can exchange information about a common interest. Check your browser's help system for the scoop on how to participate in newsgroups with your particular software.

Then check out these groups in particular:

- ✔ `rec.photo.digital`: For all the latest gossip on the topic of digital photography — as well as some good, solid advice from experienced digital imaging gurus — subscribe to the `rec.photo.digital` newsgroup. (Subscription to a newsgroup doesn't involve any fees, contracts, or forms — you simply tell your browser the name of the newsgroup that you want to follow.) Folks in this newsgroup discuss the pros and cons of different models of digital cameras, exchange ideas for creating better digital images, and even ask others to critique their images at times.

- ✔ `comp.periphs.printers`: Although you see some discussion of printers and printing issues in `rec.photo.digital`, subscribe to `comp.periphs.printers` for more in-depth exchanges of information. If you're in the market for a new printer, definitely watch the newsgroup postings for information about models you're considering. You can find out what sort of problems people are having with a particular brand or model, which printers offer the best output for certain types of print jobs, and even find out the best places to buy printing equipment online.

  In addition, you can get feedback on what brand or type of paper delivers the best results with your printer, get suggestions for troubleshooting printer problems, and find out about issues like refilling inkjet cartridges, cleaning print heads, and so on.

- ✔ `comp.periphs.scanners`: This newsgroup is the scanner equivalent of the printers newsgroup. These folks can answer all your questions about buying and using scanners — a topic that the scanner marketing gurus would have you believe is simple and straightforward but is fraught with complication and confusion.

Keep in mind that information shared on newsgroups isn't always dead-on from a technical standpoint. People share their opinions and ideas about how certain things work, but those notions aren't always correct. Verify anything presented as "fact" before you follow the poster's advice. (And for information on resolution, refer to this book, not the newsgroups!)

Part V
Appendixes

The 5th Wave   By Rich Tennant

In this part . . .

*J*ust when you thought you reached the end of the book . . . you haven't — not by a long shot. "But wait! With this set of knives you also get much, much more!"

The next several pages contain two brief but information-packed appendixes. If you haven't already installed PhotoDeluxe on your computer, look to Appendix A for assistance in doing so. The installation process is simple, but you do have to make some choices about which program components to install. Don't worry — I'll be there every step of the way to guide you through the process.

In Appendix B, you can read about all the extra goodies included on the CD at the back of this book. The Appendix also tells you everything you need to know to access the CD contents. The CD includes some great stuff — sadly, no miracle knife that can cut through aluminum cans like they were butter, but some terrific products all the same.

Appendix A
Installing PhotoDeluxe

*P*hotoDeluxe provides a program installer that eases the process of putting the program on your system. Still, you need to make a few choices along the way, which this chapter helps you do.

If you received your copy of PhotoDeluxe with a digital camera, printer, or scanner, your installation may work a little differently than outlined in this appendix. Your copy of PhotoDeluxe may also include some options that the standard, store-bought version doesn't offer. So consider the information in this chapter as a general guideline to installation and don't panic if what you see on-screen doesn't match exactly what is described here. Check your camera, printer, or scanner manual for details about any special installation instructions.

Does Your Computer Have What It Takes?

Before you install PhotoDeluxe — actually, before you *buy* PhotoDeluxe — make sure that your system has the amount of RAM and free hard drive space that the program requires. In case you received your copy of PhotoDeluxe with a digital camera, scanner, printer, or other device and can't track down those system specifications, they are as follows:

- **Version 2, Windows:** You must be running Windows 95 and have at least 16MB of RAM and 70MB of free hard drive space.

- **Version 2, Macintosh:** Mac users must be running OS 7.1 or later and need a minimum of 16MB of RAM and 70MB of hard disk space. Adobe recommends that your system have a 68040 or PowerPC processor.

- **Business Edition and Version 3:** The Business Edition and Version 3 cooperate with Windows 95, 98, and NT 4.0 with Service Pack 3 or later. If you're running Win 95 or 98, you need a minimum of 16MB of RAM to run the Business Edition and 32MB of RAM for Version 3. NT users need 32MB to kick the Business Edition into gear and 64MB to keep Version 3 humming. For all three operating systems, the program requires 140MB of free hard disk space to be happy.

Be sure to close any open programs before you install PhotoDeluxe. Also turn off any virus-checking programs. And if you use Quarterdeck CleanSweep Version 3.0.7, upgrade to version 3.0.8 to avoid potential conflicts with PhotoDeluxe.

Windows Installation

The following sections outline the installation procedure for all the various versions of PhotoDeluxe if you're using Windows as your operating system.

Version 2

If you're installing Version 2, point and click like so:

1. **Shut down all open programs (except Windows, of course).**

2. **Slip the PhotoDeluxe CD-ROM in your CD-ROM drive.**

   If the autoplay feature is enabled for your CD-ROM drive, the installation program appears automatically on your screen. If you don't see the screen, use Windows Explorer or My Computer to look for a file named Autorun.exe or Setup.exe on the PhotoDeluxe CD. Double-click either file to launch the installer. If an installer for a program other than PhotoDeluxe appears, you clicked the wrong file — search for another and try again.

   PhotoDeluxe displays a screen asking you to indicate the country in which you bought the software.

3. **Click on the appropriate country and click Next.**

4. **Read the software license agreement and click Accept to signify your total agreement and move on.**

   PhotoDeluxe displays a three-panel dialog box. The first panel contains options for installing PhotoDeluxe, certain fonts and Adobe Type Manager, Acrobat Reader 3.0.1, and AT&T WorldNet Service.

   The other tabs contain options that enable you to view the online documentation and to install demo versions of other Adobe products.

5. **Click the Documentation tab and click the Read Me First item.**

   Most programs these days include a Read Me file that tells you about any last-minute installation news, including potential problems that you may encounter and how to fix them. Make it a habit to check out the Read Me files to avoid problems down the road.

   After you read the information, click the window's close box or choose File⇨Exit to return to the installer.

6. **Click the Applications tab and then click the Adobe PhotoDeluxe 2.0 item.**

    PhotoDeluxe installs some setup files and then displays a dialog box warning you to shut down any other open programs and reminding you about international software copyright laws.

7. **Click Next.**

    The Setup Type dialog box appears. Here, you can choose whether you want to perform a custom installation or automatic installation.

8. **Click the Custom button.**

    I recommend that you choose the Custom option, because the typical option installs Internet Explorer 3.02. If you want to connect to the Internet and download additional Guided Activities projects from inside PhotoDeluxe, you need to use Explorer to do it. But the version of Explorer on the PhotoDeluxe Version 2 CD-ROM is not the most current version of the browser. Download the browser from the Microsoft Web site if you want to use Explorer. Be sure to also download the IE 4 updater from the Adobe File Library at www.adobe.com/ supportservice/custsupport/download.html.

9. **Set the installation directory.**

    At the bottom of the Setup Type dialog box, PhotoDeluxe indicates the default location on your hard drive for installing the program. In most cases, this location is perfectly fine. But if you want to change it for some reason — perhaps to install the program on a second hard drive, for example, click the Browse button and select the location from the dialog box that appears. Click OK to return to the Setup Type dialog box.

10. **Click Next to display the Select Components dialog box.**

11. **Choose the components that you want to install.**

    If you see a check mark in the box next to the component name, that component will be installed. Click the box to toggle the option on and off.

    You absolutely need to check the Adobe PhotoDeluxe 2.0 Files box. You already know my feelings about the Microsoft Internet Explorer 3.02 Files option, so turn that option off.

    The Adobe Fonts option is a little confusing. PhotoDeluxe requires certain fonts, as well as Adobe Type Manager, in order to make its Guided Activities templates run properly. Version 4.0 of ATM is included on the CD and available for you to install separately from PhotoDeluxe. If you already have this version or a later version on your computer, you certainly don't need to install it again, but you do need to install the required fonts, which is what checking the Adobe Fonts option accomplishes. After you finish installing PhotoDeluxe, you need to manually install the fonts into ATM (follow your ATM documentation for the how-to). The fonts are stored in the AdobeFonts folder in the same folder where you install PhotoDeluxe.

If you don't already have ATM Deluxe installed or want to install Version 4.0, *don't* select the Adobe Fonts option. You install ATM and the required fonts later.

At the bottom of the dialog box, the installer indicates how much hard drive space the selected components will consume and also how much free hard drive space is available. If the Space Required value is higher than the Space Available value, you're in trouble. You won't be able to install the program properly until you free up some hard drive space (by deleting files or other programs). If you're in this leaking boat, click Cancel to escape the installer and go on a search-and-destroy mission to remove some files from your hard drive. If not, move ahead to Step 12.

12. Click Next.

PhotoDeluxe asks for some user information, including your name, company name, and serial number. Do as you're told and fill in the blanks. You can find the serial number on the registration card that came with your copy of PhotoDeluxe. Or, if you got your copy with a printer, scanner, digital camera, or other product, look on the CD sleeve or case for the serial number.

13. Click Next.

The installer displays a summary screen showing the registration information you entered in the preceding step. If everything looks okay, click Yes. If you want to change something, click No to return to Step 12.

After you click Yes, PhotoDeluxe displays a summary of your installation decisions. If everything is as it should be, move on to the next step. Otherwise, click the Back button to work your way back through the installation routine to fix whatever problem you spotted.

14. Click Next.

Now PhotoDeluxe actually starts installing stuff. A progress bar appears at the bottom of the screen to show you that something is really happening. When all files are copied to your hard drive, PhotoDeluxe may display an alert box saying that you have to install the required fonts and ATM. Click OK to say that you get the picture.

The installation completes itself, and PhotoDeluxe offers you the option of registering electronically, via modem. If you want to do so, check the PhotoDeluxe 2.0 online registration box if it's not already selected. Then click Finish and follow the instructions on the registration wizard.

If you want to register some other time, deselect the registration check box and click Finish.

15. Restart or keep going.

PhotoDeluxe displays a dialog box asking whether you want to restart your computer. If you need to install ATM or want to install Acrobat

Reader, a program you use to view the online documentation on your computer, skip the restart for now and move on to Step 16. Otherwise, go ahead and restart.

16. **Install ATM and/or Acrobat Reader.**

As explained earlier, you need to install Adobe Type Manager and a collection of fonts, all provided on the PhotoDeluxe CD-ROM, in order to use the templates provided with PhotoDeluxe. If you already have ATM on your machine and you checked the Adobe Fonts option earlier, you don't have to install ATM again. If you don't already have ATM, you must install it now.

Acrobat Reader is a program that enables you to view the online documentation included on the CD-ROM. This program is provided on the PhotoDeluxe CD as well.

Before you install either program, though, make sure that a more current version doesn't already exist on your computer. Many programs install ATM and Acrobat automatically, so you may already have a copy. The Version 2 PhotoDeluxe CD-ROM provides Version 4.0 of ATM and Version 3.0.1 of Acrobat Reader.

To install either program, click the Applications tab in the first PhotoDeluxe installer screen and then click the name of the program that you want to install. Use the default installation settings recommended by Adobe. You must restart your system after installation to complete the install process.

Business Edition

To install the Business Edition, follow these eye-popping steps:

1. **Shut down all open programs (except Windows, of course).**

2. **Slip the PhotoDeluxe CD-ROM in your CD-ROM drive.**

If the autoplay feature is enabled for your CD-ROM drive, the installation program appears automatically on your screen. If you don't see the screen, use Windows Explorer or My Computer to look for a file named Setup.exe or Autorun.exe on the PhotoDeluxe program CD. Double-click the file to launch the installer. Note that your CD may have several files with the setup.exe name. If an installer for a program other than PhotoDeluxe appears, cancel out of the installation and try another setup.exe file.

PhotoDeluxe plays a little animated start-up screen and then displays the main installation screen.

3. **Click the Step 1 button.**

This button takes you to the installation wizard.

4. **Click the Install Guide button.**

A document containing last-minute tips and information regarding installation and using PhotoDeluxe appears. Always read this stuff — you never know what headaches you can avoid. To close the document, choose File⇨Exit or click the window's Close button.

5. **Click the Read Me button.**

Here's another document full of vital information. Give it the once-over and then close the document window. Now you're ready to move on.

6. **Click the Install PhotoDeluxe Business Edition button.**

After PhotoDeluxe loads some necessary installation files, the Setup window appears. In the window, PhotoDeluxe displays a dialog box warning you to shut down any other open programs and reminding you about international software copyright laws.

7. **Click Next.**

The Setup Type dialog box appears.

8. **Click the Custom button.**

I recommend that you choose the Custom option because the Typical option installs several programs that you may not want to install. By using the Custom option, you're the king of your computer.

9. **Set the installation directory.**

At the bottom of the Setup Type dialog box, PhotoDeluxe indicates the default location on your hard drive for installing the program. In most cases, this location is perfectly fine. But if you want to change it for some reason, click the Browse button and select the location. Click OK to return to the Setup Type dialog box.

10. **Click Next to display the Select Components dialog box.**

11. **Choose the components that you want to install.**

If you see a check mark in the box next to the component name, that component will be installed. Click the box to toggle the option on and off.

The components are as follows:

- **Adobe PhotoDeluxe Business Edition 1.0 Files:** These are the program files. You need them, so make sure that this box is checked.

- **Adobe Fonts:** Check this option *only* if you already have Adobe Type Manager (ATM) Version 4.0 or later already installed in your system. This option installs just the necessary PhotoDeluxe fonts without installing ATM. You must then run ATM separately to load the new fonts, which are stored in the AdobeFonts folder in the folder where you installed PhotoDeluxe.

- **Adobe Acrobat Reader 3.0.1 Files:** Acrobat Reader is used to view online documentation such as that provided on the PhotoDeluxe CD-ROM. If you don't already have Version 3.0.1 or later installed on your system, check this box.

- **Adobe ATM 4.0 Files:** This option installs Adobe Type Manager, Version 4.0, as well as fonts required to use the PhotoDeluxe templates. Unless you already have Version 4.0 or later installed, check this box. (If you uncheck this box, check the Adobe Fonts box.)

- **Digital Camera Access Files:** Check this option if you own a digital camera. The files enable you to view thumbnail images of photos stored in some brands of digital cameras. (Not all copies of the Business Edition include this option.)

- **Microsoft Internet Explorer 4.01 Files:** In order to use the Internet features that come with PhotoDeluxe, you need to use Microsoft Internet Explorer. If you have a version of Explorer that's more current than 4.01, deselect this check box. Otherwise, select the option to install Explorer and take advantage of the PhotoDeluxe Internet functions.

At the bottom of the dialog box, the installer indicates the amount of hard drive space the program components will consume and how much empty hard drive space is available on your system. If the Space Available value is larger than the Space Required value, move on to Step 12. If you don't have enough hard drive space, click Cancel to exit the installer and dump unneeded files from your hard drive to free up some space.

12. **Click Next.**

PhotoDeluxe displays a list of file formats. The list indicates the types of files the program can open. By default, all the file types are checked. Go ahead and keep them all checked — deselecting a file type doesn't save you much room on your hard disk, anyway.

13. **Click Next.**

Enter your name, company name, and program serial number in the appropriate blanks. Look for your serial number on the CD sleeve or case or on the program registration card.

14. **Click Next.**

PhotoDeluxe asks you to confirm that the information you just entered is correct. If so, click Yes; if not, click No and enter the correct data.

After you click Yes, a summary of your installation decisions appears. To change any options, click the Back button to return to preceding screens. Otherwise, move on to Step 15.

15. Click Next.

PhotoDeluxe begins copying files to your hard drive and displays a progress bar to show you the status of the installation.

After the main program files are installed, installer dialog boxes for other programs may appear, depending on what choices you made in Step 11. Install these other programs using the default settings unless you know what you're doing. Just follow the on-screen prompts to work your way through the installations.

After the installation is done, you can register electronically by modem if you like. To do so, check the online registration box if it's not already selected. Then click Finish and follow the instructions on the registration wizard. To skip the registration, deselect the registration check box and click Finish.

PhotoDeluxe then runs a multimedia tour of the program. The Adobe folks went to a lot of trouble to create the tour, but if you want to snub them and bypass it, just click the tour window's close box (the "x" in the upper-right corner of the window).

16. Restart your computer.

PhotoDeluxe displays a dialog box asking you whether you want to restart your computer. The installation isn't complete until you do, so go ahead and restart.

Version 3

Installing Version 3? Follow these laugh-a-minute instructions:

1. Shut down all open programs except Windows.

2. Put the PhotoDeluxe CD-ROM in your CD-ROM drive.

If the PhotoDeluxe installation program doesn't appear after a few seconds, click the Windows Start button, click Run, and enter the following into the text box: **D:\autoplay.exe.** (If your CD-ROM drive is set up to use some other drive letter than D, enter that letter rather than D.) Then click OK.

PhotoDeluxe politely inquires as to where you bought your software.

3. Select the country and click Next.

4. Study the software license agreement and click Accept if you're okay with its terms.

Assuming that you did in fact agree to the agreement, a new window, containing three buttons, appears.

5. Click the ReadMe & Guides button.

You can now read any last-minute information about installing and using PhotoDeluxe. Click the window close button after you read the documentation.

6. Click the Install button.

A Welcome screen appears. Read the contents and click Next. The Setup Type dialog box appears.

7. Click the Custom option.

You're a big kid now; you can decide for yourself which components of PhotoDeluxe you want to install.

8. Choose an installation directory.

At the bottom of the dialog box, PhotoDeluxe tells you where it wants to put the program — this is the Destination Directory information. Unless you have some good reason for changing the destination directory, leave well enough alone. But if you want to install the program to some other spot, click the Browse button and specify the folder and drive for the installation. Then click OK to return to the Setup Type dialog box.

9. Click Next.

The Select Components dialog box appears. Here's where you can specify which programs you want to install. See my recommendations in Step 11 of the Business Edition installation instructions for information on what you should and shouldn't select from the available options. The first option, Adobe PhotoDeluxe Home Edition 3.0 Files, is a must-install if you want to use PhotoDeluxe.

10. Click Next.

Type in your name, rank, and program serial number. You can find the serial number on your program registration card or program CD case or sleeve.

11. Click Next.

PhotoDeluxe feeds back the information you just entered. Click Yes to verify that everything looks correct. Or click No to go back and change something, if you want.

After you click Yes, PhotoDeluxe displays a summary of all your installation choices. Click Back to change your installation options. Otherwise, click Next. The program then begins installing in earnest.

After the main PhotoDeluxe files are installed, other installation dialog boxes may appear, depending on what options you selected in Step 9. Follow the on-screen prompts and select the default options unless you know what you're doing and have good reason to fool around with things.

When all the selected files are installed, PhotoDeluxe announces that the setup is complete and asks whether you want to register via modem. If you do, click Finish and follow the on-screen prompts to complete the registration. To skip the registration, deselect the registration check box and click Finish.

Macintosh Installation

To avoid installation troubles, be sure that you close down all other programs before you begin the installation, especially virus-checking software. Then travel down this installation highway:

1. **Put the PhotoDeluxe CD in your CD-ROM drive.**

   A PhotoDeluxe CD icon appears on your desktop.

2. **Double-click the PhotoDeluxe icon.**

   The PhotoDeluxe window opens.

3. **Double-click the English icon.**

   The English-language version of the installation window opens.

4. **Double-click the Read Me icon.**

   This step enables you to peruse the latest information from Adobe regarding any potential installation conflicts and how to resolve them. Close the Read Me window after you finish reading.

5. **Double-click the Adobe PhotoDeluxe install icon.**

   The installer asks you to kindly indicate the region in which you purchased the software. Click the appropriate country and then click OK. A new window opens, revealing the software license agreement that Adobe is proposing. To show that you're happy with the terms of the agreement, click OK. The main Adobe PhotoDeluxe installer screen appears next.

6. Click Continue.

Choose the hard drive where you want to install the program from the Install Location pop-up menu.

7. Select an installation option from the pop-up menu in the upper-left corner of the window.

You have two options: Easy Install and Custom Install. Custom install enables you to select whether or not to install certain PhotoDeluxe components — the program itself, QuickTime 2.5, a Read Me file and SimpleText, and some Adobe Fonts. I recommend that you choose the Easy Install option unless you have reason to do otherwise. This option installs everything that Adobe figures a typical user would want to install.

The only reason not to select a typical install is if you have versions of QuickTime or SimpleText that are more current than the ones that ship with PhotoDeluxe. In that case, select the Custom option and choose the components that you want to install. An "x" in a box next to an item installs that item. Click the box to turn the "x" on and off. Note that you must install the Adobe fonts for the program templates to work correctly.

8. Click Install.

An information window appears, asking you to enter your name and other information. You must enter this information to continue, so go ahead and press fingers to keyboard.

9. Click Next.

The program asks you to confirm the information that you just entered. If everything is okay, click Install Now. If you made a mistake, click Back to fix things.

If you have any other applications running, PhotoDeluxe warns you that you need to shut them down. Click the Continue button to automatically close any running programs, or click Cancel to exit the installation routine and close the applications yourself.

An installation progress window appears on your screen. After the installation is complete, PhotoDeluxe informs you that you next need to install Adobe Type Manager in order to use the templates included with the program.

10. Click Continue.

The PhotoDeluxe registration screen appears, asking you to select the region in which you live (again). If you don't want to register the program right now or don't have a modem to perform the electronic registration, click Cancel. Otherwise, click Next and follow the onscreen prompts to register via modem.

If you click Cancel. PhotoDeluxe asks whether you really, really want to exit the registration process. Click Yes if you do, click No if you changed your mind.

PhotoDeluxe displays a message that says that the installation was successful but that you need to restart your machine. Click Restart to do so.

11. **Install Adobe Type Manager.**

If you don't already have Adobe Type Manager (ATM) installed on your system, you need to install the version that ships with PhotoDeluxe in order for the PhotoDeluxe templates to work properly.

To install the program, double-click the PhotoDeluxe CD icon on the desktop, double-click the ATM folder, double-click the Fonts and Font Utilities folder, and double-click the Installer icon. When the installer window opens, follow the on-screen prompts to complete the installation.

Appendix B
About the CD

*G*lued to the inside back cover of this book is a special bonus from IDG Books: a CD-ROM full of demos, trial versions, and even full working versions of some popular programs related to image editing and PhotoDeluxe.

The following paragraphs give you a brief preview of the goodies on the CD and also explain how to use the CD.

System Requirements

Make sure that your computer meets the minimum system requirements listed below. If your computer doesn't match up to most of these requirements, you may have problems using the contents of the CD.

- ✔ A PC with a 486 or faster processor, or a Mac OS computer with a 68030 or faster processor.

- ✔ Microsoft Windows 95 or later, or Mac OS system software 7.5 or later.

- ✔ At least 16MB of total RAM installed on your computer.

- ✔ At least 128MB of hard drive space available to install all the software from this CD. (You need less space if you don't install every program.)

- ✔ A CD-ROM drive — double-speed (2x) or faster.

- ✔ A sound card for PCs. (Mac OS computers have built-in sound support.)

- ✔ A monitor capable of displaying at least 256 colors or grayscale.

- ✔ A modem with a speed of at least 14,400 bps.

If you need more information on the basics, check out *PCs For Dummies,* 4th Edition, by Dan Gookin; *Macs For Dummies,* 4th Edition by David Pogue; *Windows 95 For Dummies* by Andy Rathbone; or *Windows 98 For Dummies* by Andy Rathbone (all published by IDG Books Worldwide, Inc.).

Using the CD with Microsoft Windows

To install the items from the CD to your hard drive, follow these steps.

1. **Insert the CD into your computer's CD-ROM drive.**

2. **Windows 95 users: Click Start⇨Run.**

3. **In the dialog box that appears, type** D:\SETUP.EXE.

   Replace *D* with the proper drive letter if your CD-ROM drive uses a different letter. (If you don't know the letter, see how your CD-ROM drive is listed under My Computer in Windows 95.)

4. **Click OK.**

   A license agreement window appears.

5. **Read through the license agreement, nod your head, and then click the Accept button if you want to use the CD — after you click Accept, you'll never be bothered by the License Agreement window again.**

   The CD interface Welcome screen appears. The interface is a little program that shows you what's on the CD and coordinates installing the programs and running the demos. The interface basically enables you to click a button or two to make things happen.

6. **Click anywhere on the Welcome screen to enter the interface.**

   Now you're getting to the action. This next screen lists categories for the software on the CD.

7. **To view the items within a category, just click the category's name.**

   A list of programs in the category appears.

8. **For more information about a program, click the program's name.**

   Be sure to read the information that appears. Sometimes a program has its own system requirements or requires you to do a few tricks on your computer before you can install or run the program, and this screen tells you what to do, if necessary.

9. **If you don't want to install the program, click the Go Back button to return to the previous screen.**

   You can always return to the previous screen by clicking the Go Back button. This feature enables you to browse the different categories and products and decide what you want to install.

10. **To install a program, click the appropriate Install button.**

    The CD interface drops to the background while the CD installs the program you chose.

11. **To install other items, repeat Steps 7 through 10.**

12. When you've finished installing programs, click the Quit button to close the interface.

You can eject the CD now. Place it back in the plastic jacket of the book for safekeeping. Unless, of course, you're afraid that some nefarious neighbor or coworker might lift the thing. In that case, take the CD promptly to the bank and put it in a safety deposit box.

In order to run some of the programs on the *Adobe PhotoDeluxe For Dummies* CD-ROM, you may need to keep the CD in your CD-ROM drive. This is a Good Thing. Otherwise, the installed program would have required you to install a very large chunk of the program to your hard drive, which may have kept you from installing other software.

Using the CD with Mac OS

To install the items from the CD to your hard drive, follow these steps.

1. Insert the CD into your computer's CD-ROM drive.

In a moment, an icon representing the CD you just inserted appears on your Mac desktop. Chances are, the icon looks like a CD-ROM.

2. Double-click the CD icon to show the CD's contents.

3. Double-click the Read Me First icon.

The Read Me First text file contains information about the CD's programs and any last-minute instructions you may need in order to correctly install them.

4. To install most programs, just drag the program's folder from the CD window and drop it on your hard drive icon.

Other programs come with installer programs — with these, you simply open the program's folder on the CD, and then double-click the icon with the words "Install" or "Installer."

Sometimes the installers are actually self-extracting archives, which just means that the program files have been bundled up into an archive, and this self-extractor unbundles the files and places them on your hard drive. This kind of program is often called a .sea. Double-click anything with .sea in the title, and it runs just like an installer.

After you install the programs you want, you can eject the CD.

What You'll Find on the CD

Here's a summary of the software on this CD arranged by category. If you use Windows, the CD interface helps you install software easily. (If you have no idea what I'm talking about when I say "CD interface," flip back a page or two to find the section, "Using the CD with Microsoft Windows.")

If you use a Mac OS computer, you can take advantage of the easy Mac interface to quickly install the programs.

Image cataloging and management tools

PhotoRecall, from G&A Imaging

For Windows. Get image clutter under control by organizing your pictures in digital photo albums with PhotoRecall. You can add keywords and other image information data to simplify the process of tracking down a specific image.

A 30-day trial version of PhotoRecall Version 1 is included on the CD. Version 2, available via the PhotoRecall Web site, offers additional features, including the capability to publish your albums online. For more information, point your browser to www.photorecall.com.

PolyView, from Polybytes

For Windows. PolyView is a shareware program that you can use to organize your image files and view thumbnails of images in a format resembling Windows Explorer. The program also offers some image-editing tools and a batch file conversion feature (so you can convert files saved in one format to another format quickly).

PolyView is shareware, so you can try it for free, but you're honor-bound to pay the registration fee if you decide to keep the program. For more information, go to the Polybytes Web site, www.polybytes.com.

Portfolio, from Extensis
For Windows and Macintosh. Formerly known as Fetch, Portfolio is a popular image cataloging program that enables you to browse through thumbnails of all your images. If you have tons of image files, you'll appreciate the program's ability to search for specific images by keywords or other file data. Portfolio can also catalog multimedia files, audio files, and drawings.

The CD includes a 60-day trial version of Portfolio. You can find out more about the program by visiting the Extensis Web site at www.extensis.com.

Presto! PageManager, from NewSoft

For Windows. PageManager is an image cataloging and management program with a twist. In addition to enabling you to organize and preview image files, the program is designed to interact directly with your scanner. You can scan directly into PageManager and then print the image, e-mail it to friends, or create slide shows and more with the click of an icon.

In addition, you can drag any thumbnail to a PhotoDeluxe icon to open and edit the image (you can open the image in other programs in the same fashion as well). A built-in OCR (Optical Character Recognition) engine enables you to scan brochures and other documents and turn them into editable text, too.

A 15-day trial version is provided on the CD. For more information about the product, click on over to the NewSoft Web site at `www.newsoftinc.com`.

Presto! Photo Album, from NewSoft

For Windows. True to its name, Presto! PhotoAlbum makes it easy to create photo albums on your computer. You place your images on digital "pages" and then can add captions, shadows, frames, and clip art graphics to jazz up the pages. An image browser and organizer is also included. After you finish creating an album, you can post it on your Web page or share it with friends and family via e-mail.

The CD contains a 15-day trial version, and you can find out more about the program features at the NewSoft Web site, `www.newsoftinc.com`.

ThumbsPlus, from Cerious Software, Inc.

For Windows (and coming soon for the Mac). Another shareware program, ThumbsPlus also enables you to view thumbnails using a Windows Explorer-like layout. ThumbsPlus can also be used to organize movie files, fonts, and other multimedia files.

Like PolyBytes, ThumbsPlus is shareware; be a good human being and pony up the registration fee if you like the program. For more information about ThumbsPlus, visit the Cerious Software site at `www.thumbsplus.com`.

Panorama software

PhotoVista and Live Picture Viewer, from Live Picture

For Windows and Macintosh. PhotoVista enables you to stitch two or more images together to create panoramic scenes and, if you're a Macintosh user, QuickTime VR movies. The Live Picture Viewer is an add-on for your Web browser. With the viewer installed, you can explore PhotoVista panoramas that may be included in a Web site.

Give PhotoVista a look-see by installing the trial version included on the CD. The Live Picture Viewer is free; you can add it to your browser by clicking the install button in the interface and following along with the installer, which will auto-detect your browser.

For more information and online examples, visit the Live Picture Web site, www.livepicture.com.

Spin Panorama, from PictureWorks Technology, Inc.

For Windows. Spin Panorama also enables you to combine several images into a panoramic picture or a 360-degree QuickTime VR movie. You can see the program in action in Chapter 13.

PictureWorks Technology, the manufacturer of Spin Panorama as well as many other digital imaging productivity tools, supplied a fully functional version of Spin Panorama 1.0 on the CD. For more information about this product, including details about upgrading to Version 2, visit the company's Web site at www.pictureworks.com.

Puzzle makers

BrainsBreaker, from Juan Trujillo Tarradas.

For Windows. BrainsBreaker enables you to create an on-screen jigsaw puzzle out of your image. After "breaking" your image into a zillion puzzle pieces, you can work the puzzle on-screen. *Warning:* This program is addictive! A demo program is included on the CD; to get the full working version, visit www.jtrujillo.pair.com/.

Jigsaw Deluxe, from Captain's Software, Inc.

For Macintosh. With Jigsaw Deluxe, Mac users can also get in on the jigsaw puzzle fun. Try out the program using the demo on the CD, then head to www.unboxed.com/MoreInfo/CaptainsSoftware/JigsawDeluxe.html to purchase the full version.

ULead plug-ins

ULead Systems offers a variety of *plug-ins* — image-editing functions that you can add to PhotoDeluxe. (Actually, the plug-ins were created for use with Adobe Photoshop, but they work with PhotoDeluxe as well.)

To use the plug-ins, install them to the PlugIns folder, which is inside the main PhotoDeluxe folder. You can install them by simply clicking the Install button in the interface. Be sure to specify the PlugIns folder when the installation program asks you to "Specify the Plug-In Folder of your Adobe Photoshop compatible program" and "Specify Destination Folder." After installation, open PhotoDeluxe and click the Effects menu. You should see a Ulead submenu at the bottom of the Effects menu. If you don't see an Effects menu, choose File⇨Preferences⇨Long Menus or, in Version 3, click the Advanced Menus button (see Chapter 1 for more information). The CD includes 15-day trials of the following plug-ins, which are for Windows only. You can find out more about these and other plug-ins at the ULead Web site, www.ulead.com. Look for a link to the ULead Photoshop plug-ins.

✔ **Type.Plugin:** Use this plug-in to create special text effects that are either impossible or difficult to do with the PhotoDeluxe Text tool.

✔ **Particle.Plugin:** Add fire, bubbles, clouds, stars, smoke, and more to your images with Particle.Plugin.

✔ **ArtTexture.Plugin:** With this cool tool, you can fill a selection with sample patterns or edit existing patterns to create your own designs. You can even animate patterns if you want.

✔ **FantasyWarp.Plugin:** Take an image or selection and warp it into a kaleidoscope-like version of its former self. You can output the results as a still image or an animated GIF images for use on a Web page.

Web authoring tools

Dreamweaver, from Macromedia

For Windows and Macintosh. A high-powered, professional Web authoring tool, Dreamweaver offers page-creation and site management tools that have won rave reviews. Dreamweaver offers both a visual page creation tool and HTML-editing capabilities.

A 30-day trial is included on the CD; point your Web browser to www.macromedia.com for more information.

HomeSite, from Allaire

For Windows. Another popular offering for those who create and manage Web sites, this award-winning Web authoring tool enables you to create and edit HTML (the language used to create Web pages).

An evaluation copy of this shareware program is included on the CD. For more information about the product, visit www.allaire.com.

BBEdit 4.5 Demo and BBEdit 4.0 Lite, from Bare Bones Software

For Macintosh. These two demos introduce you to the power of BBEdit as an HTML text editor. BBEdit 4.0 Lite offers basic text-editing tools, while BBEdit 4.5 offers all the features in BBEdit 4.0 Lite plus many other useful features. (The full version of Dreamweaver includes BBEdit and provides fully integrated editing so that you can move easily between the two programs.) For more on BBEdit, visit www.barebones.com.

Web links page

The great folks at IDG who developed the CD for this book have created a Web page containing all the links mentioned in Chapter 17 as well as links to software companies included in this appendix. To use the page, simply run it directly from the CD. After connecting to the Internet and starting your browser, choose File⇨Open and open the Web page file, LINKS.HTM, located at the root of your CD. You can then just click a link to jump to the corresponding Web site. Cool!

If You've Got Problems (Of the CD Kind)

I tried my best to compile programs that work on most computers with the minimum system requirements. Alas, your computer may differ, and some programs may not work properly for some reason.

The two likeliest problems are that you don't have enough memory (RAM) for the programs you want to use, or you have other programs running that are affecting the installation or running of a program. If you get error messages like Not enough memory or Setup cannot continue, turn off any anti-virus software that you have on your computer. Installers sometimes mimic virus activity and may make your computer incorrectly believe that it is being infected by a virus. Also, close all running programs. The more programs you're running, the less memory is available to other programs. Installers also typically update files and programs; if you keep other programs running, installation may not work properly.

If you still have trouble installing the items from the CD, please call the IDG Books Worldwide Customer Service phone number: 800-762-2974 (outside the U.S.: 317-596-5430).

Index

● *G* ●

● *H* ●

Create Personalized Photo Albums & Scrapbooks!

Do More with Your Photos!

Take photos with your digital camera or scan your favorite print photos, from

- Vacations, holidays, special events...

- Birthdays, parties, graduations...

- Weddings, anniversaries, baby showers...

- Reunions, get-togethers, farewell parties, bon voyage parties, retirement parties...

- Picnics, BBQs, celebrations, sleep-overs...

Make Digital Photo Albums!

Add photos from digital cameras & scanners to Presto! PhotoAlbum for Windows 95!

- Share with family and friends via disk, e-mail or post on the Internet!

- Create custom or template albums.

- View thumbnails quickly with Photo Browser.

- Drag-and-drop photos, frames, clip art, shadows, and more! 200+ clip art included!

Digital Photos!

So, you've bought (or are thinking of buying) a digital camera? Great!! But what do you do if you want a real photograph from your digital camera file?

Simple! Send it to Firehouse!

Firehouse's new digital photo printer produces actual photographic prints directly from your digital files!

Best of all, you can e-mail your files to us without leaving your home or office!

1. Shoot your images.
2. View them on your computer.
3. e-mail them to Firehouse:
   mail@fire-house.net
4. Receive your photos.
5. Amaze your family and friends.

FIREHOUSE
IMAGE CENTER
1030 E. Washington St.
Indianapolis, IN 46202
800-382-9179

IDG Books Worldwide, Inc., End-User License Agreement

READ THIS. You should carefully read these terms and conditions before opening the software packet(s) included with this book ("Book"). This is a license agreement ("Agreement") between you and IDG Books Worldwide, Inc. ("IDGB"). By opening the accompanying software packet(s), you acknowledge that you have read and accept the following terms and conditions. If you do not agree and do not want to be bound by such terms and conditions, promptly return the Book and the unopened software packet(s) to the place you obtained them for a full refund.

1. **License Grant.** IDGB grants to you (either an individual or entity) a nonexclusive license to use one copy of the enclosed software program(s) (collectively, the "Software") solely for your own personal or business purposes on a single computer (whether a standard computer or a workstation component of a multiuser network). The Software is in use on a computer when it is loaded into temporary memory (RAM) or installed into permanent memory (hard disk, CD-ROM, or other storage device). IDGB reserves all rights not expressly granted herein.

2. **Ownership.** IDGB is the owner of all right, title, and interest, including copyright, in and to the compilation of the Software recorded on the disk(s) or CD-ROM ("Software Media"). Copyright to the individual programs recorded on the Software Media is owned by the author or other authorized copyright owner of each program. Ownership of the Software and all proprietary rights relating thereto remain with IDGB and its licensers.

3. **Restrictions on Use and Transfer.**

   (a) You may only (i) make one copy of the Software for backup or archival purposes, or (ii) transfer the Software to a single hard disk, provided that you keep the original for backup or archival purposes. You may not (i) rent or lease the Software, (ii) copy or reproduce the Software through a LAN or other network system or through any computer subscriber system or bulletin-board system, or (iii) modify, adapt, or create derivative works based on the Software.

   (b) You may not reverse engineer, decompile, or disassemble the Software. You may transfer the Software and user documentation on a permanent basis, provided that the transferee agrees to accept the terms and conditions of this Agreement and you retain no copies. If the Software is an update or has been updated, any transfer must include the most recent update and all prior versions.

4. **Restrictions on Use of Individual Programs.** You must follow the individual requirements and restrictions detailed for each individual program in Appendix B of this Book. These limitations are also contained in the individual license agreements recorded on the Software Media. These limitations may include a requirement that after using the program for a specified period of time, the user must pay a registration fee or discontinue use. By opening the Software packet(s), you will be agreeing to abide by the licenses and restrictions for these individual programs that are detailed in Appendix B and on the Software Media. None of the material on this Software Media or listed in this Book may ever be redistributed, in original or modified form, for commercial purposes.

5. Limited Warranty.

(a) IDGB warrants that the Software and Software Media are free from defects in materials and workmanship under normal use for a period of sixty (60) days from the date of purchase of this Book. If IDGB receives notification within the warranty period of defects in materials or workmanship, IDGB will replace the defective Software Media.

(b) IDGB AND THE AUTHOR OF THE BOOK DISCLAIM ALL OTHER WARRANTIES, EXPRESS OR IMPLIED, INCLUDING WITHOUT LIMITATION IMPLIED WARRANTIES OF MER-CHANTABILITY AND FITNESS FOR A PARTICULAR PURPOSE, WITH RESPECT TO THE SOFTWARE, THE PROGRAMS, THE SOURCE CODE CONTAINED THEREIN, AND/OR THE TECHNIQUES DESCRIBED IN THIS BOOK. IDGB DOES NOT WARRANT THAT THE FUNCTIONS CONTAINED IN THE SOFTWARE WILL MEET YOUR REQUIREMENTS OR THAT THE OPERATION OF THE SOFTWARE WILL BE ERROR FREE.

(c) This limited warranty gives you specific legal rights, and you may have other rights that vary from jurisdiction to jurisdiction.

6. Remedies.

(a) IDGB's entire liability and your exclusive remedy for defects in materials and workmanship shall be limited to replacement of the Software Media, which may be returned to IDGB with a copy of your receipt at the following address: Software Media Fulfillment Department, Attn.: *Adobe PhotoDeluxe For Dummies,* IDG Books Worldwide, Inc., 7260 Shadeland Station, Ste. 100, Indianapolis, IN 46256, or call 800-762-2974. Please allow three to four weeks for delivery. This Limited Warranty is void if failure of the Software Media has resulted from accident, abuse, or misapplication. Any replacement Software Media will be warranted for the remainder of the original warranty period or thirty (30) days, whichever is longer.

(b) In no event shall IDGB or the author be liable for any damages whatsoever (including without limitation damages for loss of business profits, business interruption, loss of business information, or any other pecuniary loss) arising from the use of or inability to use the Book or the Software, even if IDGB has been advised of the possibility of such damages.

(c) Because some jurisdictions do not allow the exclusion or limitation of liability for conse-quential or incidental damages, the above limitation or exclusion may not apply to you.

7. U.S. Government Restricted Rights. Use, duplication, or disclosure of the Software by the U.S. Government is subject to restrictions stated in paragraph (c)(1)(ii) of the Rights in Technical Data and Computer Software clause of DFARS 252.227-7013, and in subparagraphs (a) through (d) of the Commercial Computer–Restricted Rights clause at FAR 52.227-19, and in similar clauses in the NASA FAR supplement, when applicable.

8. General. This Agreement constitutes the entire understanding of the parties and revokes and supersedes all prior agreements, oral or written, between them and may not be modified or amended except in a writing signed by both parties hereto that specifically refers to this Agreement. This Agreement shall take precedence over any other documents that may be in conflict herewith. If any one or more provisions contained in this Agreement are held by any court or tribunal to be invalid, illegal, or otherwise unenforceable, each and every other provision shall remain in full force and effect.

Using the Adobe PhotoDeluxe
For Dummies CD

● ●

*T*he *Adobe PhotoDeluxe For Dummies* CD-ROM includes demos, trial versions, and some full working versions of popular programs related to image-editing and PhotoDeluxe.

You can use the CD-ROM included with this book on your PC with Microsoft Windows or with a Macintosh computer.

For details about the contents of the CD-ROM and instructions for installing the software from the CD-ROM, see Appendix B (About the CD).

Playing games is really fun... The Dummies Way™!

Pressman®
©1998 Pressman Toy Corporation, New York, NY 10010

Crosswords For Dummies™ Game

You don't have to know how to spell to have a great time. Place a word strip on the board so that it overlaps another word or creates a new one. Special squares add to the fun. The first player to use up all their word strips wins!
For 2 to 4 players.

Trivia For Dummies™ Game

You're guaranteed to have an answer every time! Each player gets 10 cards that contain the answer to every question. Act quickly and be the first player to throw down the correct answer and move closer to the finish line!
For 3 or 4 players.

Charades For Dummies™ Game

Act out one-word charades: when other players guess them, they move ahead. The special cards keep the game full of surprises. The first player around the board wins.
For 3 or 4 players.

...For Dummies and The Dummies Way are trademarks or registered trademarks of IDG Books Worldwide, Inc.

IDG BOOKS WORLDWIDE BOOK REGISTRATION